The Synagogue in Late Antiquity

Contributors to this volume:

Lee I. Levine, editor
Hebrew University, Jerusalem

Shaye J. D. Cohen
The Jewish Theological Seminary, New York

Gideon Foerster
Hebrew University, Jerusalem

Joseph Gutmann
Wayne State University, Detroit, Michigan

Reuven Kimelman
Brandeis University, Waltham, Massachusetts

A. T. Kraabel
Luther College, Decorah, Iowa

Eric M. Meyers
Duke University, Durham, North Carolina

Bezalel Narkiss
Hebrew University, Jerusalem

Lawrence H. Schiffman
New York University, New York

Avigdor Shinan
Hebrew University, Jerusalem

Morton Smith
Columbia University, New York

Yoram Tsafrir
Hebrew University, Jerusalem

J. Yahalom
Hebrew University, Jerusalem

The Synagogue in Late Antiquity

Edited by Lee I. Levine

**A Centennial Publication of
The Jewish Theological Seminary of America**

A CENTURY OF ACHIEVEMENT

1886–1986
תרמ״ו–תשמ״ו

Published by
The American Schools of Oriental Research
Philadelphia, Pennsylvania

Library of Congress Cataloging in Publication Data

The Synagogue in Late Antiquity.

   Papers from a conference sponsored by the Center for
Synagogue Studies, The Jewish Theological Seminary of
America and held at the Seminary Oct. 21–24, 1984.
   "A Centennial Publication of The Jewish Theological Seminary
of America."
   Includes bibliographies and index.
   1. Synagogues—Congresses. 2. Synagogues—Near East—
Congresses. 3. Synagogue architecture—Near East—
Congresses. 4. Synagogue art—Near East—Congresses.
5. Judaism—Liturgy—Congresses. 6. Jewish art and
symbolism—Near East—Congresses. 7. Jews—Antiquities
—Congresses. I. Levine, Lee I. II. Jewish Theological
Seminary of America. Center for Synagogue Studies.
BM653.S89 1986   296.6'5'0901   86-14069
ISBN 0-89757-510-5
ISBN 0-89757-509-1 (pbk.)

Contents

Foreword

Among the great privileges of a scholarly institution are the opportunities it has to serve as a home for scholars and scholarly resources, as a magnet for students, and as a forum to stimulate serious study in areas related to its central message. The conference at which the articles in this volume were first presented provided such an opportunity for The Jewish Theological Seminary of America.

Professor Lee I. Levine, a graduate of the Seminary and a distinguished scholar who has done much research on the rabbinic age, raised profound questions about the early synagogue. It was clear that these questions were important and that the search for answers would advance our understanding of the period and provide insights into the origin and development of the synagogue ritual.

The Seminary was able to convene this conference thanks to the Stroock Institute for Rabbinic Studies, an endowment established for just such purposes. Scholars from Israel and from the West gathered in the new Boesky Family Library Building to address Professor Levine's questions and to raise new ones. The assembled experts included students of architecture and Jewish art, as well as those involved with liturgy and the form and content of worship in the ancient synagogue. As often happens when gifted scholars gather, there was a cross-fertilization of ideas, enabling each discipline to broaden its understanding of its own field by applying to it the insights gained in related areas. This stimulating exchange was as evident in the critiques and discussion that followed each presentation as in the papers. However, the papers themselves, by the very juxtaposition of their diverse subject matter, will suggest many of the parallels first revealed at the conference. In addition, those who were present will doubtless continue to be inspired by the insights gained there, and their future research and writing will inevitably reflect that stimulation.

In conclusion, the Seminary is indebted to Professor Levine for suggesting and organizing this fertile meeting of great minds, and to Professors Ismar Schorsch and Raymond Scheindlin who, as successive provosts of the Seminary, did so much to facilitate it. The Seminary is proud that one of its graduates conceived of this conference, that several of the experts who presented papers were also associated with this institution, either presently or in the past, and that it had the resources, both financial and in personnel, to organize the conference and to assemble the scholars, both present and future, best equipped to profit from its deliberations.

This volume, like the conference from which it derived, testifies to the Seminary's commitment to Jewish tradition and to the devotion to critical scholarship which has won it recognition in the American academic establishment. It constitutes a rewarding investment of those resources, one which I hope will be replicated often in the future.

Gerson D. Cohen

Acknowledgments

It is my pleasant duty to acknowledge those responsible for the conference and this publication. First and foremost, thanks are due to the Chancellor of The Jewish Theological Seminary, Dr. Gerson D. Cohen, whose receptivity to the idea of the conference and whose full support of its implementation were crucial for success. The Stroock Institute for Rabbinic Studies is to be thanked for its generous support. In addition, warm appreciation is due the two successive provosts of the Seminary, Professors Ismar Schorsch and Raymond Scheindlin, whose terms of office overlapped the planning and execution of these events. Each gave unstintingly of his time and energies to guarantee our success. We are also pleased to acknowledge the cooperation of the American Schools of Oriental Research and its First Vice President for Publications, Professor Eric Meyers, in the publication of these proceedings. Finally, thanks are due to those who helped in the preparation of the manuscript and in seeing it through the various stages of publication: Hani Davis in Jerusalem and Jean Highland in New York.

Lee I. Levine
Jerusalem

October 1986
Tishri 5747

List of Abbreviations

B	Babylonian Talmud
CChr	Corpus Christianorum: Series Latina
CDC	Cairo Geniza: Zadokite Documents
CSEL	Corpus Scriptorum Ecclesiasticorum Latinorum
CT	Codex Theodosianus
GCS	Die griechischen christlichen Schriftsteller
J	Jerusalem Talmud
PG	Patrologiae Cursus Completus: Series Graeca
PL	Patrologiae Cursus Completus: Series Latina
RSV	Revised Standard Version
T	Tôseptā'

List of Illustrations

Introduction

Lee I. Levine

Several years ago The Jewish Theological Seminary organized The Center for Synagogue Studies under the auspices of the Stroock Institute for Rabbinic Studies. One of the first activities undertaken by the Center was the sponsoring of a conference devoted to the study of the ancient synagogue. The purpose of this conference was to bring together scholars whose fields of research are related to the synagogue in antiquity and to create an atmosphere that would be conducive to fruitful scholarly interchange. Participants were invited from Israel and America and included those who specialize in the study of the material culture (archaeology and Jewish art), as well as others whose research focuses primarily on the manifold Jewish and non-Jewish literary sources. Phenomena relating specifically to the Jews of Israel were treated at this conference, as well as those relating to Diaspora Jewry. Topics such as prayer, *piyyût*, Jewish art and architecture, the Torah-reading ceremony, and sermons in the ancient synagogue were discussed. The conference was held at the Seminary on October 21–24, 1984. The studies included in this volume were originally delivered at these sessions.

The first two studies focus on evidence of the Second Temple period. My own paper emphasizes the range and diversity that seem to characterize the early synagogue, both architecturally and functionally. I suggest that this may be the result of the relative newness of the institution, of the fact that it served mainly as a community center, and of the necessity to cater to the different needs of various far-flung Jewish communities. Lawrence H. Schiffman focuses on recently published evidence from Qumran. These texts appear to attest to a regular cycle of prayers and hymns, as well as to supplicatory prayers and possibly a marriage ritual. Parallels to later rabbinic texts are noted, and we are left pondering some far-reaching questions: what is the precise connection between Qumran and the post-70 C.E. era as reflected in rabbinic literature? Did one influence the other? Were the Pharisees at the time behaving in a fashion similar to the Qumran community, and how reflective are these Qumran patterns of Jewish practice generally during the Second Temple period?

Two papers deal exclusively with the Diaspora synagogue. Basing his remarks primarily on the material remains of six synagogues, A. T. Kraabel portrays the Diaspora synagogue community as a fusion of Jewish and non-Jewish elements. On one hand there were various Greco-Roman forms of social and religious organization, and on the other there were inherited Jewish communal patterns. Kraabel posits a kind of exile or Diaspora theology that facilitated the establishment and flourishing of these communities outside the Homeland. Joseph Gutmann offers a review of the major issues that have engaged scholars this past half century regarding the synagogue of Dura Europos. Despite the plethora of evidence and many conflicting theories, it is suggested that at least one dominant theme is the centrality of the ark and Temple and that these scenes reflect the procession and Torah-reading ceremony so central in the synagogue ritual. Foreign influences on the art of Dura Europos are noted, and the ties between this art and midrashic literature are presented.

Several studies deal with synagogue prayer, focusing on the *Šĕmaʿ* and its accompanying blessings. Reuven Kimelman traces the evolution of these paragraphs from their first appearance as part of the Temple ritual through the period of late antiquity when they acquired a form similar to the one used today. The common thread running through the three accompanying blessings and the three sections of the *Šĕmaʿ* is carefully traced, and the process of interpolation of additional themes into the original composition is traced. Morton Smith distinguishes between two basic types of ancient Jewish prayer: the Deuteronomic-inspired expressions that focus on the God of history and national redemption on one hand, and the celestial, transcendent Deity of the cosmos who is praised by the angels in a mystic, other-worldly setting on the other. The latter type of prayer appears in the *Yôṣēr* benediction of the *Šĕmaʿ*, as well as in several other compositions that are recited daily.

Several other papers deal with the various religious activities associated with the synagogue. Avigdor Shinan points to the wide range of practices relating to the reading of the Torah. Besides several explicit references to these practices in our sources, traces of additional customs are also noted in ancient homilies. Moreover, attention is given to the setting, function, and form of these early synagogue sermons. J. Yahalom discusses the ancient *piyyûṭ* from a literary perspective, indicating its uniqueness vis-à-vis earlier types of Jewish poetry. He notes some of the more important *payṭānîm* of the Byzantine period and points to the similarities between the ancient *piyyûṭ* and contemporary Christian liturgical compositions.

Three studies focus on the material remains of the ancient synagogue. Eric M. Meyers summarizes the state of the field regarding the Galilean synagogue, to which he himself has made considerable contributions. He emphasizes that a number of conceptions that had become well-nigh axiomatic in synagogue studies of the past are now being seriously called into question. The coupling of typology and chronology, that is, the idea that certain architectural and artistic styles are to be associated with specific historical periods, is untenable in light of recent finds. Moreover, contrary to accepted opinion, many Galilean synagogues indeed had a *bîmâ* and with it a permanent place for the Torah. Finally, regional diversity as well as the flourishing state of the Palestinian community throughout the period of late antiquity necessitates a reappraisal of the state of the Jewish community in Byzantine Palestine. Gideon Foerster and Yoram Tsafrir have together presented a comprehensive and convincing picture of the architectural and artistic dependence of the synagogue on the material culture of the Roman-Byzantine world. Foerster offers a wide-ranging survey of various architectural elements of the Galilean synagogue and their ties to motifs and styles in late Roman architecture of the second and third centuries. Tsafrir focuses on the "basilica"-type synagogue, noting the remarkable similarities between the Christian basilica and the synagogue during the Byzantine period, including various modes of artistic expression and the use of chancel screens and apses with benches for the seating of the elders of the community.

A unique view of the ancient synagogue is afforded by Shaye J. D. Cohen's examination of pagan and Christian sources as they relate to the synagogue. Some of the information garnered corroborates what is already known from Jewish material. In many cases, however, the data available are different and at times most thought-provoking in their implications. Cohen has carefully analyzed these sources, summarized previous opinion, and offered more than a few suggestive insights of his own.

The last paper is devoted to the study of several aspects of Jewish art during this period. Bezalel Narkiss addresses the various influences on the art of the ancient synagogue. He marshals a wide range of examples relating to pagan motifs and art forms that were adopted (and adapted) for synagogal usage. The parallel adaptation of such forms in Christian art is likewise noted. In addition, Narkiss touches upon the ties between early Jewish art and midrashic literature.

No less stimulating than the papers themselves were the lively and engaging exchanges that followed their original presentations. The discussions included not only constructive critiques of each paper, but time and again the participants succeeded in focusing on implications derived from one discipline or one set of sources to others similarly concerned with the ancient synagogue. Archaeologists and art historians found that some of their conclusions were concomitant with similar developments in the study of the *piyyût* or the development of prayer. The opposite was true as well. Although we were clearly dealing with bodies of evidence that at first glance appeared quite disparate, it soon became apparent that certain basic characteristics of the synagogue in antiquity found expression in different types of evidence.

One fact that became quite clear from the outset of our discussions was that throughout antiquity the synagogue as an institution, along with its rituals, was constantly developing. Both its external forms and internal patterns continued to evolve from century to century, if not from generation to generation. Some impetus for this development was related directly or indirectly to the dramatically changing political, social, and religious circumstances of the Jewish people, particularly between the first and fourth centuries. In addition, it was driven home by speaker after speaker that in any given generation the range and variety of expression connected with the synagogue was stunning. This conclusion, which has become commonplace in the study of the archaeology of the synagogue, was now perceived to apply to its rituals as well.

Finally, a number of speakers raised the issue of the Hellenizing influences that may have shaped the ancient synagogue. Here, again, what has been an accepted fact in the fields of art and architecture—namely, that the material culture of the synagogue was heavily indebted to the surrounding culture—was perceived to be an important and relevant issue even in other, more "spiritual," dimensions of the institution.

Beyond the particular study of the ancient synagogue, one of the wider implications of our deliberations was the awareness of the continued vigorous development within Judaism in late antiquity. Whereas previous generations have assumed that the Jews in general and the Jewish community of Palestine in particular entered a long period of decay and decline in the third and fourth centuries, the evidence discussed at our conference pointed to the fourth to seventh centuries as a period of material prosperity, spiritual creativity, and continued fruitful contact with the surrounding world.

Issues germane to the study of the ancient synagogue that were not accorded special treatment, or that were only tangentially discussed in the course of our conference, also deserve mention. Time and again the question of the social and communal implications of the evidence we were discussing arose. Rarely were we in a position to make a firm determination. What, for example, were the social and religious implications of a multiplicity of customs regarding the recitation of prayers, the reading of the Torah, or reciting *piyyûṭim*? What, if anything, does the recital of *piyyûṭim* tell us about the intellectual, cultural, and religious condition of the local Jewish community? Another issue concerns the relationship of the rabbis to the synagogue: were they integrally involved or only occasionally present, since their focus was the Bêt Midraš? In other words, how rabbinic was the ancient synagogue, religiously, socially, and organizationally? Finally, it was felt that much work needed to be done in order to gain proper perspective on the uniqueness and centrality of the ancient synagogue. Were there similar institutions within pagan culture at the time? If so, what was their relationship to the synagogue? To what degree was the synagogue influenced by external factors, and to what degree was it mainly an internal Jewish development? Where and to what degree did these two lines of influence meet and interact?

Moreover, a proper perspective on the synagogue within ancient Judaism still requires much study. The domestic setting of Judaism was always central, as was the tradition of learning represented by the academy. Where did the synagogue fit in? Did it express a Judaism different from or similar to that found in other institutions? There was little question among the participants of this conference that much needs to be done in these and other areas. By the interdisciplinary nature of our discussions, which has been regarded as important and innovative, we hope to have made a modest contribution towards this end.

1. The Second Temple Synagogue: The Formative Years

Lee I. Levine

By the end of the Second Temple period the synagogue had become a central institution in Jewish life. It could be found everywhere, in Israel and the Diaspora, east and west, in cities as well as in villages. The synagogue filled a wide variety of functions within the Jewish community and had become by the first century a recognized symbol of Jewish presence.[1]

There can be no doubt that the appearance of the synagogue centuries earlier had been of cardinal significance in the development of Judaism. The synagogue universalized official Jewish ritual practice while democratizing worship by taking it out of priestly hands. Thus the way was opened for any Jew anywhere to participate and officiate in the recognized communal ritual. Moreover, the synagogue radically changed the content of this ritual, shifting the focus from sacrifice and libation to Torah study and prayer. Finally, the synagogue welcomed within its confines the presence of the congregation as a whole, unlike the Temple where people were kept at a distance, often far removed from the scene of the ritual.

Given the extent of the revolution caused by the synagogue, our ignorance of its origins is all the more lamentable. Most extant evidence dating from the Second Temple period derives from the first century C.E.; by then, as noted, the synagogue had already become a well-developed communal and religious institution throughout Israel and the Diaspora (Levertoff 1932: 60–77; Billerbeck 1964: 143–61). Clearly such an institution had not developed overnight; its evolution was inevitably long and complex. Moreover, it would likewise be gratuitous to assume that the late Second

Temple synagogue functioned as its successor in the talmudic era. Just as the formation of the ancient synagogue was gradual, so, too, the continuation of this process in the post-70 C.E. era brought significant changes (Lerle 1968: 31–42; Kimelman 1981: 226–44; Segal 1977: 98–108, 152–55; Katz 1984: 63–76).

In this regard, a word of caution on methodology may be called for. Since both literary and archaeological material relating to the synagogue in late antiquity, that is, the post-70 C.E. era, is rich and abundant, there has been a tendency among some to assume that what was true of the second to fourth centuries probably held true, in one form or another, for the pre-70 period as well. If the synagogue emerged sometime during the course of the Second Temple era, then surely, it is argued, by the first century C.E. the basic forms characteristic of the later synagogue would have already crystallized and developed. Such an assumption, however, is unwarranted. There can be no question that the destruction of the Temple and Jerusalem in 70 C.E. had a profound impact on Jewish life generally and on the development of the synagogue in particular, as did the emergence of new centers of Jewish life in the Galilee and Babylonia during late antiquity. The synagogue was not the same for these changes. Expressed archaeologically, the buildings and artistic expression of Capernaum, Hammat Tiberias, Sardis, and Dura bear social, communal, and religious implications far different from those of the earlier, more modest, and unadorned settings at Delos, Masada, and even Gamla. The inner development of the synagogue displayed a similar progression: in every realm of activity—prayers, the Torah reading, sermons, and later the development of the *piyyût* (poems written for synagogue liturgy)—the synagogue continued to reflect a wide variety of customs and an ever-changing repertoire of practices. Therefore it is of paramount importance to exercise caution in using later material when drawing conclusions for an earlier period.

In the following study we will focus our attention on the emergence and development of the synagogue in the period preceding 70 C.E. and, despite the relative paucity of sources, we will attempt to describe and characterize this institution during the period when the Temple in Jerusalem continued to function and flourish.

The origins of the synagogue are shrouded in mystery. Was it a product of Israel or the Diaspora? Did it first emerge in the late First Temple period or at the beginning of the Second? Or perhaps only later during the Hellenistic period? Was it originally a social-communal institution or a religious one? Did the impetus to create such an institution come from the outside world, from factors and stimuli originating in the surrounding culture, or from internal needs and pressures? Or perhaps from a combination of the two?[2]

Not only are we in the dark as regards the origins of the synagogue, but also as regards its initial stages of development. Except for a few scattered references from the Diaspora,[3] nothing is known of this institution until the first century C.E. Despite the absence of sources, we will attempt to sketch, albeit in very general terms, the emergence and development of the synagogue as an institution in its early stages.

It might be advisable first to define the term *synagogue*. During the Second Temple period this term had two possible meanings: a group of people, a community; or a building, an institution. These two meanings, however, were far from being mutually exclusive. As a matter of fact, the existence of one practically presupposes the existence of the other. Every community undoubtedly had a regular place of worship, while any building referred to as a synagogue obviously served as a meeting place for the community of individuals that it served. Nevertheless, at the very beginning of its development, the synagogue, or whatever it might have been called, almost surely did not refer to a specific building, but to a group of people that met regularly for religious purposes not connected with the Temple and sacrifices.

It seems quite likely that the synagogue as an additional or alternative form of divine worship to the Temple first began at the very end of the First Temple period or, at the latest, during the exilic period. Religious frameworks other than the Temple itself were already operative in the pre-586 B.C.E. era, as attested to in the story of the Shunamite woman (2 Kings 4) or in the discovery of numerous altars and local sanctuaries in Israelite archaeological sites. Undoubtedly the reforms of Josiah, if indeed they remained in effect during the years following his death, would have compelled those living outside of Jerusalem to seek new nonsacrificial ways of worshipping God. Perhaps an indication of such an alternative during this period can be found in the phrase "they have burned all God's assembly-places [or tabernacles] in the land" (Psalms 74:8), a difficult verse that probably refers to events surrounding the destruction of the First Temple.[4]

During the Restoration period and in conjunction with limited Jewish settlement in the immediate area of Jerusalem, the Temple again became the main, and probably exclusive, focus for divine worship. The ceremonial reading of the Torah in the time of Ezra and Nehemiah took place there (Nehemiah 8:1, 3:26; Ezra 10:3),[5] and several centuries later, in describing Jewish ritual practice (which included devoting the entire Sabbath to prayer), the Greek writer Agatharchides spoke only of the Temple precincts (*Apion* 1.22 [209–10]; Ezra 10:9).[6] To whatever extent religious ceremonies did take place in the towns and villages of Judaea, they appear to have been held outside, in the local square or plaza near the city gate. From later sources, which nevertheless may reflect practices from the Second Temple era as well, we learn that prayers for rain were offered in the town square and a

Torah-reading ceremony was conducted there while the local priestly course served in Jerusalem (Mishna Ta'anît 2:1; Mishna Bikkûrîm 3:2, Mishna Ta'anît 4:2; Hoenig 1979).[7] Thus, for this period there is no reason to assume that the synagogue had already developed into a place of assembly or into a specific physical setting.

On the basis of our extant sources, the first appearance of buildings intended for religious and communal purposes was in the Diaspora during the third century B.C.E. Such buildings are documented in Egypt for the third and subsequent centuries. In Israel, the synagogue probably first made its appearance during the Hasmonean or Herodian periods, during the first century B.C.E. Such a development was the result of the dramatic expansion of Jewish territory and the enormous increase in Jewish population, together with the Hellenistic proclivity to erect buildings for communal purposes. The earliest evidence for a synagogue building in Israel is the Theodotus inscription from Jerusalem which indicates the existence of such an institution at the end of the first century B.C.E. The Gamla building dates to the first century C.E. and those at Masada and Herodium to the time of the First Revolt. The subsequent development of the synagogue following the destruction of the Temple is well documented. Rabbinic sources as well as archaeological data contain much information about the synagogue during this later period, as regards both its physical appearance and the functions and activities therein.

The Second Temple synagogue was a heterogeneous institution in its size and plan and in its function and role within the Jewish community. Even before the destruction of the Temple, the synagogue was considered a central institution in the life of the people, although it never competed with the Temple in terms of sanctity and cosmic significance (Cohen 1984) and although it might have differed radically from place to place. It is impossible to explain these differences chronologically, that is, that one type preceded another. One can discern significant differences at any given time with regard to the status, location, and activities of the synagogue. As we will presently see, one cannot speak at this time of a crystallized and homogeneous institution in either Israel or the Diaspora.

The diversity among synagogues is evident from even the small amount of physical remains and from the various names given this institution. Let us begin our examination of the synagogue with the archaeological data (figure 1.1). Four buildings regarded as synagogues have been dated to the pre-70 C.E. era: Gamla, Masada, and Herodium in Israel, and Delos in the Diaspora. Of these, scholars agree most on the identification of the Masada synagogue. The finds there include scrolls and ostraca, in addition to the building itself; all seem to indicate that the site was indeed a synagogue.[8] The building at Herodium on the other hand, taken by itself, gives little indication that it functioned as a synagogue. Only by comparison with Masada (both were remodelled at the same time, under the same circumstances, and by the same people—presumably for a similar purpose) does such an identification seem likely.[9]

Over the past half-century much controversy has focused on the identification of the Delos synagogue.[10] The pagan decorations on the many oil lamps found there seem, at first glance, to preclude the possibility that this was indeed a synagogue. On the other hand, the inscriptions repeatedly mention a *proseuche* and "the most high God," terms usually reserved for a Jewish context, and other architectural features likewise argue for a Jewish identification. As a result, scholarly consensus today regards this building as an early synagogue, and recent finds of a Samaritan inscription and possibly a ritual bath nearby have strengthened this conviction (Bruneau 1982: 465–504; Kraabel 1984: 44–46).

The main building at Gamla has also been identified as a synagogue, although the evidence here remains somewhat more inconclusive (Gutman 1981: 30–34).[11] The orientation of the building towards Jerusalem, the proximity of what has been identified as a ritual bath, and the reputation of the town during the war as a hotbed of nationalistic fervor have been the main factors in favor of the identification of the building as a synagogue.

Of these four buildings, Delos is the oldest, dating from the mid-first century B.C.E. (and perhaps earlier); Gamla was presumably built in the mid-first century C.E.; and both Masada and Herodium were transformed into synagogues during the war years (66–74 C.E.). There have been lately several attempts to delineate a typology of the Second Temple synagogue on the basis of these buildings (or at least of the three found in Israel): columns in the center, benches on four sides with a focus on the center of the room, the proximity of ritual baths—and, in the case of Delos, the sea itself (Foerster 1973: 224–28, note 11; Ma'oz 1981: 35–41). However, such attempts must be deemed futile. Whatever common elements exist can be attributed to Greco-Roman architectural traditions generally, and not to particular synagogue styles. Moreover, the differences between these buildings are remarkable and, taken together, provide a strong argument against the assumption of a single typology:

> *Entrances* At Delos there were three entrances from the south and one from the east (this refers to the second stage of the building; in the first stage there were three entrances from the east). At Herodium there were three entrances from the east. However, at Masada there was only one entrance to the east, and at Gamla there was a main entrance from the southwest and a side entrance from the east.

Orientation   At Herodium one would have to face a long side wall to the right as one entered the building in order to be facing Jerusalem; at Masada, the Jerusalem orientation was opposite the entrance; and in Gamla the entrance itself faced Jerusalem. At Delos the focus was toward the single eastern entrance with the three southern entrances off to the side.

Benches   Gamla and Masada had benches on four sides of the hall, Herodium on three (possibly four), and Delos on two. Likewise, the number and organization of these benches differed. At Delos there was a single bench, at Herodium two, an aisle and a single bench against the wall on three sides. Masada had four benches on three sides and a single one on half of the fourth. Gamla had the most extensive layout, with four benches on four sides, an aisle in back, and a single bench against the northeastern wall.

Main Hall   In three of these buildings the main hall was rectangular, and at Masada an additional storeroom protruded into the sanctuary area.

Seat of Moses   Quite well known from literary sources, such a seat was found at Delos, yet nothing comparable was found at any of the other three buildings (Bacher 1897: 299–301; Sukenik 1934: 57–61; Renov 1955: 262–67; Roth 1949: 100–11).

Bîmâ   No traces of a *bîmâ* or a Torah shrine were found in any of these structures. At Gamla a single row of stones was laid in the middle of the floor; its purpose, however, remains enigmatic.

Setting   Each of these synagogues was built in a different setting. The Delos synagogue had formerly been a private home near the sea, and at Gamla the synagogue was located in the one large public building of the city (at least of those heretofore excavated) near the city wall. The other two synagogues were built in Herodian complexes: at Masada in a former reception hall of the king outside the area of the two palaces, at Herodium in the dining area (triclinium) of the king's palace atop the mountain.

On the basis of these differences, it would appear quite unjustified to speak of a single type of Second Temple synagogue. What we have, in fact, is a wide variety of buildings that might have served such a purpose. Moreover, at this time a synagogue was usually an all-purpose communal building. It was not built exclusively, or perhaps even primarily, for religious activities. Communal religious rituals, which took place in these buildings primarily on Sabbaths and holidays, made use of existing facilities; such activities probably had little if any effect on the plan and design of such structures. Qumran may be an excellent case in point. Communal prayer and study were conducted there daily. There is even a reference in the scrolls to a בית השתחות, a place of worship (Zadokite Fragments [CDC] 11: 21–22). However, archaeological evidence indicates that no special room was constructed for such purposes.

Moreover, the above examples were drawn from archaeological remains. Were we to add the several literary sources that refer specifically to a synagogue building, the spectrum would expand even further. Apion knew of synagogue worship under the open sky. He claimed that such buildings were to be found throughout Jerusalem and were oriented eastward (*Apion* 2.2 [10]; Stern 1974–84: volume 1, 394–95). According to the Tôseptā', the main Alexandrian synagogue resembled a basilica, with a wooden *bîmâ* in the center along with seventy richly decorated chairs for the elders of the community (Sûkkâ 4, 6 in Lieberman 1962a: 273; Lieberman 1962b: volume 4, 889–92).[12] Elsewhere the Tôseptā' preserves traditions requiring synagogues to have their entrances facing east (towards the Temple in Jerusalem) and to be built on the highest spot in the city (Měgîllâ 3, 22–23 in Lieberman 1962a: 360). Neither the Gamla nor the Delos synagogues, the two pre-70 C.E. buildings from urban settings, followed these directives. Philo speaks of richly ornamented Alexandrian synagogues whose decorations included shields, golden crowns, and inscriptions (*Embassy* 20 [133]; Krauss 1966: 161–64).[13] No such remains have been found in the four synagogues excavated to date. Finally, Josephus and the New Testament mention the practice (at least in the Diaspora) of building synagogues near bodies of water (*Antiquities* 14.10.23 [258]; Acts 16:13).

The diversity of synagogue buildings may also be reflected in the numerous terms used in ancient sources concerning the synagogue. Most often the building is referred to as a συναγωγή, synagogue (place of gathering), or a προσευχή, *proseuche* (place of prayer). However, it is also called a τὸ ἱερόν, sanctuary (*Apion* 1.22 [209]; *War* 7.3.3 [45]; 4.7.2 [408]; 7.5.5 [144]; 3 Maccabees 2:28); τὸ ἅγιος τόπος, a holy place (Frey 1936–52: volume 1, 505, number 694; volume 2, 153, number 966); εὐχεῖον, a place of prayer (Tcherikover, Fuks, and Stern 1957–64: volume 2, 223); σαββατεῖον, a Sabbath meeting place (*Antiquities* 16.6.2 [164]; Tcherikover, Fuks and Stern 1957–64: volume 3, 46; Krauss 1966: 26–27); or a διδασκαλεῖον, a place of instruction (Philo, *Special Laws* 2.62). Terms such as *amphitheater* (Applebaum 1979: 161, 164–67) and *templum* (Tacitus 5.5.4; Stern 1974–84: volume 2, 43) are also used in connection with the synagogue.

This plurality of names clearly indicates a wide variety of perceptions regarding the essential nature of this institution; clearly it meant different things in various locales. Sometimes the synagogue is referred to on the basis of its particular architectural plan (amphitheater), or in reference to a certain kind of activity (*proseuche* or *didaskaleion*) or to a specific day of the week when the community met for religious purposes (*sabbateion*). Even the two most popular terms—*proseuche* and *synagogue*—may reflect varying types of institutions. Finally, in Rome synagogues might be named after famous people, neighborhoods, places of origin, or even professions (Leon 1960: 135–66).

What exactly took place in the ancient synagogue? What functions did the institution fulfill? First, it is certain that the synagogue functioned in many capacities and served a wide range of activities within the Jewish community.[14] It was, in fact, a center for the entire community, serving as a place for study (*Antiquities* 16.2.4 [43]; Mark 1:21, 6:2; Genesis Rabbâ 65, 22 in Theodor and Albeck 1965: 734–35; J Měgîllâ 3.1.73d),[15] for law courts (Matthew 23:34; Acts 22:19; Mishna Makkôt 3:12),[16] for the collection of local charity funds (Matthew 6:2; T Šabbāt 16, 22 in Lieberman 1962a: 79; T Těrûmôt 1, 10 in Lieberman 1955: 109; T Baḇâ' Batrā' 8, 14 in Zuckermandel 1963: 409; B Kětûbbôt 5a; Stern 1974–84: volume 2, 99, 158), as well as funds destined for the Temple in Jerusalem (Philo, *Embassy* 23.156; *Antiquities* 16.6.4 [167–68], 14.10.8 [215]), as a hostel (see Theodotus inscription below; B Pěsāḥîm 100b–101a; J Měgîllâ 3.4.74a) and also as a place for social and political gatherings (*Life* 54 [276–82]). Banquet halls are mentioned in connection with synagogues, and although their precise usage remains somewhat unclear, it would appear that these banquets had religious as well as social implications (*Antiquities* 14.10.8 [214–16]; 16.6.1 [164] and comment by Marcus and Wikgren 1963: 273; Mark 12:31; Matthew 23:6). Both the Essenes in Qumran and the Therapeutae in Egypt converted their meals into a distinctly sacred context (Manual of Discipline [1QS] 6:2–8; Rule of Congregation [1QSa] 2:17–22; Philo, *Contemplative Life* 8–9, 67–74; Schiffman 1979: 45–56; Bokser 1984: 55–62). In late antiquity a triclinium, banquet hall, is mentioned in connection with several synagogues (Lifshitz 1967: 18–19, 51–52; Hengel 1966: 167–72).[17]

On occasion we hear about activities of a more exceptional nature associated with the early synagogue: one building in Egypt is referred to as a place of refuge (Tcherikover, Fuks, and Stern 1957–64: volume 3, 144, number 1449), others are mentioned (in a later period) as places for taking oaths (Pěsîqtā' Rabbātî 22 in Friedman 1880: 113a). The Jews of Sardis were given permission to offer sacrifices, a privilege whose significance remains elusive to this day (*Antiquities* 14.10.24 [260–61]). Does it mean that sacrificial rites were part of the synagogue worship in that city? And if so, did such activity take place elsewhere as well? (Bickerman 1958: 137–64). We know of sacrifices that were offered outside of Jerusalem during the Second Temple period in Samaria and Egypt (and there are those scholars who would add Qumran and 'Arāq 'el-'Āmîr in Transjordan to this list, for example, Campbell 1979: 159–67). However Sardis stands alone as a synagogue community that is specifically mentioned in this connection.

The discernible differences among ancient synagogues are many. Among them were large and imposing structures such as in Tiberias (*Life* 54 [276–82]) and Alexandria (Philo, *Flaccus* 6 [41–43]; T Sûkkâ 4, 6 in Lieberman 1962a: 273); others were quite modest. The locations of the synagogue likewise varied greatly; at times it was located in the main communal building of the town or city as in Gamla, or in a special structure as in the large urban centers of Alexandria and Caesarea (*War* 2.14.4–5 [285–91]). In several instances the synagogue was erected near the sea, as in Delos or Antioch of Pisidia (*Antiquities* 14.10.23 [258]; Acts 16:13), in the center of the city, as in third-century C.E. Sardis (Seager 1981: 178–84) and perhaps in Alexandria, or in a district where the immediate neighbors were gentiles, as in Caesarea (*War* 2.14.4 [285–86]).

The range of people frequenting the synagogue also varied greatly from place to place. The social composition of the urban synagogues might have been on a neighborhood basis, by profession, or by country of origin. In several cities a number of such groups merged to form a synagogue (Leon 1960: 135–66; T Měgîllâ 2, 17 in Lieberman 1962a: 352). In the villages and towns of Israel, all worshipers were local residents or hailed from the immediate surroundings. In the Diaspora, and especially in the larger cities, however, a greater variety of people, including gentiles, proselytes, and semi-proselytes (*sebomenoi; metuentes*) frequented the synagogue. In several sources the presence of women among the worshipers is emphasized (Acts 13–14, 16–18; *War* 7.3.3 [45]).

Despite the plethora of communal activities that occurred in the ancient synagogue, the institution served first and foremost as a place for religious worship. It is in this context that it is most often mentioned in our sources. The question remains, however, as to what indeed was the nature of this religious activity. Once again, diversity appears to have been no less pronounced than uniformity.

A perusal of the sources leads to the inescapable conclusion that the reading of the Torah and its accompanying rituals constituted the main and, at least in Israel, exclusive function of synagogue worship. All of our sources—Josephus, Philo, rabbinic literature, the New Testament, and archaeological evidence—attest to this fact. According to Josephus, for example:

He [Moses] appointed the Law to be the most excellent and necessary form of instruction, ordaining, not that it should be heard once for all or twice or on several occasions, but that every week men should desert their other occupations and assemble to listen to the Law and to obtain a thorough and accurate knowledge of it, a practice which all other legislators seem to have neglected. (*Apion* 2.17 [175])

Philo speaks in a similar vein:

He [Augustus] knew therefore that they have houses of prayer [*proseuche*] and meet together in them, particularly on the sacred sabbaths when they receive as a body a training in their ancestral philosophy. (*Embassy*, 23 [156])

And . . . you sit in your conventicles and assemble your regular company and read in security your holy books, expounding any obscure point and in leisurely comfort discussing at length your ancestral philosophy. (*Dreams* 2.18 [127])

The New Testament affords a similar picture. In the numerous traditions which report on Jesus' and Paul's visits to synagogues, we invariably hear about the reading or exposition of the Torah or the Prophets:

And he came to Nazareth, where he had been brought up; and he went to the synagogue, as his custom was, on the Sabbath day. And he stood up to read; and there was given to him the book of the prophet Isaiah. He opened the book and found the place where it was written. . . . And he closed the book, and gave it back to the attendant, and sat down; and the eyes of all in the synagogue were fixed on him. And he began to say to them, "Today this scripture has been fulfilled in your hearing." (Luke 4: 16–22 [RSV])

And on the Sabbath day they went into the synagogue and sat down. After the reading of the Law and the prophets, the rulers of the synagogue sent to them, saying, "Brethren, if you have any word of exhortation for the people, say it." So Paul stood up, and motioning with his hand said. . . . (Acts 13: 13–16 [RSV])

Rabbinic sources likewise speak of this activity, and this activity only, with regard to the synagogue. In an early series of traditions regarding synagogue ritual the Tôseptā' notes the reading of the Torah and the delivering of homilies (Měgĭllâ 3 in Lieberman 1962a: 353–64). Likewise, the famous description of the Alexandrian synagogue, referred to above, focuses exclusively on the Torah-reading ceremony:

And a wooden *bîmâ* was to be found in the center [of the hall], and the *hazzān* of the synagogue would stand in the corner [of the *bîmâ*] with kerchiefs in his hand. When one came and took hold of the scroll to read [a section from the Torah], he [the *hazzān*] would wave the kerchiefs and all the people would answer "Amen" for each blessing. He would [again] wave the kerchiefs and all the people would respond "Amen." (T Sûkkâ 4, 6 in Lieberman 1962a: 273; Lieberman 1962b: 889–92)

Finally, archaeological evidence confirms this point. In what constitutes the most important epigraphic evidence from Second Temple Jerusalem, the Theodotus inscription—dating from the first century C.E.—has the following to say about one ancient Jerusalem synagogue:

Theodotus, son of Vettenos the priest and archisynagogos, son of an archisynagogos and grandson of an archisynagogos, built the synagogue for reading the Law and studying the commandments, and as a hostel with chambers and water installations to provide for the needs of itinerants from abroad, which [that is, the synagogue] his fathers, the elders and Simonides founded. (Schwabe 1956: 362–65; Frey 1936–52: volume 2, 332–35)

Thus, the synagogue of Theodotus functioned primarily in three areas: it was a place for the reading of the Torah, for instruction of the commandments, and it also served as a hostel. Its omission of any mention of prayer is striking. Was prayer excluded because of the proximity of the Temple Mount (the inscription was discovered in the City of David and the synagogue was presumably located there)? Or was prayer not yet a regular communal religious activity of the Jewish community? Whatever the case, it cannot be denied that the Torah-reading ceremony was central to the synagogue. One religious framework, dominated by the reading of the Torah to the exclusion of prayer, took place during the week when the local priestly course went to Jerusalem to officiate in the Temple. Those remaining behind would gather daily (perhaps in a local synagogue) and read the opening sections of Genesis. Nothing was ever said about the recitation of prayers at this time (Mishna Ta'anît 4:2).

By the first century C.E., a number of supplementary activities had crystallized which served to deepen and broaden the learning experience connected with the Torah reading. By the end of the Second Temple period not only the Jews of the Roman Diaspora, but also those of Israel, required translations of the Hebrew text of the Bible into the vernacular (Fitzmyer 1970: 501–31; Rabin 1976: volume 2, 1007–39). In Alexandria and in most other urban centers of the Roman world, the spoken language of the Jewish community was Greek. In Israel and in many places throughout the

East, Aramaic was widespread, and we have evidence that some Jews in these areas, particularly those living in large urban centers, may have been more comfortable with Greek (Sevester 1968; Mussies 1976: 1040–64).[18] According to tannaitic sources, the Torah was translated verse by verse; with regard to the reading from the Prophets, up to three verses could be read at once and then translated (Mishna Měgîllâ 4:4; T Měgîllâ 3, 20 in Lieberman 1962a: 359; Patte 1975: 49–86). As a result of the extended reading, the amount covered each week was limited, and about three to three and one-half years were required to complete the Torah-reading cycle (Heinemann 1968: 41–48).

The New Testament sources are of particular value in that they describe the Sabbath-morning ritual, focusing on two activities in addition to the Torah reading. One is the reading of the haftarah (that is, from the Prophets), which Jesus was asked to recite when he visited the Nazareth synagogue (Luke 4: 16–22), as well as Paul when he came to the synagogue in Antioch of Pisidia (Acts 13: 13–16).[19] A second activity is the delivering of a homily in connection with the Torah reading. Such a sermon might have preceded or followed the reading on Saturday morning, although later sources mention sermons on Friday night and Saturday afternoon as well (J Sôṭâ 1.4.16a; Yalqût Šimʿônî–Proverbs 964). Taken together with the ceremonial introduction and the removal of the Torah scroll from the ark before and after its reading, these activities constituted the main, if not exclusive, ingredient of synagogue worship (T Měgîllâ 3, 21 in Lieberman 1962a: 356–60).

In light of the archaeological data, and on the basis of what is known from our literary sources about the centrality of the Torah-reading ceremony, it may well be asked why there are no remains of a permanent Torah shrine in any of the four extant pre-70 C.E. synagogues?[20] In the talmudic period, for example, beginning with the third century and becoming even more widespread from the fourth century on, the Torah shrine became a permanent fixture in practically every synagogue. The most plausible answer to our question is that the widespread use and multipurpose nature of the synagogue did not allow for the permanent introduction of Torah scrolls into the main hall. Despite the importance of the religious component of the synagogue, the building itself had to remain as "neutral" as possible. The need to define the large central room as a sanctuary by building a permanent installation to house the scrolls emerged only several centuries after the destruction of the Second Temple and was related to the increasing tendency of the people to define itself more and more in religious terms. The increased usage of Jewish symbols in this later period—the menorah, Torah shrine, *lûlāb*, shofar, etc.—further attests to this need. The reasons for this development are not entirely clear. Perhaps they were contingent upon the increasing importance of Christianity, at least in certain locales.

Perhaps there is even a connection between the diversity of extant pre-70 C.E. synagogue buildings and the emphasis on the Torah-reading ceremony. Synagogues require a specific orientation and thus a degree of uniformity only when prayer is one of the focal activities. From biblical times prayer was said facing Jerusalem and the Holy Temple. However, there is no such requirement regarding the reading of the Torah. Consequently, one can understand the enormous diversity in synagogue building plans of this period. The lack of uniformity, particularly in regard to orientation, a cardinal factor in later synagogues, would seem to indicate the relative unimportance of prayer as a required congregational activity.

Nevertheless, the place of prayer in the ancient synagogue remains in question. Prayer per se was of course well known from biblical times, both in its spontaneous individual and in its institutionalized form (Greenberg 1976: 57–92; 1982: 896–922; 1983). The latter was largely restricted to the Temple setting (Haran 1979: 182–85), the former might have found expression on any occasion. Prayer appears regularly in the late biblical and apocryphal books written during the Second Temple period (Johnson 1948). Some of the prayers that later formed the backbone of Jewish synagogue liturgy had already made their appearance, albeit often in embryonic form, by the late Second Temple period. The *Šĕmaʿ* (Deuteronomy 6: 4–9, 11: 13–21; Numbers 15: 37–41) was already being recited daily in the Temple, as was a very partial and primitive form of what were to become its accompanying paragraphs. So, too, were several sections of what later became the *ʿAmîdâ*, the basic prayer in the synagogue liturgy. Only in Yabneh did the *ʿAmîdâ* undergo a final (or almost final) redaction under the leadership of Rabban Gamaliel II (B Bĕrākôt 28b; Cohen 1983). Behind this redaction lay a long period of formulation that spanned generations and perhaps centuries.

Ben Sira states many of the same themes (chapters 36 and 51 in Segal 1959: 355–57), and Baer (1955: 30–36) as well as Bickerman (1962) have pointed out some remarkable Hellenistic parallels. Marmorstein (1943–44) has called attention to a papyrus of liturgical content where many ideas of the *ʿAmîdâ* are to be found, Talmon (1960; 1978) and Weinfeld (1975–76; 1979) have pointed out certain similar themes from Qumran, as has Levi (1896) with regard to the Psalms of Solomon. Liebreich (1961) has suggested that many basic patterns of Jewish prayer are already expressed in the Prayer of the Levites found in Nehemiah 9, yet four hundred years later the Qumran material reflects very little of such a crystallized prayer. Indeed, no text of any synagogue prayer is datable to the Second Temple period, and although such a consideration is not in and of itself decisive, it ought not be totally disregarded in our historical reconstruction.

When the *'Amîdâ* came to be formulated largely as we have it today is a matter of conjecture. There is no way of determining whether the major redaction was indeed Yabnean or somewhat earlier. However, even if one assumes a pre-70 C.E. date for this redaction, it is gratuitous to assume that such a prayer was then part of synagogue liturgy. Given the fluidity of the elements of the *'Amîdâ*, the centrality of the Torah-reading ceremony, and the absence of even one contemporary reference to the existence of synagogue prayer, we must conclude that neither the *'Amîdâ*, nor probably any other prayer, was an established part of synagogue worship at the time (Elbogen 1972: 20–32, 192–93; Alon 1980: 265–72; Cohen 1983; Heinemann 1977: 123–55; Zeitlin 1964: 230–31).

Was there then any sort of organized communal prayer before 70 C.E.? Yes, but as far as the Jews of Israel are concerned, only in very specific and highly defined circumstances. One circumstance was that the early morning Temple ritual for officiating priests included a series of fixed prayers.

> The officer said to them, "Recite the benediction." They recited the benediction and recited the Ten Commandments, the *Šěma'*, and "It shall come to pass," and "And the Lord spoke to Moses." They pronounced three benedictions with the people: "True and certain," and "'Aḇôdâ," and the Priestly blessing, and on the Sabbath they pronounced a further benediction for the outgoing course of priests. (Mishna Tāmîd 5:1)[21]

Prayer also appears to have been an established pattern for at least some of the sects at this time. The Essenes apparently recited prayers several times throughout the day (*War* 2.8.5 [128–29]; Talmon 1960; 1978), and a similar pattern was followed by the Therapeutae of Egypt (Philo, *Contemplative Life* 3 [27–28]; Schürer, Vermes, and Millar 1979: 591–97; Simon 1967: 120–30). Of the Pharisees and Sadducees we know nothing in this regard.[22]

However, the importance of communal prayer finds expression not in Israel but in the Diaspora. The fact that a great many synagogues of the Diaspora (including the one in Tiberias) were called *proseuche*, house of prayer, indicates the important role that prayer played in local Jewish ritual. While we know nothing of the actual prayers recited in these synagogues, it is reasonable to assume that many, if not most, were taken from the Bible or from the practice of the Temple.

A number of suggestions have been offered to explain the difference in the terms *synagogue* and *proseuche* (Schwank 1955: 267–78; Hengel 1975: 39–41). According to one opinion, the difference between them is chronological: *proseuche* was the term in vogue from the third century B.C.E. until the first century C.E. However, even before the common era the term *synagogue* had made its appearance, and by the second century C.E. it had replaced its predecessor. There is an element of truth in this distinction, although it is doubtful whether this can constitute a fully satisfactory explanation. Moreover, the paucity of sources from the Hellenistic era on one hand, and from the Diaspora in the period following the Second Temple destruction on the other, compels us to be extremely cautious in this regard. In another vein, it has been suggested that the *proseuche* was a simpler, more primitive building, as opposed to the synagogue which might have been a basilica in form (at least in Alexandria, according to the Tôseptā'). However, some scholars have argued that the *proseuche* was a large and imposing structure in Tiberias (*Life* 54 [276–82]) and in Alexandria (Philo, *Embassy* 20 [133]), while the contemporary synagogue was far more modest.

More recently, Hengel has suggested a geographical differentiation for these terms. According to him, the term *proseuche* refers to a Diaspora setting, while *synagogue* is characteristic of Judaea (1975: 41–54). Thus, Egyptian Jewish sources (both epigraphic and literary) as well as Greco-Roman authors employ the term *proseuche*, while Josephus, the New Testament, and rabbinic sources almost always use the term *synagogue* when referring to a Judaean context.

None of the above explanations is above criticism. The chronological distinction does not apply in many cases, and certainly not in the critical first century C.E. when both terms were in use. And if indeed the chronological distinction is valid, what caused the change in nomenclature? Was the change totally bereft of any religious or social significance? The claim that the distinction indicated a more or less ornate building is meaningless, since our sources are contradictory on this point. An imposing Alexandrian synagogue is called *proseuche* by Philo, but another, no less imposing one (or was it the same one?) is called *synagogue* in rabbinic sources. Or, for example, the imposing Tiberias structure was referred to by Josephus as a *synagogue*, while the far more modest structure at Delos bore the same name. In the end, the geographic distinction by Hengel appears to be the most convincing, although even here there are some exceptions that might undermine the rule. It seems all too clear that originally *proseuche* did not carry a geographical connotation. Rather it seems to have reflected a difference with regard to the ritual conducted therein.

We have seen that the Torah-reading ceremony with its accompanying activities constituted the main and, at times, exclusive ingredient of synagogue worship in Israel. The place of prayer was more problematic. It differed from place to place, and we can assume that it played a more central role in the *proseuche*, as the name itself indicates. Moreover, it is clear that Jerusalem synagogues did not have formal congregational services. Those wishing to pray in a public context would do so at the Temple at the appointed times, as evidenced in the New Testament (Acts 3:1). It is probably for this reason that prayer was omitted in the list of synagogue activities recorded in the Theodotus inscription. The role of prayer in synagogues outside Jerusalem, in Judaea proper, the Galilee, Transjordan, and along the coast is more complex. For those coming to Jerusalem infrequently, it is likely that some form of organized prayer took place in the synagogues (Matthew 6:5), although the Torah reading always remained focal.[23]

Three factors may account for the difference between the synagogue and *proseuche*. First, it is likely that the distance from the Temple and the inability to visit on a regular basis may have induced Diaspora Jewry to create a fuller religious experience than what was deemed necessary or desirable by most Jews living in Israel. Second, the use of hymns and prayers by Hellenistic religious associations may have influenced the customs and practices of Diaspora Jewry, which included prayers and hymns as an integral element in their worship, in addition, of course, to the reading and study of the Torah (Hengel 1975: 33–35). Finally, Jews living in the Diaspora, among a gentile population, may have wished to give their main communal institution a name with a more clearly religious connotation —*proseuche* rather than *synagogue*—in order to highlight its uniqueness vis-à-vis the surrounding culture.

In Israel, on the other hand, the proximity of the Temple, the somewhat less-intense contact with non-Jewish surroundings (except for those Jewish communities in the large Hellenistic cities), and the traditional conservatism of the farmer (who composed the vast majority of the Jewish population in the country as opposed to the largely urban-dwelling Diaspora), almost certainly minimized the need to expand the religious expression in the synagogue. Moreover, it is generally recognized that, at least in Israel, many elements of the nonsacrificial Temple religious practice were transferred to the synagogue. Among other things, this refers to the recitation of the *Šĕma‘* sections of the ‘*Amîdâ*, the *Hallēl*, confessions and the *Taḥanûn* prayer, various psalms (including those for the different days of the week), the priestly blessing, blowing the shofar on Rosh Hashanah when it falls on the Sabbath, using the *lûlāḇ*, and reciting *Hôšā‘nôt* throughout the Sukkoth holiday (Heinemann 1977: 123–55).[24] The above constituted a significant part of the worship service in the synagogue during the talmudic period. When this transference took place is unknown. Chances are that much, if not most, was appropriated only after 70 C.E. As noted above, we have no evidence for these practices in a synagogue setting prior to the destruction of the Second Temple. In that case either earlier patterns of worship in the pre-70 synagogue were lost, or such patterns never existed and only after the Second Temple destruction were Temple practices adopted to create a new synagogue liturgy. The latter alternative is more likely.

We have returned to the starting point of our study. Once again, the distinction between *proseuche* and *synagogue* emphasizes the multifarious character of the synagogue during the Second Temple period. It is reasonable to assume that this variety was especially noticeable among synagogues in different regions, particularly in the Diaspora. This was the result, in part, of local influences on the size, shape, and, at times, form of the particular synagogue. An example of such variety, albeit from a slightly later period, can be found in the third-century synagogues of Dura Europos and Sardis (Seager 1972; 1973; Kraabel 1981: 79–91). Moreover, on the basis of our limited first-century sources from Cyrenaica and Rome, one can also point out significant differences and widely varying practices in each locale (Applebaum 1979; Leon 1960).

Parallels between the Egyptian *proseuche* and local pagan shrines are illuminating and provide us with rich data regarding the nature and extent of local influence. As was the case with these pagan institutions, local Jewish houses of worship were dedicated to the Ptolemaic royal family, and at least one served as a place of asylum. Many appear to have been planned similarly to pagan temples, and synagogue officials sometimes bore titles very like those of their pagan counterparts. Here, of course, we must be careful not to overstate the elements of dependency and imitation. Borrowing was always selective, and the uniqueness of the *proseuche* was evident not only in what was not borrowed but also in the adaptation of what was indeed adopted. For instance, the Jewish sanctuary was not named after a deity, as were the Serapeion, Isieion, and Apolloneion; it was simply called a *proseuche*. Ptolemaic rulers were indeed mentioned in synagogue inscriptions, however they never appear with their divine epithets as they do in pagan contexts (Hengel 1975: 35; Dion 1977: 45–55).

The variety that characterized the early synagogue strengthens one of the suggestions presented at the outset of this paper. At the end of the Second Temple period the synagogue was still a relatively young institution, whose outward forms, patterns, rules, and rituals were far from crystallized. Throughout this period the synagogue was in the process of gradual development, and, as a result, its form and nature differed from place to place. The first-century synagogue was the product of initiatives and innovations that had occurred over many generations (if not centuries) and was widespread over many lands. In a sense this process never really ended, although the rate of change and range of diversity, both internally and externally, diminished somewhat in the centuries following the destruction of the Temple. Even then, however, the synagogue continued to develop, and by the end of antiquity it had a crystallized form and structure far different from what had existed in the pre-70 C.E. era.

Notes

1 It is noteworthy that attacks on Jewish communities both in Israel and the Diaspora were directed in many cases against their main institution, the synagogue. Such was the case in Alexandria (Philo, *Flaccus* 6 [41–43]), Caesarea (*War* 2.14.4–5 [285–91]), and Dor (*Antiquities* 19.6.3 [300–3]).

2 Despite the absence of data, there has been no dearth of attempts to establish a date for the origin of the synagogue. Such theories are usually based on a biblical statement taken to imply the existence of a nonsacrificial religious framework, a likely historical *sitz im leben* for the emergence of such an institution, or later indirect evidence (inscriptions and rabbinic traditions). Opinions have ranged over some five centuries, from the seventh to the second centuries B.C.E. Convenient summaries of the many opinions put forward on these questions can be found in Krauss 1966: 52–66; Schrage 1971: 810–12; Gutmann 1972: 36–40.

3 Practically all evidence prior to the first century C.E. comes from Hellenistic Egypt. Most of it is epigraphic. See Tcherikover, Fuks, and Stern 1957–64: volume 3, 138–44 as well as 3 Maccabees 3:7. The only building that served as a synagogue during this period was found at Delos.

4 Although there is much controversy over the phrase "God's assembly-places," it probably refers to temporary religious frameworks that existed in Judaea just prior to the destruction of the First Temple in 586 B.C.E., and that might have become more firmly crystallized as a result of Josiah's reforms in 622 B.C.E. However, the influence of these assembly places on the later development of the synagogue appears to have been slight, if any. Many, however, have assumed that this psalm refers to the persecution of the Jews by Antiochus, a suggestion that appears unlikely for a number of reasons. See, for example, Momigliano 1975: 107; Gelston 1984: 82–87; Donner 1972: 41–49; Johnson 1979: 132–33.

5 The precise location of the water gate is unclear. It would be natural to assume that a gate with such a name would be located immediately above the Gîḥôn spring. However, the designation in Nehemiah seems to indicate a point further north, closer to the Temple precincts. Most scholars have chosen the latter conclusion (Burrows 1934: 130; Vincent 1954: 248–49; Avi-Yonah 1954: 247; Simons 1952: 246).

6 The following short titles are used in this article to refer to the works of Josephus: *Apion* for *Against Apion*; *Life* for *The Life*; *War* for *The Jewish War*; and *Antiquities* for *Jewish Antiquities*.

7 For those general readers who are unfamiliar with rabbinic literature, there are many good books on the subject; see, for example, Strack 1969.

8 Rectangular in plan, the Masada synagogue is located at the northwestern edge of the summit and measures 12.5 by 10.5 meters. The main hall had four tiers of benches, except for the northwest side, which had one. The entrance was in the middle of the southeast side. The building had two rows of columns, one row on the south side with three columns, and one row on the north with two. A small room (3.6 by 5.5 meters) was in the northwest corner, where the scrolls used in the synagogue service were stored (Yadin 1966: 181–91; 1977: 809–10; Hüttenmeister and Reeg 1977: 314–15).

9 The Herodium synagogue was rectangular, 10.6 by 15.15 meters. Its roof was supported by four columns, and it had three entrances to the east. Benches were found on three, possibly four, sides, and a *miqḇe*, or ritual bath, was located just outside the entrance (Foerster 1976: 509; 1981: 24–29; Hüttenmeister and Reeg 1977: 173–74).

10 Located by the sea in a residential area of the city, the main room was 16.90 by 14.40 meters, and was later divided into two smaller ones. A single marble bench lined most of the western and northern walls, with a large ornate chair in the middle of the western one.

This may well be an example of the "Seat of Moses" mentioned in our literary sources. In the second stage of the building one entrance faced the courtyard to the east and three opened to a room on the south (Mazur 1935: 15–24; Goodenough 1953–68: volume 2, 71–75; Bruneau 1970: 480–93; 1982: 465–504; Kraabel 1979: 491–94; 1984: 44–46).

11 The proposed synagogue measures 19.6 by 15.10 meters and has four rows of columns and a main entrance from the southwest. It is lined on four sides with benches.

12 These references, however, are to post-70 C.E. synagogues, as are the many references in Aramaic synagogue inscriptions to אתרה קדישה, "the holy place" (Naveh 1978: 34, 48, 77, 95, 99, 100).

13 The following short titles are used in this article to refer to the works of Philo: *Embassy* for *The Embassy to Gaius*; *Contemplative Life* for *On the Contemplative Life*; *Special Laws* for *On the Special Laws*; and *Dreams* for *On Dreams*.

14 For a summary of these functions, see Krauss 1966: 182–98; Schrage 1971: 821–28; Levine 1981: 3–4. On the origin of the synagogue as a communal-"secular" institution, see Löw 1884: 97 and following; Krauss 1966: 53–56; Zeitlin 1930–31: 69–81. Compare also the reservations of Landsberger 1949: 149–55.

15 See also Schürer, Vermes, and Millar 1979: volume 2, 417–20; Safrai 1976: volume 2, 945–58.

16 For a later period, J Bĭkkûrîm 1.5.64a; Epiphanius, *Panarion* 30, 11.

17 As reflected in rabbinic literature, see J Bĕrākôt 2.5d; J Šabbāt 1.3a. On the parallel with Hellenistic religious associations, see Roberts, Skeat, and Nock 1936: 47–48.

18 For two remarkable rabbinic reports on the knowledge of Greek in the second and third centuries, see B Sôṭâ 49b; J Sôṭâ 7.21b.

19 Regarding the canonization of the Scriptures in the Hasmonean period, and not essentially in Yabneh, see Leiman 1976; Patte 1975: 39–42.

20 It is important to remember that, archaeologically speaking, we are dealing with small communities (Masada, Herodium, and even Gamla). It is quite possible that in urban centers the synagogue was one of several large buildings and was more geared to the religious dimension, that is, there may have been a permanent Torah shrine therein. However, this is only speculative at this point, owing to the total absence of urban synagogal remains.

21 See also Mishna Yômā' 7:1; T Yômā' 3, 18 in Lieberman 1962a: 247 and parallels.

22 See, for example, T Bĕrākôt 3, 3 in Lieberman 1955: 15 and parallels.

23 The Mishna (Nĕdārîm 2:4) informs us of certain differences between the Galilee and Judaea regarding the population's awareness of the Temple and its ritual. In the Galilee such awareness was far less prevalent. Perhaps the same holds true for synagogue practice, particularly as regards those elements which were often associated with the Temple.

24 This fundamental dependence on Temple practice is likewise reflected in the *taqqānôt* of Rabban Yoḥanan ben Zakkai (Mishna Rosh Hashanah 4: 1–4; B Rosh Hashanah 21b, 31b) and by the dictum, "Prayers were instituted in place of sacrifices" (B Bĕrākôt 26b; J Bĕrākôt 4.1.7b).

Bibliography

Alon, G.
  1980   *The Jews in Their Land in the Talmudic Period*. Translated by G. Levi, from Hebrew, 1957–58. Jerusalem: Magnes.

Applebaum, S.
  1979   *Jews and Greeks in Ancient Cyrene*. Leiden, The Netherlands: Brill.

Avi-Yonah, M.
1954   The Walls of Jerusalem – A Minimalist View. *Israel Exploration Journal* 4: 239–48.
Bacher, W.
1897   Le siège de Moïse. *Revue des études juives* 34: 299–301.
Baer, Y. F.
1955   *Israel among the Nations.* Jerusalem: Bialik (Hebrew).
Bickerman, E.
1958   The Altars of the Gentiles: A Note on the Jewish "ius sacrum." *Revue Internationale des Droits de l'Antiquité* 5: 137–64.
1962   The Civic Prayer of Jerusalem. *Harvard Theological Review* 55: 163–85.
Billerbeck, P.
1964   Ein Synagogengottesdienst in Jesu Tagen. *Zeitschrift für Neutestamentlichen Wissenschaft* 55: 143–61.
Bokser, B.
1984   *The Origins of the Seder.* Berkeley, Calif.: University of California Press.
Bruneau, P.
1970   *Recherches sur les cultes de Délos à l'époque hellénistique et à l'époque impériale.* Paris: Boccard.
1982   Les Israélites de Délos et la juiverie Délienne. *Bulletin de Correspondence Hellénistique* 100: 465–504.
Burrows, M.
1934   *Nehemiah 3: 1–32 as a Source for the Topography of Ancient Jerusalem.* Series: *Annual of the American Schools of Oriental Research* 14: 115–40.
Campbell, E. F.
1979   Jewish Shrines of the Hellenistic and Persian Periods. In *Symposia Celebrating the Seventy-fifth Anniversary of the Founding of the American Schools of Oriental Research (1900–1975),* edited by F. M. Cross, pages 159–67. Cambridge, Mass.: American Schools of Oriental Research.
Cohen, N.
1983   The Nature of Shim'on Hapakuli's Act. *Tarbiz* 52: 547–55 (Hebrew).
Cohen, S. J. D.
1984   The Temple and the Synagogue. In *The Temple in Antiquity,* edited by T. G. Madsen, pages 151–74. Provo, Utah: Brigham Young University.
Dion, P. E.
1977   Synagogues et temples dans l'Egypte hellénistique. *Science et Esprit* 29: 45–75.
Donner, H.
1972   Argumente zur Datierung des 74. Psalms. In *Wort, Lied, und Gottesspruch: Beiträge zu Psalmen und Propheten: Festschrift für Joseph Ziegler,* edited by J. Schreiner, pages 41–49. Würzburg, Germany: Echter.
Elbogen, I.
1972   *Prayer in Israel.* Translated by J. Heinemann, from German, 1931. Jerusalem: Dvir (Hebrew).
Fitzmyer, J.
1970   Languages of Palestine in the First Century A.D. *Catholic Biblical Quarterly* 32: 501–31.
Foerster, G.
1973   The Synagogues at Masada and Herodium. *Eretz Israel* 11: 224–28 (Hebrew).
1976   Herodium. In *Encyclopaedia of Archaeological Excavations in the Holy Land,* volume 2, edited by M. Avi-Yonah and E. Stern, pages 502–10. Jerusalem: Israel Exploration Society and Massada Press.

1981   The Synagogues at Masada and Herodium. In *Ancient Synagogues Revealed*, edited
          by Lee I. Levine, pages 24–29. Jerusalem: Israel Exploration Society.

Frey, P. J.-B.
1936–52   *Corpvs Inscriptionvm Ivdaicarvm*. Rome: Pontificio Instituto di Archeologia
          Christiana.

Friedmann, M., editor
1880   *Pesikta Rabbati*. Vienna: Kaiser.

Gelston, A.
1984   A Note on Psalm LXXIV 8. *Vetus Testamentum* 34: 82–87.

Ginsburger, M.
1931   La chaire de Moïse. *Revue des études juives* 90: 161–65.

Goodenough, E.
1953–68   *Jewish Symbols in the Greco-Roman Period*. 13 volumes. New York: Pantheon.

Greenberg, M.
1976   On the Refinement of the Conception of Prayer in Hebrew Scriptures. *AJS
          Review* 1: 57–92.

1982   Prayer. In *Encyclopedia Biblica*, volume 8, edited by B. Mazar, pages 896–922.
          Jerusalem: Bialik (Hebrew).

1984   *Biblical Prose Prayer*. Berkeley, Calif.: University of California Press.

Gutman, S.
1981   The Synagogue at Gamla. In *Ancient Synagogues Revealed*, edited by Lee I. Levine,
          pages 30–34. Jerusalem: Israel Exploration Society.

Gutmann, J.
1972   The Origin of the Synagogue. *Archäologischer Anzeiger* 87: 36–40.

Haran, M.
1979   Priest, Temple and Worship. *Tarbiz* 48: 175–85.

Heinemann, J.
1968   The Triennial Lectionary Cycle. *Journal of Jewish Studies* 19: 41–48.

1977   *Prayer in the Talmud: Forms and Patterns*. Berlin: de Gruyter.

Hengel, M.
1966   Die Synagogeninschrift von Stobi. *Zeitschrift für Neutestamentlichen Wissenschaft* 57:
          167–72.

1975   Proseuche und Synagoge. In *The Synagogue, Studies in Origin, Archeology and Archi-
          tecture*, edited by J. Gutmann, pages 27–54. New York: Ktav.

Hoenig, S. B.
1979   The Ancient City-Square: The Forerunner of the Synagogue. In *Aufstieg und
          Niedergang der römischen Welt*, part 2, volume 19.1, edited by H. Temporini and
          W. Haase, pages 448–76. Berlin: de Gruyter.

Hüttenmeister, F.; and Reeg, G.
1977   *Die antiken Synagogen in Israel*. 2 volumes. Wiesbaden, W. Ger.: Reichert.

Johnson, A. R.
1979   *The Cultic Prophet and Israel's Psalmody*. Cardiff, U.K.: University of Wales.

Johnson, N.
1948   *Prayer in the Apocrypha and Pseudepigrapha*. Philadelphia, Pa.: Society of Biblical
          Literature.

Katz, S.
1984   Issues in the Separation of Judaism and Christianity after 70 C.E.: A Reconsidera-
          tion. *Journal of Biblical Literature* 103: 63–76.

Kimelman, R.
1981   Birkat Ha-Minim and the Lack of Evidence for an Anti-Christian Jewish Prayer
         in Late Antiquity. In *Jewish and Christian Self-Definition*, volume 2, edited by J. A.
         Sanders et al., pages 226–44. Philadelphia, Pa.: Fortress.
Kraabel, A. T.
1979   The Diaspora Synagogue: Archeological and Epigraphic Evidence since Sukenik.
         In *Aufstieg und Niedergang der römischen Welt*, part 2, volume 19.1, edited by
         H. Temporini and W. Haase, pages 477–510. Berlin: de Gruyter.
1981   Social Systems of Six Diaspora Synagogues. In *Ancient Synagogues: The State of
         Research*, edited by J. Gutmann, pages 79–91. Chico, Calif.: Scholars.
1984   New Evidence of the Samaritan Diaspora has been Found in Delos. *Biblical
         Archaeologist* 47: 44–46.
Kraeling, C.
1979   *The Excavations at Dura Europos – The Synagogue*. Reprint. New York: Ktav.
Krauss, S.
1966   *Synagogale Altertümer*. Reprint. Hildesheim, W. Ger.: Olms.
Landsberger, F.
1949   The House of the People. *Hebrew Union College Annual* 22: 149–55.
1959   The Sacred Direction in Synagogue and Church. *Hebrew Union College Annual* 28:
         181–203.
Leiman, S.
1976   *The Canonization of Hebrew Scripture: The Talmudic and Midrashic Evidence*. Hamden,
         Eng.: Archon.
Leon, H.
1960   *The Jews of Ancient Rome*. Philadelphia, Pa.: Jewish Publication Society.
Lerle, E.
1968   Liturgische Reformen des Synagogengottesdienstes als Antwort auf die Juden-
         christliche Mission des ersten Jahrhunderts. *Novum Testamentum* 10: 31–42.
Levertoff, P.
1932   Worship in the First Century. In *Liturgy and Worship*, edited by W. K. L. Clarke,
         pages 60–71. London: Society for Promoting Christian Knowledge.
Lévi, I.
1896   Les dix-huit bénédictions et les Psaumes de Salomon. *Revue des études juives* 32:
         161–78.
Levine, L. I.
1981   Ancient Synagogues – A Historical Introduction. In *Ancient Synagogues
         Revealed*, edited by Lee I. Levine, pages 1–10. Jerusalem: Israel Exploration
         Society.
1984   The Roman Period from the Conquest of Pompey to the End of the Second
         Temple Period. In *The History of Eretz Israel*, volume 4, edited by M. Stern, pages
         9–281. Jerusalem: Keter (Hebrew).
Lieberman, S.
1955   *The Tosefta – Zera'im*. New York: Jewish Theological Seminary.
1962a   *The Tosefta – Mo'ed*. New York: Jewish Theological Seminary.
1962b   *Tosefta Ki-Fshutah*, volume 4. New York: Jewish Theological Seminary.
Liebreich, L.
1961   The Impact of Nehemiah 9: 5–37 on the Liturgy of the Synagogue. *Hebrew Union
         College Annual* 32: 227–37.
Lifshitz, B.
1967   *Donateurs et fondateurs dans les synagogues juives*. Paris: Gabalda.

Löw, L.
1884   Der synagogale Ritus. *Monatschrift der Geschichte und Wissenschaft des Judentums* 33: 97 and following.

Ma'oz, Z.
1981   The Synagogue of Gamla and the Typology of Second-Temple Synagogues. In *Ancient Synagogues Revealed*, edited by Lee I. Levine, pages 35–41. Jerusalem: Israel Exploration Society.

Marcus, R., and Wikgren, A., translators
1963   *Josephus VIII: Jewish Antiquities, Books XV–XVII.* Cambridge, Mass., and London: Harvard and Heinemann.

Marmorstein, A.
1943–44 The Oldest Form of the Eighteen Benedictions. *Jewish Quarterly Review* 34: 137–59.

Mazur, B.
1935   *Studies on Jewry in Greece.* Athens: Hestia.

Momigliano, A.
1975   *Alien Wisdom: The Limits of Hellenization.* Cambridge, Eng.: Cambridge University.

Mussies, G.
1976   Greek in Palestine and the Diaspora. In *The Jewish People in the First Century*, volume 2, edited by S. Safrai and M. Stern, pages 1040–64. Philadelphia, Pa.: Fortress.

Naveh, J.
1978   *On Mosaics and Stone.* Jerusalem: Israel Exploration Society (Hebrew).

Patte, D.
1975   *Early Jewish Hermeneutic in Palestine.* Missoula, Mont.: Scholars.

Rabin, C.
1976   Hebrew and Aramaic. In *The Jewish People in the First Century*, volume 2, edited by S. Safrai and M. Stern, pages 1007–39. Philadelphia, Pa.: Fortress.

Renov, I.
1955   The Seat of Moses. *Israel Exploration Journal* 5: 262–67.

Roberts, C.; Skeat, T.; and Nock, A. D.
1936   The Gild of Zeus Hypsistos. *Harvard Theological Review* 29: 39–87.

Roth, C.
1949   The "Chair of Moses" and its Survivals. *Palestine Exploration Quarterly* 81: 100–11.

Safrai, S.
1976   Education and the Study of Torah. In *The Jewish People in the First Century*, volume 2, edited by S. Safrai and M. Stern, pages 945–70. Philadelphia, Pa.: Fortress.

1983   *The Late Second Temple and Mishnaic Periods.* Jerusalem: Ministry of Education and Culture (Hebrew).

Safrai, Z.
1981   Communal Functions of the Synagogue in Eretz Israel during the Mishnaic and Talmudic Periods. In *Festschrift for M. Wizer*, edited by S. Schmidt, pages 230–48. Yabneh (Hebrew).

Schiffman, L.
1979   Communal Meals at Qumran. *Revue de Qumran* 10: 45–56.

Schrage, W.
1971   "συναγωγή". *Theological Dictionary of the New Testament.* Grand Rapids, Mich.: Eerdmans.

Schürer, E.; Vermes, G.; and Millar, F.
1979   *The History of the Jewish People in the Age of Jesus Christ.* Revised edition, volume 2. Edinburgh, Scotland: Clarke.

Schwabe, M.
1956   Greek Inscriptions. In *Sepher Yerushalayim* (*The Book of Jerusalem*), volume 1, edited by M. Avi-Yonah, pages 362–65. Jerusalem and Tel Aviv: Bialik and Dvir (Hebrew).
Schwank, B.
1955   Qualis erat forma synagogarum Novi Testamenti. *Verbum Domini* 33: 267–78.
Seager, A.
1972   The Building History of the Sardis Synagogue. *American Journal of Archeology* 76: 425–35.
1973   The Architecture of the Dura and Sardis Synagogues. In *The Dura Europos Synagogue*, edited by J. Gutmann, pages 79–116. Missoula, Mont.: Scholars.
1981   The Synagogue at Sardis. In *Ancient Synagogues Revealed*, edited by Lee I. Levine, pages 178–84. Jerusalem: Israel Exploration Society.
Segal, A.
1977   *Two Powers in Heaven*. Leiden, The Netherlands: Brill.
Segal, M.
1959   *The Complete Book of Ben Sira*. Jerusalem: Bialik (Hebrew).
Sevester, J. N.
1968   *Do You Know Greek?* Leiden, The Netherlands: Brill.
Simon, M.
1967   *Jewish Sects at the Time of Jesus*. Philadelphia, Pa.: Fortress.
Simons, J.
1952   *Jerusalem in the Old Testament*. Leiden, The Netherlands: Brill.
Stern, M.
1974–84 *Greek and Latin Authors on Jews and Judaism*. 3 volumes. Jerusalem: Israel Academy for Sciences and the Humanities.
Strack, H. L.
1969   *Introduction to the Talmud and Midrash*. New York: Atheneum.
Sukenik, E. L.
1934   *Ancient Synagogues in Palestine and Greece*. London: Milford.
Talmon, S.
1960   The "Manual of Benedictions" of the Sect of the Judaean Desert. *Revue de Qumran* 8: 475–500.
1978   The Emergence of Institutionalized Prayer in Israel in the Light of the Qumran Literature. In *Qumran: sa piété, sa théologie, et son milieu*, edited by M. Delcor, pages 265–84. Paris: Duculot.
Tcherikover, V.; Fuks, A.; and Stern, M.
1957–64 *Corpus Papyrorum Judaicarum*. 3 volumes. Cambridge, Mass.: Harvard University Press.
Theodor, J., and Albeck, C., editors
1965   *Midrash Bereshit Rabba*. Jerusalem: Wahrmann.
Vincent, H.
1954   *Jérusalem de l'ancien Testament*, volume 1. Paris: Gabala.
Weinfeld, M.
1975–76 Traces of Qĕdûšat Yôṣēr and Pĕsûqê dĕ-Zimrâ in the Qûmrân Literature and in Ben Sirā'. *Tarbiz* 45: 15–26 (Hebrew).
1979   The Prayers for Knowledge, Repentance and Forgiveness in the "Eighteen Benedictions" – Qumran Parallels, Biblical Antecedents and Basic Characteristics. *Tarbiz* 48: 186–200 (Hebrew).

Yadin, Y.
  1966   *Masada.* New York: Random House.
  1977   Masada. In *Encyclopaedia of Archaeological Excavations in the Holy Land,* volume 3, edited by M. Avi-Yonah and E. Stern, pages 793–816. Jerusalem: Israel Exploration Society.
Zeitlin, S.
  1930–31 The Origin of the Synagogue. *Proceedings of the American Academy for Jewish Research* 2: 69–81.
  1964   The Tefillah, the Shemoneh Esreh: An Historical Study of the First Canonization of the Hebrew Liturgy. *Jewish Quarterly Review* 54: 230–31.
Zuckermandel, M. S., editor
  1963   *Tosephta.* Jerusalem: Wahrmann.

2. The Dead Sea Scrolls and the Early History of Jewish Liturgy

Lawrence H. Schiffman

One of the most serious problems confronting the student of the Dead Sea Scrolls is evaluating the significance of the scrolls for the reconstruction of the history of Judaism. The Qumran scrolls, emanating from the Hasmonean and Herodian periods, are the earliest postbiblical Hebrew texts that throw light on the varieties of Judaism during the Second Commonwealth. On one hand, much of what is encountered in the Dead Sea Scrolls can be explained as the result of the peculiar ideology of the Qumran sect. On the other hand, much of the material may represent the common beliefs and practices of the Judaism of the time.

How can we determine if given practices are, in fact, typical for Jews of the period, or if they belong only to the sectarians of Qumran? It would be easy to answer this question if we possessed documents from the Pharisees, Sadducees, or the large group later termed the *'Am Hā-'āreṣ* which would allow us to make comparisons. However, for the period in which the Qumran scrolls were authored, we have only the account of Josephus and the scanty traditions of the *tannā'îm*. In both cases, the material must be closely evaluated in terms of date and tendentiousness. Even more important, differences between religious groups constituted a subject of interest, whereas common beliefs and practices did not, so the latter naturally tended to be deemphasized by authors while the former were often stressed.

It is in the methodological context just outlined that we approach the question of liturgy as reflected in the Qumran scrolls and the significance of these scrolls for the early history of Jewish liturgy. We shall attempt to evaluate the liturgical patterns in evidence at Qumran and to compare them with what is known of the early rabbinic traditions. When we have assembled a handsome list of parallels, we shall ask what their significance is and what conclusions may be drawn from them. The first part of this study will summarize the observations that emerge from the more well-known texts. The second will concentrate on the recently published materials from Cave 4.

Temple and Synagogue

The sect that left us the Dead Sea Scrolls removed itself voluntarily from Hellenistic Jerusalem, most probably out of protest against the Hasmonean takeover of the high priesthood. Among its initial leaders were certainly members of the House of Ṣādôq, the priestly family that had dominated the high priesthood during virtually all the years of the First and Second Temples (see Schiffman 1975: 72–75). These priests, together with those who followed them to Qumran in the Judaean desert, forswore participation in the Jerusalem cult because of the manner in which it was conducted. They maintained that violations of the Law marred the Temple and that its priests were illegitimate (Cross 1971: 75–89). Presumably, the founders of the sect believed that the Jerusalem cult no longer served as a vehicle for contact between Israel and its God, and they therefore saw no value in their continued participation in it. Retiring to Qumran, they had to live a Judaism devoid of Temple and cult, a Judaism in which prayer, purity, study, and sectarian life itself served as a replacement for the Temple. Therefore, the sect viewed itself as a sanctuary that brought its members into the very same forms of contact with the Lord that they formerly experienced through cultic worship (Gärtner 1965). Despite some claims to the contrary, sacrifices were not performed at Qumran (Schiffman 1983: 201).

The situation that faced the *tannā'îm* in the early Yabnean period was very similar. Judaism had long been based on sacrificial worship in which Israel's relationship with God was secured through the proper and orderly conduct of the rites required by the levitical codes. Now, in the aftermath of the Great Revolt of 66–74 C.E., there was no longer any cult. The priest no longer sacrificed; the Levite no longer sang; Israel no longer made pilgrimages to the holy Temple. Henceforth, only prayer and the life of rabbinic piety could ensure Israel's continued link to its Father in Heaven.

It is naive to assume that this eventuality came upon Pharisaic-rabbinic Judaism with no warning. Indeed, our historical hindsight allows us to see that throughout the Second Commonwealth period, cult was on the wane, and prayer and liturgy were on the rise. Gradually, prayer was making more and more inroads even in the Temple. Those distant from the Temple turned increasingly to prayer in the Second Commonwealth period. Pharisaism, in translating Temple purity to the home and table, had helped to free the later sages from the inexorability of cult. But what seems most important to us in the context of this study is that the Qumran sect had long ago demonstrated how to live a Jewish life without a Temple. They had, as we shall see, developed both a liturgy and an ideology to accommodate their absence from the Temple (see Bokser 1977; 1984: 4–13).

Nevertheless, throughout its days the sect yearned not for the restoration of the Temple, since in their view it continued to function (albeit improperly), but for the return of their own priestly leaders to dominance of the cult. This, to them, was tantamount to its restoration. It would mean the establishment of the New Jerusalem (Barthélemy and Milik 1955: 134–35; Baillet, Milik, and de Vaux 1962: 84–89, 184–93) and of the ties that would then unite Israel and the God of Israel. In the end of days, the priests of the sect would officiate at the Temple, guaranteeing its efficacy and ensuring its utmost purity. Until that day, the sectarians would have to be satisfied with the efficacy of prayer and with the study of texts dealing with the worship and cult of the Temple at which they would neither serve nor offer sacrifice.

The Zadokite Fragments (CDC) 11: 21–22 make reference to some kind of place of worship:

וכל הבא אל בית השתחות אל יבא טמא כבום

And anyone who enters the house of prostration let him not come in a state of impurity requiring washing *(ṭĕmē' kībbûs)* . . .

The remainder of the passage is quite difficult. Nonetheless, this text seems to indicate that the sectarians who were scattered in the towns and cities of Palestine established permanent places of sanctity for the conduct of sacred services. However, there is no evidence of the establishment of a synagogue or anything like it, in the sense of a fixed place of prayer, among the archaeological remains from Qumran. In fact, the Qumran settlement predates the earliest excavated synagogues in Palestine. It seems, therefore, that community prayers, certainly part of the life of the Qumran sectarians, were conducted in premises used for other purposes, perhaps in the dining hall. A special building for worship would not be necessary at the sectarian center at Qumran since the entire settlement was dedicated to this purpose. Such a house of worship would be needed only by those who lived elsewhere in the Land of Israel.

The Liturgical Texts

Based on a detailed study of the poem which concludes the Manual of Discipline, S. Talmon (1958–59; 1959–60) has suggested that there was a detailed series of prayer texts for the various times of prayer of the sect. He maintained that the sect prayed three times each day and three times each evening, a matter to which we will return. Talmon identified allusions to the reading of the *Šĕmaʿ* and a proto-ʿ*Amîdâ*. He also found evidence for specific rituals for festivals, new moons, Sabbaths, the Day of Atonement, Sabbatical and Jubilee years. While we will see that there is reason to question his conclusions regarding the six daily prayer times, liturgies for the various occasions he listed have now been identified in Cave 4.

A text that may bear on the question of organized liturgy at Qumran is 11QPsa (Sanders 1965; 1967). This scroll contains canonical and non-canonical psalms, as well as numerous other interesting poetic texts. This text, when originally identified, was regarded as a scroll of psalms (Sanders 1971). It is, in fact, a liturgical collection (compare Talmon 1965–66: 215; Skehan 1973, 1975). Many of the canonical psalms in this text are exactly the same as those utilized in the later rabbinic liturgy. Even the organization of the psalms in the scroll seems to parallel the conceptual framework of the later rabbinic prayerbook. Most important, many of the selections that figure in talmudic discussions as part of the prayer services appear here with liturgical responses included in them. Clearly, these very same psalms, most notably Psalm 145, were used in liturgical context by the Qumran sect.

It is tempting to see the Hôdāyôt Scroll (Sukenik 1954–55; Licht 1957) as a series of hymns for public worship. In fact, there is no evidence for the liturgical nature of this material. These poems are individual plaints, perhaps composed by a leader of the sect, maybe even the teacher of righteousness, and they concentrate on serious matters of theology and belief. These poems are certainly not part of a regular order of prayers (contrast Holm-Nielsen 1971: 1047).

Numerous fragments found in the Qumran caves have been classified by scholars as liturgies. While many of these fragments are at best insubstantial, the material recently published in *Discoveries in the Judaean Desert*, volume 7 (Baillet 1982) will change this picture radically. These texts show that numerous rituals and liturgies, similar in scope to those of tannaitic tradition, existed among the sectarians of Qumran. We must also note here the presence of fragments of Ben Sîrāʾ at Qumran (51:13–20; 30 in Sanders 1965: 79–85; and the fragmentary 2Q 18 in Baillet, Milik, and de Vaux 1962: 75–77). A poem substantially parallel to the conclusions of the blessings of the later tannaitic Eighteen Benedictions was appended in some Hebrew versions (at 55:12) to the last chapter of Ben Sîrāʾ (Segal 1971–72: 355–57; Academy of the Hebrew Language 1973: 55). We do not know if this passage was part of the Qumran recension of Ben Sîrāʾ.

Finally, numerous phylacteries *(tĕfillîn)* have been found at Qumran. The phylacteries are associated with liturgical practice in the rabbinic tradition. At Qumran, these ritual objects also bear witness to variations of custom, especially as regards the order and content of the biblical passages included in them (Habermann 1953–54; Vermes 1959; Yadin 1969). The entire matter is in need of reevaluation in light of the most recently published exemplars (Milik 1977: 34–79).

Common Liturgical Motifs

There are certain motifs found in later rabbinic traditions that have important parallels in the Qumran texts. Among the fragments from Caves 4 and 11 is the Angelic Liturgy (Serek Šîrôt ʿÔlat Ha-ŝabbāt, in Strugnell 1959; van der Woude 1982, Masada fragment in Newsom and Yadin 1984) that describes the angelic praise of God. This composition is to be seen as a *merkābâ* text (Schiffman 1982), and, indeed, this term itself appears in the work. It constitutes a description of the regular praise of God in the heavens by the angelic hosts. They are seen as praising Him on a daily basis according to fixed rituals (see Newsom 1982). This concept also appears in the rabbinic *qĕdûšâ* prayers (Elbogen 1972: 47–53) and is more fully developed in the early *Hēkālôt* literature (Altmann 1946).

M. Weinfeld (1975–76) has argued that elements of liturgical language found later in the rabbinic prayers are preserved already among the texts of the Qumran corpus. Among the most prominent is the parallel with the rabbinic *qĕdûšâ* in the Hymn to the Creator found in 11QPsa (Sanders 1965: 89–91). This poem is certainly similar to the *Hēkālôt* hymn ʾĒl ʾAdôn which found its way into the rabbinic liturgy (Amram Gaon 1971: 71; Baer 1956–57: 211–12; Elbogen 1972: 87).

What is essential to our question is the methodological dilemma posed by these materials. How are we to account for the presence of these common motifs in the Qumran and rabbinic traditions? Are we to assume that the Qumran materials directly influenced the *Hēkālôt* which, in turn, influenced the rabbinic liturgy? Or, perhaps, ought we even to assume direct influence? On the contrary, we might also be dealing with a simple case of parallel development. Perhaps, if we had Pharisaic texts from this period, we might discover that some of the Pharisaic sages were involved in the very same kinds of speculation.

The Daily Prayers

Among the texts recently published in *Discoveries in the Judaean Desert*, volume 7, 4Q503 is one of extreme importance. This manuscript, dated by the editor, M. Baillet (1982: 105), to the Hasmonean period (100–75

B.C.E.), consists of a series of prayers to be recited on the various days of the month. Specific texts are designated for evening *('ereb)*, and morning *(ṣē't ha-šemeš)*, although no specific nighttime prayer appears to be included here. The material for each day of the month constitutes a literary unit, and the days are numbered according to lunar months. Each day's entry begins:

> ובא לחודש בערב יברכו וענו ואמרו ברוך אל ישראל אשר. . . .
> שלום עליכה ישראל

On the x of the month, in the evening *(bā-'ereb)*, they shall bless, recite and say: Praised be the God of Israel Who . . . . May peace be upon you, O Israel

Then the text takes up the morning prayer:

> ובצאת השמש להאיר על הארץ יברכו וענו ואמרו ברוך אל
> ישראל. . . . .

When the sun goes forth to illumine the earth they shall bless, recite and say: Praised be the God of Israel . . . .

Most interesting is the benediction:

> [ברוך אל ישראל א]שר בח[ר] בנו מכול [ה]גוים

[Praised be the God of Israel w]ho cho[se] us from among all [the] nations. (Baillet 1982: 111)

Prominent phrases are *'ôr ha-yômām* in the morning prayer (3:10, page 106; 4:1, page 108; 11:2, page 116; fragment 15–16:6, page 110), and *diglê laylâ* (8:11, 19, page 113; compare fragment 39:3 [*dig*]*lê 'ereb)* and *gôrālê ḥōšek* (fragment 76, page 127; fragment 215, page 135) in the evening selections. Each day is described as having so many *ša'arê 'ôr,* gates of light, (4:2, page 108; 8:10, page 113; fragment 19:2, page 110) that seem to be equivalent to the number of the day in the lunar month.

The editor has observed that this text seems to depart from the calendar of solar months and years which scholars previously identified as that of the Qumran sect (Baillet 1982: 105–6). Here we have a calendar of lunar months, probably synchronized by leap years, similar to those known from tannaitic tradition (Herr 1976: 843–57). Baillet sees the text as starting with the month of Nisan, so that the festival described in fragment 24 (column 7) as occurring on the fifteenth of the month seems to him to be Passover. The text describes this day as *mô['ēd] mānôaḥ wĕ-ta'anûg* (fragment 24–25:5, page 111). *Mānôaḥ* describes other days (12:15, page 118; fragment 41:3, page 119) that must have been Sabbaths or festivals (compare 1QM 2:8–9 [the War Scroll]; 1QpHab. 11: 6–7, 8 [the Habakkuk Commentary]).[1]

The liturgical materials found here are too short to have constituted the entire liturgy. These appear to have represented a small section of the worship service which, in the ritual of the authors, changed on a daily basis throughout the month and, perhaps, throughout the year. In view of the content of these prayers, it is most likely that the benedictions preserved here constituted an expansion upon a precursor of the first benediction before the *Šěma'* (Elbogen 1972: 12–15). We do not mean to assert that this passage proves the recitation of the *Šěma'* at this date, although the Mishna attributes it to Temple times (Tāmîd 5:1). This same passage in the Mishna indicates that some benediction was already associated with the *Šěma'* in Temple times in the view of the *tannā'îm* (compare B Běrāk̲ôt 11b–12a; J Běrāk̲ôt 1.5). Some early version of the blessing on the heavenly lights must have been in use (compare Mann 1925: 273, 292, 323; Sa'adyah Gaon 1970: 13, 26). Although in rabbinic tradition this benediction was variable only for morning and evening, with later additions for Sabbaths and festivals, at Qumran it varied by the day. Further, the very idea of "gates" or portals occurs in the rabbinic morning benediction (Amram Gaon 1971: 71). Much of the vocabulary of these prayers is found in rabbinic liturgy as well.

Our text speaks of twice daily prayer, morning and evening (late afternoon). Amoraic tradition saw prayer as a substitute for the Temple sacrifices once the Temple had been destroyed (B Běrāk̲ôt 26a). Nonetheless, it was argued by some *tannā'îm* that the very same services had already been conducted in the Second Temple period, at which time the service could merely be said to have been instituted to correspond with the times of the daily sacrifices (T Běrāk̲ôt 3, 1). While still others argued that the prayers were instituted by the patriarchs (Daniel prayed thrice daily [Daniel 6:11]), the *amôrā'îm* explained that even this view admitted that the exact times for the services depended on the times for sacrificial worship (B Běrāk̲ôt 26b; J Běrāk̲ôt 4.1.7b).

The link with sacrificial worship was apparently basic. Otherwise, how can we explain the fact that the nighttime service was a matter of debate throughout the tannaitic period? Indeed, it was eventually decided that in halakhic terms the nighttime service was optional (B Běrāk̲ôt 27b; J Běrāk̲ôt 4.1.7c–d). The only reasonable explanation is that since there was no nighttime sacrifice, this prayer had an inferior status. Even the rabbinic explanation that the burning of limbs and fats throughout the night constituted the equivalent of a nighttime sacrifice was not sufficient to elevate the nighttime prayer to the status of a required daily service.

Our Qumran text mentions only the two required prayer times, testifying to a period when, at least for some Jews, only twice daily prayer was normative. In fact, our text supports the view of the *tannā'îm* that originally twice daily prayer was the norm. The system of two daily prayers in this text is in marked contrast to the six daily prayer times that Talmon (1958–59; 1959–60) finds mentioned in the poem at the end of the Manual of Discipline. Several explanations are possible. First, it may be that Talmon's interpretation of the poetic material takes too literally the imagery and that, as A. Dupont-Sommer (1952: 232) has claimed, only two prayer times are in fact referred to in the poem. Second, it may be the texts describe the ritual practices of different communities or different stages in the history of one community. These are all matters that only the publication of additional material can clarify.

The Qumran Supplication Texts

4Q 501 is entitled "Lamentation" by the editor. In Baillet's opinion (1982: 79) it is written in a Herodian hand, around 50–25 B.C.E. This text appeals to God to remember the downtrodden position and disgrace of Israel and not to hand over the land *(naḥalâ)* to foreigners. God is asked to avenge the wrongs that the nations have perpetrated against His nation.

Although this text is extremely fragmentary, it contains parallels in theme and content to the rabbinic supplication, the *Taḥanûn* for Mondays and Thursdays (*Wĕ-hû' Raḥûm*, Amram Gaon 1971: 55–58; Sa'adyah Gaon 1970: 24–25; Baer 1956–57: 112–16; Elbogen 1972: 58–62). This prayer, in its present form, has been dated to the Middle Ages. Most notable is the dependency of both texts on Joel 2:17.

A similar composition is the 4Q *Dibĕrê Ha-mĕ'ôrôt*, which has been preserved in three copies (4Q 504–6). The name of the text actually appears in the manuscript (4Q 504, Baillet 1982: 138), a rare phenomenon in the Qumran library. J. Starcky (1956: 66), who first worked on these texts, considered it to be a "recueil d'hymnes liturgiques." Baillet has suggested that this document provides material intended for use on specific days of the week. Indeed, Wednesday, which he terms "day of the Covenant," and the Sabbath (Saturday), "the day of praise," are explicitly mentioned. What precedes this Sabbath material he assumes refers to Friday, "the day of confession of Sins." He takes the absence of sectarian character as well as the date of the earliest exemplar, which in his opinion is around 150 B.C.E., to indicate that this text stems from the *Ḥasîdîm* of whom, he says, the Essenes are the spiritual heirs (Baillet 1982: 137).

Based on the preliminary publication of this material (Baillet 1961), M. R. Lehmann (1964; 1982) has taken issue with this analysis. He points to the large number of parallels between the *Dibĕrê Ha-mĕ'ôrôt* and the

Taḥanûn. According to him, the earliest forms of the *Taḥanûn* go back to the time of the Second Temple, and this prayer is termed *dĕḇārîm* in tannaitic usage (T Bĕrāḵôt 3, 6; compare Lieberman 1955: 31). Lehmann questions the reading *mĕ'ôrôt* and notes that this word is found in the first blessing before the *Šĕmaʿ*. An extensive and impressive list of linguistic parallels is then presented by him. He therefore classifies the *Diḇĕrê Ha-mĕ'ôrôt* as the supplications of an individual to be recited after the priest has completed the service and goes even further to conclude that the length of this prayer requires us to see it as intended for Monday and Thursday. He states that the text is more appropriate to Monday and Thursday than to the days that Baillet has suggested. In his final, official publication, Baillet (1982: 137) simply notes that he gives the same explanation he had given previously, despite the work of Lehmann.

It is indeed surprising that Lehmann's analysis totally ignores the testimony of the text itself which explicitly mentions Wednesday and Saturday. Baillet's suggestion that there are preserved here prayers for each day of the week is quite convincing, despite the absence of references to other days. On one hand, the fragmentary nature of the text allows us to presume that the mention of the other days of the week would have appeared in the lacunae. On the other hand, the substantial list of parallels assembled by Lehmann seems to require attention.

In summary, therefore, we are suggesting that the above text be identified as a series of daily supplications for liturgical use for each day of the week and that certain topics judged improper for the Sabbath day were apparently avoided (see Schiffman 1975: 87–90). This text would have been recited as part of an organized ritual. It is not possible to tell if the particular text was written for Temple service or for worship away from the Temple. Nonetheless, if used at Qumran, it would undoubtedly have been part of an organized liturgy.

Moreover, the texts we have examined show that some Jews, whose works are preserved at Qumran, were already reciting prayers with motifs similar to the rabbinic *Taḥanûn* as part of their prayer services in the first century B.C.E. By the time of the composition of the 4Q *Diḇĕrê Ha-mĕ'ôrôt*, the uniqueness of the Sabbath and the inappropriateness of certain of these motifs on this holy day led to the inclusion of a special version for the Sabbath.

Festival Prayers

Prayers for festivals are preserved in three manuscripts from Cave 4 (4Q 507–9) and, indeed, the very same text is found in 1Q 34 and 34 bis (Barthélemy and Milik 1955: 136 and 152–55). The Cave 4 manuscripts have been dated by Baillet to the beginning of the first century C.E. (4Q 507, Baillet 1982: 175), the early first century C.E. (4Q 508, page 177), and to the end of the Hasmonean period, about 70–60 B.C.E. (4Q 509, page 184). The text specifically mentions the Day of Atonement and the Day of First Fruits (Shavuot). Baillet has made a plausible reconstruction, according to which the text proceeds through the entire Jewish ritual calendar, beginning with the New Year on the first of Tishri, followed by the Day of Atonement, Tabernacles, Offering of the 'Omer or Barley Harvest, possibly the Second Passover, and Shavuot. The New Moon is also mentioned. (A reference to Passover has not been identified in the preserved portions of the text.)

The exact reconstruction of the ritual calendar of this text and of the prayers for each occasion is impossible, since the state of preservation of the manuscripts does not allow for it. In addition, it cannot be determined whether the ritual calendar of this text is similar to that known from tannaitic Judaism, or to the expanded calendar of the Temple Scroll (see Yadin 1983, volume 1, 89–142).

One line that particularly stands out in this text reads:

ואספתה נדחינו למועד . . . ונפוצותינו תקבץ לתקופת. . . .

And may You assemble our banished at the time of . . . and our dispersed ones may You soon gather. . . . (Yadin 1983, volume 1, 1: 3–4, page 186; compare Isaiah 11–12)

The parallel to the festival Mûsaf (additional service) of later rabbinic tradition is so clear that it suggests the prayer for the restoration of the Diaspora to the Land of Israel recited on festivals (Amram Gaon 1971: 126; Sa'adyah Gaon 1970: 151; Baer 1956–57: 352) may go back as early as the first century B.C.E.

It is not possible to determine the exact function of these prayers. They do not mention the sacrificial system, so as to suggest that they were a substitute for it. Nor can we find any indication that they were intended to be recited along with sacrificial rites. Happiness and rejoicing are explicitly mentioned, so it is possible that they were meant to be recited as part of the celebration of these festivals at Qumran or elsewhere.

The last three texts examined here contained prayers for each day of the month (to be recited morning and evening), daily supplicatory prayers, and, now, specific prayers for each festival. These constituted together a cycle of prayer texts that indicates a fairly developed liturgy. We cannot be sure if all three were recited by the same people, but it does seem likely that they constituted a unit, a part of the liturgy of the sect.

The Marriage Ritual

The next two texts contain rituals for specific occasions. The first, 4Q 502, is an extensive text that Baillet (1982: 81) has taken as a ritual for marriage. J. M. Baumgarten (1983) has disputed this interpretation. He sees the text as celebrating the place of honor accorded to elderly couples who joined the sect. Despite some claims that the sectarians of Qumran, identified as Essenes, were celibate, the Qumran texts speak of a society in which marriage is the norm (Schiffman 1983: 214–15; compare Cross 1961: 97–100, 237–38). Our text contains a direct parallel with the treatise of two spirits of the Manual of Discipline which undoubtedly constitutes part of the sectarian corpus (Baillet 1982: 81; compare fragment 16, page 86 and 1QS 3:13–4:26). Furthermore, the clearly sectarian terms *běnê ṣedeq* (fragment 1:10, page 82) and *těʿûdôt* (8:9, page 83; fragment 43:1, page 91; 9:16, page 83 [restored]) are used.

Baillet suggests that 4Q 502 might have been part of a longer book of happy occasions, including marriage, circumcision, and bar mitzvah. This, however, is impossible. In the Rule of the Congregation we have a list of the ages of sectarian life (see Schiffman 1984). While ten is the age of passage from the status of *ṭaf* (1QSa 1:8), there is no mention of bar mitzvah in the sectarian corpus. Further, the list of stages does not mention circumcision, even though the biblical command of circumcision (Genesis 17:23–27; Leviticus 12:3; see Schiffman 1985: 23–25) must have been fulfilled at eight days among the sectarians.

The text contains a series of prayers, apparently to be uttered by the principals in the ceremony. Each begins *bārûk ʾēl yiśrāʾēl ʾāšer...*, "Blessed be the God of Israel Who..." (fragment 19:6, page 86; fragment 24:2, page 88). The appearance of such phrases as *bānîm û-bā[nôt]*, "sons and daugh[ters]" (fragment 14:6, page 85), *raʿayātô*, "his wife" (fragment 1:7, page 82), *pěrî beṭen*, "the fruit of the womb" (partially restored in fragment 20:3, page 87 and fragment 163:3, page 99), *la-ʿaśôt zerāʿ*, "to reproduce" (fragment 1:4, page 82), *śimḥat yaḥad*, "mutual happiness" (partially restored in fragment 4:3, page 82, and fragments 105 and 106:2, page 95), [ʾa]bî ha-naʿarâ, "the [fa]ther of the girl" (fragment 108:3, page 95; see Judges 19:3) would suggest that this is a marriage ritual. In addition, a fragmentary allusion indicates that it was a seven-day feast (fragment 97:2, page 94), as was the case also in biblical and talmudic traditions.

No perceptible parallels between this Qumran text and the marriage benedictions described in amoraic sources (B Kětûbbôt 7b–8a) could be found. This text is totally unrelated to the liturgical traditions of the tannaitic period and therefore differs from the other liturgical materials from Qumran that we have examined.

The Purification Ritual

The final manuscript to be considered here, 4Q 512, has been dated to the early first century B.C.E. Baillet (1982: 262) has identified the following aspects discussed in this text: sexual impurities, purity of the cultic servitors, the laws of *ṣāraʿat* for both persons and houses, and contact with the dead. In addition, there is explicit mention of the obligation to purify oneself for Sabbaths and festivals, for the equinoxes and solstices, and for the harvest festivals and the New Moon. This description seems to accord with the so-called sectarian calendar, based upon solar months and solar years (Talmon 1958).

Examination of the halakhic regulations found in this text will have to await more thorough study of the law of ritual purity and impurity in the scrolls. What concerns us is the liturgical aspect. Each person in association with his or her purification ritual recited a prayer beginning with the clause: *bārûk ʾatâ ʾēl yiśrāʾēl ʾašer . . .*, "Blessed be You God of Israel Who . . . " (fragment 41:3, page 274; fragment 42–44:3, page 275). This series of recitations has a definite purpose. One of the criticisms often levelled against the Jewish laws of ritual purity and impurity has been the apparent lack of concern with the ethical and religious dimension. The claim has been made that these rites are mechanical at best and that they represent taboos. This group of Jews by at least the first century B.C.E. emphasized that these rituals have an important spiritual and religious meaning, that the purification from impurity must be preceded and accompanied by an inner turning, a dedication to the goals and aspirations that Judaism seeks. Indeed, this very idea is enshrined in the Manual of Discipline which commands that only those who have done proper repentance may be permitted to enter the waters of purification (1QS 2:26–3:12). Purification is a deep spiritual process of self-improvement, not a mere cultic rite.

Conclusion

The study of Qumran liturgy is in its infancy. The liturgical texts are only now beginning to appear and definitive results are still forthcoming. At the same time, while we tend to think of tannaitic liturgy as well known and established, we actually have a long way to go before we will be able to speak of the status of the liturgy in the early years after the destruction of the Second Temple. When it comes to actual texts, we are so dependent on later material that almost all of our conclusions must remain tentative.

If we may judge from the fragments found at Qumran, the sect practiced a regular order of prayer. Special texts were recited for each day of the month, morning and evening. Supplicatory prayers similar to the rabbinic *Taḥanûn* were used for the various days of the week. Special festival prayers were also recited. Liturgical materials accompanied the purificatory rituals, giving meaning and significance to these rites. Finally, there may have been a marriage ritual at Qumran.

By the Yabnean period the *Šĕmaʿ* and Eighteen Benedictions already formed the basis of the tannaitic liturgy, and the texts of some other important prayers must have been at least fairly fixed. Yet many disagreements existed, and much was left to be done. Clearly, the Yabnean sages were attempting to draw the community of Israel together around a common liturgy, at a time when their traditions were diverse. A look at the Qumran material can indicate the scope of this diversity, but much other Temple and non-Temple material must have existed as well. The task of the sages of Yabneh was to supplant this material and to crystallize a standardized Pharisaic-rabbinic liturgy that might serve as the basis of Jewish practice in future generations.

While many parallels exist in the area of liturgy between the practices of the Dead Sea Sect and those of the early *tannāʾîm*, the differences are such as to require that we do not assume that Qumran materials typify Second Temple Judaism in all respects. After all, Second Temple Judaism was to a large extent a set of competing alternatives grappling with one another in what ultimately became a test of the survival of the fittest. In that struggle, tannaitic Judaism prevailed. Qumran came to an end in the early years of the Revolt (de Vaux 1973: 38–41). However, in those areas in which the parallels are clear, we are dealing most probably with elements common to the varieties of Judaism known from Second Temple times. These elements, represented at Qumran, constitute part of the heritage that tannaitic Judaism received from its spiritual forebearers, the Pharisees. Some of the traditions in evidence at Qumran, common to most Second Temple Jews, therefore survived in the tannaitic tradition. Others might even have been bequeathed directly or through some intermediary to rabbinic Judaism. Many of the practices of the Qumran sect died out, and some went underground, only to emerge some seven centuries later in the Karaite consensus.

The liturgy of rabbinic Judaism, then, has its roots in the traditions of the Second Commonwealth period. Organized liturgical practices existed, at least among those Jews whose texts survived among the manuscripts of the Qumran library, already more than a century before the destruction of the Temple. Prayer and the service of the heart were already becoming increasingly important. When the destruction of the Temple brought to a close the age of sacrifice, the *tannāʾîm*, based on those inherited traditions, began to standardize and develop the system of prayer and ritual that later became embodied in the Jewish prayerbook.

Notes

1 See Barthélemy and Milik 1955 for a full listing of the abbreviations used to designate the
manuscripts found at Qumran.

Bibliography

Academy of the Hebrew Language
   1973   *The Book of Ben Sira. The Historical Dictionary of the Hebrew Language.* Jerusalem:
           Academy of the Hebrew Language and Shrine of the Book.
Altmann, A.
   1946   Šîrê Qĕdūšâ Bĕ-siprût Ha-Hēk̠ālôt Ha-qĕdûmâ. *Mĕlîlâ* 2: 8–10 (Hebrew).
Amram Gaon
   1971   *Sēder Rab̠ 'Amrām Gā'ôn.* Edited by D. S. Goldschmidt. Jerusalem: Mossad
           Harav Kook (Hebrew).
Baer, Y.
   1956–57 *Sēder 'Ab̠ôdat Yiśrā'ēl.* Tel-Aviv: Or-Torah (Hebrew).
Baillet, M.
   1961   Un recueil liturgique de Qumran, grotte 4: "Les Paroles des Luminaires." *Revue
           Biblique* 68: 195–250, plates 24–28.
   1982   *Qumrân Grotte 4.* Part 3 (4Q482–4Q520) in volume 7 of *Discoveries in the
           Judaean Desert.* Oxford: Clarendon.
Baillet, M.; Milik, J. T. ; and de Vaux, R.
   1962   *Les "Petites Grottes" de Qumran.* Volume 3 of *Discoveries in the Judaean Desert.*
           Oxford: Clarendon.
Barthélemy, D., and Milik, J. T.
   1955   *Qumran Cave I.* Volume 1 of *Discoveries in the Judaean Desert.* Oxford: Clarendon.
Baumgarten, J. M.
   1983   4Q502, Marriage or Golden Age Ritual? *Journal of Jewish Studies* 35: 125–35.
Bokser B. M.
   1977   *Philo's Description of Jewish Practices.* Protocol of the Thirtieth Colloquy. Berke-
           ley, Calif.: Center for Hermeneutical Studies in Hellenistic and Modern Culture.
   1984   *The Origins of the Seder.* Berkeley, Calif.: University of California Press.
Cross, F. M.
   1961   *The Ancient Library of Qumran and Modern Biblical Studies.* Revised edition. Grand
           Rapids, Mich.: Baker.
   1971   The Early History of the Qumran Community. In *New Directions in Biblical
           Archaeology,* edited by D. N. Freedman and J. C. Greenfield, pages 70–89. Gar-
           den City, N.Y.: Doubleday.
Dupont-Sommer, A.
   1952   Contribution à l'exégèse du Manuel de Discipline X 1–8. *Vetus Testamentum* 3:
           229–43.
Elbogen, I.
   1972   *Ha-tĕfillâ Bĕ-yiśrā'ēl Bĕ-hitpathûtâ Ha-histôrît.* Tel-Aviv: Dvir (Hebrew).
Gärtner, B.
   1965   *The Temple and the Community in Qumran and the New Testament.* Cambridge, Eng.:
           Cambridge University.
Habermann, A. M.
   1953–54 'Al Ha-tĕfillîn Bi-yĕmê Qedem. *Eretz Israel* 3: 174–77 (Hebrew).

Herr, M. D.
1976   The Calendar. In *The Jewish People in the First Century,* volume 2, edited by S. Safrai and M. Stern, pages 834–64. Philadelphia, Pa.: Fortress.
Holm-Nielsen, S.
1971   Thanksgiving Psalms. In *Encyclopaedia Judaica,* volume 5, edited by C. Roth, columns 1045–48. Jerusalem: Keter.
Lehmann, M. R.
1964   A Reinterpretation of 4Q Dibrê Ham-Me'oroth. *Revue de Qumran* 5: 106–10.
1982   *Masôt Û-Masā'ôt.* Jerusalem: Mossad Harav Kook (Hebrew).
Licht, J.
1957   *Měgillat Ha-Hôdāyôt.* Jerusalem: Mosad Bialik (Hebrew).
Lieberman, S.
1955   *Tosefta Ki-Fshuṭah, Seder Zera'im, Part 1.* New York: Jewish Theological Seminary of America.
Mann, J.
1925   Genizah Fragments of the Palestinian Order of Service. *Hebrew Union College Annual* 2: 269–338.
Milik, J. T.
1977   Tefillin, Mezuzot et Targums (4Q128-4Q157). In *Discoveries in the Judaean Desert,* volume 4, part 2 *(Qumrân Grotte 4),* pages 33–90. Oxford: Clarendon.
Newsom, C.
1982   4Q Sereḳ Širot 'Olat Haššabbat (The Qumran Angelic Liturgy). Dissertation abstract. *Harvard Theological Review* 75: 132.
Newsom, C., and Yadin, Y.
1984   The Masada Fragment of the Qumran Songs of the Sabbath Sacrifice. *Israel Exploration Journal* 34: 77–88, plate 9.
Sa'adyah Gaon
1970   *Sīddûr Rab Sa'adyah Gaon.* Edited by I. Davidson, S. Assaf, and B. I. Joel. Jerusalem: R. Mass (Hebrew).
Sanders, J. A.
1965   *The Psalms Scroll of Qumran Cave 11.* Volume 4 of *Discoveries in the Judaean Desert.* Oxford: Clarendon.
1967   *The Dead Sea Psalms Scroll.* Ithaca, N.Y.: Cornell University Press.
1971   Cave 11 Surprises and the Question of Canon. In *New Directions in Biblical Archaeology,* edited by D. N. Freedman and J. C. Greenfield, pages 113–30. Garden City, N.Y.: Doubleday.
Schiffman, L. H.
1975   *The Halakhah at Qumran.* Leiden, The Netherlands: Brill.
1982   *Merkavah* Speculation at Qumran: The 4Q *Serekh Shirot 'Olat Ha-Shabbat.* In *Mystics, Philosophers, and Politicians: Essays in Jewish Intellectual History in Honor of Alexander Altmann,* edited by J. Reinharz and D. Swetschinski, pages 15–47. Series: Duke Monographs in Medieval and Renaissance Studies 5. Durham, N.C.: Duke University Press.¹
1983   *Sectarian Law in the Dead Sea Scrolls: Courts, Testimony, and the Penal Code.* Series: Brown Judaic Studies 33. Chico, Calif.: Scholars.
1984   The Eschatological Community of the Serekh Ha-'Edah. *Proceedings of the American Academy for Jewish Research* 51: 105–29.
1985   *Who Was a Jew? Rabbinic and Halakhic Perspectives on the Jewish Christian Schism.* Hoboken, N.J.: Ktav.

48   Lawrence H. Schiffman

Segal, M. S.
1971–72   *Sēp̄er Ben Sîrā' Ha-Šālēm.* Jerusalem: Mosad Bialik (Hebrew).
Skehan, P.
1973   A Liturgical Complex in 11Q Psa. *Catholic Biblical Quarterly* 35: 195–205.
1975   Jubilees and the Qumran Psalter (11QPsa). *Catholic Biblical Quarterly* 37: 343–47.
Starcky, J.
1956   Le travail d'édition des fragments manuscrits de Qumrân. *Revue Biblique* 63: 66.
Strugnell, J.
1959   The Angelic Liturgy at Qumrân—4Q Serek Šîrôt 'Ôlat Haššabbāt. *Supplements to Vetus Testamentum* 7: 318–45.
Sukenik, E. L.
1954–55   *'Ôṣar Ha-Měgîllôt Ha-Gěnûzôt.* Jerusalem: Mosad Bialik and the Hebrew University (Hebrew).
Talmon, S.
1958   The Calendar Reckoning of the Sect from the Judaean Desert. In *Aspects of the Dead Sea Scrolls,* edited by C. Rabin and Y. Yadin, pages 162–99. Series: Scripta Hierosolymitana 4. Jerusalem: Magnes.
1958–59   "Maḥazôr" Ha-Běrākôt šel Kat Midbar Yěhûdâ. *Tarbiz* 28: 1–20 (Hebrew).
1959–60   The "Manual of Benedictions" of the Sect of the Judaean Desert. *Revue de Qumran* 2: 475–500.
1965–66   Mizmôrîm Ḥiṣônīyyîm Ba-Lāšôn Ha-Ibrît Mī-Qumrân. *Tarbiz* 35: 214–34 (Hebrew).
de Vaux, R.
1973   *Archaeology and the Dead Sea Scrolls.* The Schweich Lectures of the British Academy, 1959. London: The British Academy.
Vermes, G.
1959   Pre-Mishnaic Jewish Worship and the Phylacteries from the Dead Sea. *Vetus Testamentum* 9: 65–72.
Weinfeld, M.
1975–76   'Iqbôt šel Qědûšat Yôsēr Û-Pěsûqê dě-Zimrā' Bě-Měgîllôt Qumrân Û-ḇě-Sēper Ben Sîra'. *Tarbiz* 45: 15–26.
van der Woude, A. S.
1982   Fragmente einer Rolle der Lieder für das Sabbatoffer aus Hohle XI von Qumran (11Q SirSabb). In *Von Kanaan bis Kerala, Festschrift für J.P.M. van der Ploeg,* edited by W. C. Delsam, et al, pages 311–35. Kevelaer: Butzon and Bercker; Neukirchen-Vluyn: Neukirchener Verlag.
Yadin, Y.
1969   *Tefillin from Qumran.* Jerusalem: Israel Exploration Society and Shrine of the Book.
1983   *The Temple Scroll.* 3 volumes. Jerusalem: Israel Exploration Society, Institute of Archaeology of the Hebrew University, Shrine of the Book.

3. Unity and Diversity among Diaspora Synagogues

A. T. Kraabel

The purpose of this essay is to sketch an *hypothesis* about the Jewish Diaspora (for the primary evidence, see Kraabel 1979, 1982, and 1985). The intent of the hypothesis is to account for the survival and even the success of synagogue Judaism in the cities of the Greco-Roman world. It goes as far as I am able presently to set this phenomenon in the context of the Greco-Roman world.

Let me state the thesis at the outset: The Judaism of the synagogue communities of the Roman Diaspora is best understood, on the basis of the present evidence, as the grafting of a transformed biblical "exile" ideology onto a Greco-Roman form of social organization. The most important result of that process was not a text or a system of thought, but an architectural and social symbol, the synagogue itself—the building and the community.

With more data one could accomplish the kind of detailed treatment of community life, history, and theology that is regularly done from the texts of rabbinic Judaism or of primitive Christianity. But the evidence is severely limited when such a reconstruction is attempted for the Roman Diaspora and is usually based on the works of Philo and scraps of questionable Christian evidence; the results are not persuasive.

Only the synagogue communities can tell us anything very definitive about this Judaism. There is no lack of evidence, such as magical papyri and gems, for individual instances of the conflation of Jewish and pagan pieties by gentiles or Jews. But with the evidence of a synagogue building at Ostia or Sardis or Dura we have definitive information about the Judaism of a specific community whose members chose to establish and maintain this institution, and thus to define and express their understanding of what it meant to be Jewish in that particular situation.

The primary data for the synagogue Judaism of the Roman Diaspora are scattered and diverse. Substantial new excavations would undoubtedly bring to light new data, but none are likely in the near future. The diversity of current data was evident some years ago in the *Age of Spirituality* exhibition at the Metropolitan Museum of Art (Weitzmann 1979). The section on Judaism, under the direction of Professor Narkiss, displayed frescoes from Pompeii and Dura and fragments of a synagogue floor mosaic from Hammam-Lif in Tunisia; Rome supplied a sarcophagus and some of the famous gold glass; from Asia Minor came a seventh-century gold medallion and one of the Noah's Ark coins from third-century Apamea in Phrygia; Egypt provided an oil lamp and an incense burner; both examples of Jewish architecture were from outside the Holy Land—the Roman Diaspora's two most spectacular synagogues at Dura and Sardis. These are precious materials, of course, but insufficient for a persuasive detailed reconstruction of Diaspora existence.

My own evidence is even more restricted, since it is limited to synagogues where the sites are well preserved and excavated enough to convey some impressions of the people who maintained and used the buildings, and the gentile communities in which they lived. The six buildings differ greatly, as do their locations (Kraabel 1979, 1981). Following are summary descriptions of these sites:

> *Sardis* in Lydia (Asia Minor) was a metropolis before the Trojan War, an economic power, and a political and cultural center ruled by Croesus in the mid-sixth century, then captured by Cyrus of Persia. It surrendered to Alexander the Great in 334 B.C.E. and was controlled by his successors. In 133 B.C.E. it came under Roman control. Sardis is a powerful representative of the Lydian, the Eastern Greek, and later the Roman world, and was open to the rest of Anatolia and the east. The excavated synagogue is the latest known from that community and dates from the second or third century C.E. It was destroyed in 616 C.E.

> *Priene* on the Aegean coast (Asia Minor) was always relatively small, a Hellenistic "planned city" laid out on a regular grid-pattern. Its major deities are the Greek Zeus, Athena, Demeter, the Egyptian Isis, and the Anatolian Cybele; its culture was strongly Ionian and Greek. The synagogue here dates from the third or fourth century C.E.

> *Dura* in Syria, on the remote eastern rim of the Empire, was a small caravan- and garrison-city that was walled and fortified. Its society was

3. *Diaspora Synagogues* 51

a complex racial and religious mixture where no one tradition dominated. Its existence was often precarious: it was only intermittently under Roman authority, and then continued as a non-Roman community under the control of the Roman army. It was open to non-Roman influence from all directions. While Jews lived in Dura long before the second century C.E., its famous synagogue was established during that time and destroyed in 256 C.E.

Delos, the island birthplace of Apollo, was a crossroads in the Aegean from prehistoric times. Well known in the literature of classical antiquity, it attracted merchants, travelers, and immigrants from the eastern Mediterranean, particularly after it became a free port in the second century B.C.E. By that time a permanent community of Greek-speaking Samaritans had been established on the island (Bruneau 1982; Kraabel 1984), along with several important sanctuaries of a non-Greek type for foreign deities. The Jewish synagogue dates from the first century B.C.E. to the second century C.E.

Ostia was the port of Rome during the great expansion of trade in the early Empire. Excavations reveal a well-planned city, with harbors, large warehouses, a traders' office, guild halls, and blocks of private apartments. The community of Ostia included families from Rome and elsewhere in Italy, along with traders, slaves, and ex-slaves from the Mediterranean area. Non-Roman cults are well documented—Cybele, Bellona, Isis, and especially Mithras existed along with Judaism and Christianity. The earliest synagogue on the site may go back to the first century C.E. The latest and most developed synagogue is from the fourth century.

Stobi in Macedonia was a Roman administrative center. It flourished in the second and third centuries, and grew and prospered in the fourth and fifth centuries when three Christian basilicas were built within the city and at least two more just outside of it. The earliest building, the "Synagogue of Polycharmos," dates from the third century C.E.; the later synagogue is from the fourth century.

Detailed accounts of these buildings may be found in the published reports of these sites. The immediate task is to examine the larger social context for these Diaspora Jewish communities.

In these six examples, and in other cases, a Jewish community survived and even prospered outside the Homeland in a largely gentile environment. The Diaspora synagogue community was a successful social organization that endured and remains to this day. Some of the reasons for that success and for the shape of this new form of Judaism are reflected in ideas and themes found in postexilic Israelite religion. But they are only half of the explanation, and will be discussed in the next section, beginning on page 55. I will begin with that part of the story that comes out of the Greco-Roman world, the "gentile" world outside Palestine. It is of a piece with the profound changes that took place within Greco-Roman society itself in the period between Alexander the Great and Augustus: the expansions and movements of peoples that began with Alexander, and continued later when the armies of the Republic gave Rome its empire.

These events at the same time produced or accelerated the disintegration of the social unities of the classical world: the coherence of the *polis* ended and, somewhat later, the Roman idea of *communitas*. The Greco-Roman world responded to the demise of these large social units by creating smaller units, as the *polis* and the small town of Rome had been in their glorious pasts. Nowadays these groups are classified as economic, ethnic, cultural, social, or religious. At that time, they had differing frameworks, although the motivation for forming smaller units was the same: to create a small *cosmos* within the chaos that had replaced the former order, to cope with the sense of loss and powerlessness that most people, particularly immigrants, felt in the new ethnic melting pot. In the Hellenistic period and under the Roman Empire voluntary organization into small social units was most popular (see Ziegler, Sontheimer, and Gartner 1964–75, under "Vereinswesen" and "Berufsverein"; Klauser 1950–, under "Gemeinschaft"; Rostovtzeff 1941, in Index I, under "Associations").

For a long time classicists and ancient historians said little about these groups, since classical authors all but ignored them, for at least two reasons: The associations were usually formed by the less affluent, who are poorly represented in the literary texts; and the associations were in their greatest numbers after the "classical" period of Greek and of Latin literature. Thus, for a long time the associations were not attested to in the evidence customarily used to re-create ancient history and were assumed nonexistent. More recently, inscriptions and papyri have become available in great quantity and, together with the data from excavations, clarify the widespread popularity of voluntary organizations and clubs.

Surprisingly few of these organizations were of a religious nature. Most clubs had a patron deity, but after the time of Alexander the Great very few are attested to whose main purpose was to worship or honor a particular deity. The closest thing to a religious guild would be the *technitai* of Dionysus, found in Athens, Smyrna, and Syracuse from the third century on, whose purpose was the promotion of music and drama. They were customarily given privileged status, including exemption from taxation and military service.

Most associations, however, were more everyday affairs, made up of artisans of a particular skill—such as "the associated spikers of razorfish"
at Miletus (Dittenberger 1903-5, number 756)—or merchants or ex-
soldiers, "Old Boys" from the same school, interest groups of all sorts,
even slaves. Dining societies, mutual aid societies, and burial societies were
also common.

Such associations were always ad hoc; there was no larger national or
international structure to which they were attached. In a very real sense,
they were popular because they were local, because they offered something
of what the individual had lost in the advent of the Hellenistic and Roman
empires.

The need for community in a bewildering larger world affected people at
nearly every level of wealth and education. Among the philosophically
trained in this period, "friendship" was a topic commonly discussed. This
new emphasis reflected a new kind of social grouping where the ties were
not of blood or nationality but of intellectual affinity. Epicureans established
a community of philosophical friends, the "garden" of Epicurus, to which
men and also women and slaves were admitted. In many ways it was not so
much a philosophy as a community of like minds. Communal gatherings
were important. Memorial feasts were held regularly on the anniversary of
Epicurus's death. Centuries after his death there was still remarkably little
change in Epicurean teachings (see Klauser 1950-, under "Epikur").
It is not surprising, then, that in the preserved sayings of Epicurus,
friendship is mentioned in strong and positive terms: "The noble soul
occupies itself with wisdom and friendship: of these the one is a mortal
god, the other immortal" (*Vatican Sayings*, number 78; trans. Bailey 1926).

When immigrants from Egypt or Asia Minor entered Greece, they found
the voluntary association useful for religious and social purposes, although
it was quite different from what they had been used to in the Homeland.
They brought their deities with them: in a sense both the god and his
followers were immigrants; the private club served the needs of both. Thus,
there were organizations honoring the Egyptian Isis or the Anatolian Cybele.
There were societies with initiation rites, or mystery-rites, involving Greek
deities (like Dionysus) or foreign gods. Unlike the rites of the archaic or
classical period, these mysteries served to build a sense of belonging to the
single localized group. Those who had been initiated in the same rites
formed a kinship, a substitute for the multi-generational natural families of
earlier times.

Jews began to form their own communities in the Greco-Roman world
early in the Hellenistic period. The oldest inscriptions referring to synagogues come from Egypt and are dated to within a century of the death of
Alexander the Great (Frey 1952: 1440, 1532A). The oldest excavated syna-

gogue is not in Palestine; it is on the Greek island of Delos, dating from the first century B.C.E. Far to the west, at the same time, the Jewish community in Rome was of good size (Leon 1960), and the synagogue community in Ostia just outside of Rome dates to as early as the first century C.E.

More successfully than any other of Rome's minorities, the Jewish population was able to adapt a Hellenistic gentile social form, the private organization, to its particular social and religious purposes. The remarkable developments that occurred among the Greek-speaking Jews in the cities of the Roman world may be summarized as follows (see also Collins 1983):

> They dispensed with a priesthood, even while the Jerusalem Temple still stood. Everything we know about Diaspora synagogue organization indicates that it was led by laymen from the outset.

> They retained the Bible in a Greek translation. Their reverence for the Scripture is manifested architecturally in the Torah shrines in five of the six buildings described above, indicating a strong tie to this element of traditional Judaism. This is striking for two reasons: first, the basic pattern of the godly life found in the Scriptures assumes a very different kind of existence than was available to Diaspora Jews; and, second, although in Palestine and Babylonia influential Jews found it necessary to produce substantial, normative materials to supplement the Bible and adapt it to their times, the Jews of the Mediterranean Diaspora saw no such necessity.

> They developed a new form of community organization which was fairly uniform from one Diaspora city to the next.

> They retained essential cultic practices—food laws, circumcision, Sabbath observance—while adjusting to gentile city life.

> They developed a new architecture, based on the public architecture of the Roman Empire but adapted to liturgical use. It replaced the Temple architecture that had dominated Israelite religion for a thousand years, and it was so successful that it is still in use in Jewish, Christian, and Moslem versions.

> They developed an iconography whose symbolism often derived from the figurative language of the Bible. The use of wall paintings, mosaics, and plastic art to carry those forms was novel in a religion that in earlier periods had had a great antipathy to "graven images." Later some striking examples of this iconography appeared in the Homeland, too—the mosaics of Bêt 'Alpā', for example—but the idea seems to have begun in the Diaspora, as Jews looked for new vehicles to carry the tradition for them and their descendants (Neusner 1981).

Their community extended into the next world. If possible, Jews established their own cemeteries, separate from the graves of non-Jews. The epitaphs were usually brief, but the thought expressed was often recognizably biblical. Pagan "tombstone theology" involved a few very well-known ideas, endlessly repeated. These rarely occurred in Jewish inscriptions.

In some sense this was also a world community, the only successful example of a network of Hellenistic voluntary associations that extended beyond national boundaries. The common tie was, of course, the Homeland, not necessarily the Palestine of their own times, but the biblical Israel elevated to mythical status. It is not surprising, then, that the Diaspora synagogues placed the Torah shrine on the wall closest to Jerusalem, thus orienting the building towards the Holy City. While most Diaspora Jews had no wish to return to the Holy Land, except perhaps on a brief pilgrimage, it was and has remained the center of their world.

Despite all these changes the communities continued to see themselves as Jewish. That identification was important, and they boldly made it. Other Jewish immigrants blended into the gentile population and disappeared. These did not.

Nor were the Diaspora Jews unreflective. The changes I have mentioned need not have been accidental or unplanned. In order to survive as immigrants in a pluralistic society, Diaspora Jews expanded and adapted certain themes in their ancestral religion and abandoned others. They had been "prepared" to succeed in the Diaspora chiefly by three "external events," incursions of foreign powers into the Jewish Homeland—which indeed would have been avoided at all costs had it been possible.

The result of these events was the beginning of a worldview or theology that would make Jews ready to handle life outside the Homeland. Perhaps because other immigrant groups lacked the first—the formative events —they also lacked the second, the theology. They were not ready for the new situation in any way that would allow them to survive as religious and cultural unities.

A great deal has been written about the impact of gentile culture on Palestine, particularly after Alexander the Great. The events of this period are usually called "the Hellenization of Judaism," with the discussion centering on the rise and fall of the Maccabean kingdom in the second and first centuries B.C.E. (compare Smith 1971: 57–81). Important as these events were in Palestine, their impact was not felt in the Roman Diaspora. The Judaism with which the Diaspora Jews identified was the "Israelite religion" of the Bible and the Temple, and not that shaped and revised under the Maccabees.

Two of the three "external events" are in the Bible. The first is the capture of the northern kingdom by the Assyrians in 722 B.C.E.; the second is the Exile, beginning in 587 B.C.E. with the fall of Jerusalem to Babylonian armies under Nebuchadnezzar. In both instances, outside forces profoundly altered Israelite existence, forcing thousands of Israelites to live as captives outside the Holy Land.

After the first deportation, many Jews simply "disappeared," having merged into the gentile population of the Assyrian Empire. The second deportation, the Exile, had profoundly different results. In a very real sense Judaism was born out of that Exile. As a result of these two events, particularly the second, the Exile became a permanent element in the religion of Israel. For Jews the Diaspora became a theological issue. No other Mediterranean people has had a similar experience.

There was little in the thought and imagery of other Eastern immigrant religions that might have formed an ideological justification for life in a Diaspora and for this new kind of social organization. The worship of Cybele and especially of Isis became popular also with those who had not come from the homelands of these goddesses. But out of the large number of devotees no extensive communities were formed. No common code of religious practice nor common homeland held them together.

Judaism was different. With increasing migration in the Hellenistic period, what Israel had learned from the Exile became central to a new and often voluntary "Exile" in the Greco-Roman world. At this point "Diaspora" becomes a more appropriate term than "Exile." Indeed some Jews would never return from the East to the Holy Land, but would move directly into the Mediterranean Diaspora from Babylonia. Those who established the Jewish community at Sardis are the best documented example.

In Babylonia, desire to maintain one's Jewishness had led to the formation of cohesive communities for that purpose. Ideologically and sociologically the Babylonian exile was where the synagogue began—in its earliest sense, as a community assembly rather than a building. There is no archaeological evidence from that date, of course, and even the literary references are fragmentary. Nevertheless, it was a major innovation, the shift from a national religion of Holy Land and Temple to that of a minority community. Like many other *nova* in religion, its beginnings have left only faint traces in the historical record.

After the return from Babylonia, what might be called "Exile theology" remained a part of Jewish religious thought. Consequently, the later Diaspora of the Hellenistic and Roman periods had at hand the religious symbols, the theology, and a form of social organization sanctioned by earlier generations that would allow Jews to maintain an existence outside of the Holy Land without forfeiting their cultural and religious heritage. Of all the immigrant groups of the Roman Empire, only the Jews were prepared theologically and sociologically for Diaspora existence.

The third "external event" in Jewish history was the destruction of the Jerusalem Temple by Roman troops under Titus. This was in one sense a surprising event—unexpected, terrible, catastrophic—and yet in a very real sense the Jewish people were ready for it. Judaism had become a "larger" religion; Jews had overflowed Palestine to the point that many more of them lived outside of the Homeland than within it. A religion and ideology centering on the Holy Land and the sacrificial cult in Jerusalem were no longer of sufficient scope for what Judaism had become. The larger conception of Judaism that emerged from the Exile now came to justify and validate life outside of Palestine. It made clear how Jews might exist faithfully in a minority community in the gentile world.

In that process the "Exile theology" would itself be transformed. A more positive "Diaspora theology" began to take its place, at least for some Diaspora Jews, as one of the major themes of the "Exile theology" was transcended. I refer to the idea that somehow the displacement from the Homeland (the "Dispersion") was a punishment from God. That idea had included the presupposition that the great hope of many Jews was to escape the world of the gentile and to return to the Homeland one day.

For some Jews in the Roman world this "punishment" language could still make a great deal of sense, for example, for the prisoners of war who became Roman slaves after Jerusalem was captured. Their situation must have been no better than that of the hostages taken to Babylonia after the earlier destruction of the city.

In addition, and perhaps more important, Exile language was soon adopted by Christians in an attempt to discredit the Jews: For Christians the Jewish Diaspora was not a worthy religious way of life, but a divine punishment, an exile in the worst sense of the word (Kraabel 1982: 460–464). The Christians used this idea so extensively when rationalizing Judaism that it became the dominant interpretive symbol by which many gentiles and Jews understood Jewish existence in the Roman world outside of Palestine.

But over the centuries many Jews left the Homeland voluntarily, as did other people from peripheral areas of the Mediterranean who sought their fortunes in the centers of power of the Hellenistic and Roman world. These individuals did not understand themselves to be in exile, but rather welcomed and desired immigration as part of a new situation that was also under the control of Providence. Just as the rabbis spiritualized the Temple and its cult, so the Diaspora Jews spiritualized the Homeland. Like many immigrants in more recent times, their transplanted, transformed religion allowed them to believe that their *new* homeland was not alien. They had made the main elements of Judaism portable: the Scriptures, the symbols, and the synagogue community itself. The Diaspora was not Exile; in some sense it became a Holy Land, too.

In summary, the synagogue Judaism of the Roman Diaspora is best understood as the grafting of a biblical diaspora theology onto a Greco-Roman social organization. The shift to minority status in places outside the Homeland led to the abandonment of many elements of the ancestral religion, a new emphasis on others, and the adoption of the new environment's iconography, architecture, and organizational form.

The result could be called a new religion, differing from traditional Palestinian Judaism, "biblical religion," as much as rabbinic Judaism had. Yet at the same time it was self-consciously and sometimes enthusiastically Jewish, prepared to survive within an environment of religious pluralism by relying on resources within the tradition.

It was no accident that this is the conference's only paper to have Diaspora Judaism as its main concern. Among Jewish and gentile scholars alike, the emphasis has always been on the biblical and rabbinic literatures, and on the Holy Land. The data from the Diaspora are less accessible and, more significant, less likely to be considered by students either of history or of religion. Hypothetical reconstructions like the one attempted in this paper are difficult to test because there are so few competing hypotheses against which they might be measured. It is the responsibility of those who are dissatisfied with the story I have related here to come up with a better way of assembling the data into a coherent and meaningful whole.

When G. D. Cohen, the chancellor of the Jewish Theological Seminary in New York, wrote—in a 1973 article significantly titled "The Blessing of Assimilation in Jewish History"—that "the great ages of Jewish creativity have always been products of the challenge of assimilation and of the response of leaders who were to a certain extent assimilated themselves," he might have been describing the Jews of the Mediterranean synagogues (compare Neusner 1982: 35–48). The evidence for the synagogue Judaism of the Mediterranean Diaspora is sparse and scattered. However, there must have been at one time many more synagogues like the six specific examples I have mentioned. It is inconceivable, I believe, that communities as substantial as these could exist only in a few Roman towns.

However, the fact remains that Diaspora Judaism did not survive. Rabbinic Judaism did. My own judgment is that this does not mean that somehow rabbinic Judaism was inherently "better," "more authentic," or "more Jewish." Roman Diaspora Judaism did not survive because it succumbed to outside forces, not to any internal flaw or weakness. But that is another topic and another essay.

Bibliography

Bailey, C., editor and translator
1926   *Epicurus: The Extant Remains, with Short Critical Apparatus, Translation and Note.* Oxford: Clarendon.

Bruneau, P.
1982   Les Israélites de Délos et la juiverie délienne. *Bulletin de Correspondance Hellénique* 106: 465–504.

Cohen, G. D.
1973   The Blessing of Assimilation in Jewish History. In *Understanding Jewish Theology,* edited by J. Neusner, pages 251–258. New York: Ktav.

Collins, J. J.
1983   *Between Athens and Jerusalem.* New York: Crossroad.

Dittenberger, W., editor
1903–5   *Orientis Graeci Inscriptiones Selectae,* volumes 1 and 2. Leipzig, W. Ger.: S. Hirzel.

Frey, P. J.-B., editor
1952   *Corpvs Inscriptionvm Ivdaicarvm,* volume 2. Rome: Pontificio Instituto di Archeologia Cristiana.

Klauser, T., editor
1950–   *Reallexikon für Antike und Christentum.* Stuttgart, W. Ger.: Anton Hiersemann.

Kraabel, A. T.
1979   The Diaspora Synagogue. In *Aufstieg und Niedergang der römischen Welt,* part 2 volume 19.1, edited by H. Temporini and W. Haase, pages 477–510. Berlin/New York: de Gruyter.

1981   Social Systems of Six Diaspora Synagogues. In *Ancient Synagogues: The State of Research,* pages 79–91 and figure 19. Series: Brown Judaic Studies 22. Chico, Calif.: Scholars.

1982   The Roman Diaspora: Six Questionable Assumptions. *Journal of Jewish Studies* 33: 445–464.

1984   New Evidence of the Samaritan Diaspora Has Been Found of Delos. *Biblical Archaeologist* 47: 44–46.

1985   *Synagoga Caeca:* Systematic Distortion in Gentile Interpretations of Evidence for Judaism in the Early Christian Period. In *"To See Ourselves as Others See Us": Christians, Jews, "Others" in Late Antiquity,* edited by J. Neusner and E. S. Frerichs, pages 219–46. Chico, Calif.: Scholars.

Leon, H. J.
1960   *The Jews of Ancient Rome.* Philadelphia, Pa.: Jewish Publication Society of America.

Neusner, J.
1981   The Symbolism of Ancient Judaism: The Evidence of the Synagogue. In *Ancient Synagogues: The State of Research,* pages 7–17. Series: Brown Judaic Studies 22. Chico, Calif.: Scholars.

1982   *The Academic Study of Judaism.* Chico, Calif.: Scholars.

Nock, A. D.
1972   *Essays on Religion and the Ancient World.* Edited by Z. Stewart. Oxford: Clarendon.

Rostovtzeff, M.
1941   *The Social and Economic History of the Hellenistic World.* Oxford: Clarendon.

Smith, M.
1971   *Palestinian Parties and Politics that Shaped the Old Testament.* New York: Columbia University Press.

Weitzmann, K.
1979   *Age of Spirituality: Late Antique and Early Christian Art, Third to Seventh Century.*
         New York: Metropolitan Museum of Art.
Ziegler, K.; Sontheimer, W.; and Gärtner, H., editors
1964–75 *Der Kleine Pauly: Lexikon der Antike.* Stuttgart/Munich, W. Ger.: Deutscher
         Taschenbuch Verlag.

4. The Dura Europos Synagogue Paintings: The State of Research

Joseph Gutmann

The discovery of the third-century C.E. Dura Europos synagogue in 1932 highlights what G. Scholem (1973: xi) aptly has called "the internal censorship of the past, particularly by rabbinic tradition [which] has tended to play down or conceal many developments whose fundamentally Jewish character the contemporary historian has no reason to deny." M. Avi-Yonah (1973: 133) also felt that recent scholarship, especially on the Dura synagogue paintings had restored to Judaism a visual dimension sadly lacking before.

Scholars have raised a number of questions about the Dura Europos synagogue paintings, including: what do the individual paintings depict? Does the cycle of paintings reflect a definite and preplanned theological program of contemporary Judaism? What are the stylistic and iconographic sources of the Dura paintings? Why was the so-called Second Commandment ignored here? What influence might this painting cycle have exerted on later Jewish and Christian art? No consensus has been reached on these questions. Scholars are generally in accord on only three issues: first, that Erwin R. Goodenough's assumption that these paintings reveal a Philonic mystic Hellenistic Judaism may not be valid (Smith 1975:194–209; Avi-Yonah 1973: 117–35); second, that a scholar armed with the presumptive stern injunction of the Second Commandment would have been utterly shocked by this discovery and would have been forced to deny the Jewishness of these paintings; and, third, that the mural motifs in the Dura synagogue probably were not conceived there, but most likely stem from or reflect a program from one of the synagogues of a larger Jewish community of that region (Kraeling 1979: 391). As David Wright (1980: 8) stated, the Dura synagogue paintings "are too clumsy and provincial in execution to have been invented independently, without an iconographic model, in that desert outpost."

I have recently summarized and discussed the agreement or disagreement of scholars on what is depicted on the individual panels of the Dura synagogue (1984b: 1315–22). Of the approximately twenty-nine panels preserved, there is general agreement on what is represented in about a dozen of them. Some murals have as many as six different interpretations. For instance, the figure in wing panel III has been construed as representing Abraham, Joshua, Jacob, Moses, Enoch, and Elijah (Gutmann 1984b: 1317).

Many scenes in the Dura synagogue contain *'aggādôt* culled from such contemporary Palestinian works as the Jerusalem Targums, midrashic books like Genesis Rabbâ, the Jerusalem Talmud, and the Tôseptā'. These *'aggādôt* arose primarily in Palestine during the Amoraic period to meet the evergrowing challenge of Christianity in the Roman Empire. Christians, like Jews, sought potential converts; both shared a common sacred text —the Hebrew Bible—and resorted to similar methods of scriptural eisegesis and exegesis in preaching, writing, and art in order to reinforce their respective claims. Jewish scholars living in Parthian-Sasanian Babylonia, where Christianity never became the official religion, were not forced or challenged to produce such an immense literary genre to combat patristic scriptural interpretations (Gutmann 1984b: 1325–26; Wilken 1983: 68–83).

The Palestinian *'aggādôt* are at times found in earlier, so-called Hellenistic works from such diaspora centers as Alexandria. (It should be noted that the rabbis in Palestine, who devised the *'aggādôt*, were as subject to Hellenistic influences as the scholars of the Jewish Diaspora [Fischel 1973; Lieberman 1950].) Whether these extra-Septuagintal amplifications of the biblical narrative were known and copied by Palestinian rabbinic scholars or whether the rabbis and the "Hellenistic" scholars arrived at similar stories and interpretations without any direct influence deserves study (Gutmann 1983: 92–95).[1]

As far as the overall purpose and meaning of the entire cycle is concerned, scholars have tended to take one of three positions (Gutmann 1984b: 1322–24): first, that no unifying idea governs this painting cycle; second, that one comprehensive unified theological theme is discernible in these paintings; and, third, that several religious messages are expressed in this cycle.

As some forty percent of the cycle of paintings has been destroyed, and no similar cycle of synagogue paintings has yet been discovered, we may, at this time, not be able to unravel the full meaning of the entire cycle. However, recent research on the second, and largest, of the three bands of the Dura synagogue reveals a series of paintings that may have been analogous to contemporary Palestinian liturgical practice. The prominence given the yellow, rounded Torah ark-chest in the second band—a purposeful substitution for the ark-box described in the Bible—suggests the possibility that it was related to a liturgical hymn sung by the congregation when the Torah ark was brought from outside the synagogue, where it was kept at that time, and then led in procession around the synagogue. If this is the case, what unites all the paintings in the second band, which at first glance appear haphazardly torn from their biblical moorings, is not the biblical texts, but a contemporary Palestinian song and practice (Gutmann 1973: 148–50; Gruenwald 1980: 41, note 56).

The most important object in the synagogue is, of course, the ark containing the Torah scroll, symbolic of God's revelation to the Jewish people. The Torah is the only thing in the synagogue that possesses qĕdūšâ, holiness, and should not be touched by human hands. All other appurtenances in the synagogue are deemed expendable in times of stress or catastrophe, yet to the Torah alone is ascribed a sacred and transcendental value (Gutmann 1984a: 4).

Recent scholarship has also posited contemporary liturgical inspiration for the mosaic floors found in Palestinian synagogues dating from the fourth to the sixth centuries (Yahalom 1980: 54–56; Foerster 1981: 11–40; Gutmann 1984b: 1337–38). A similar practice was common in some later churches, for instance the fifth-century church of Santa Maria Maggiore in Rome and the sixth-century church of San Vitale in Ravenna, where some of the biblical scenes were again severed from their narrative biblical confines. Prominence in the churches was often given to the church altar—whose antitype was also the ancient biblical ark (Revel-Neher 1984: 44–67; Bloch 1963: 757–58)—the most significant object in the church, where the drama of the Mass was performed and recited. What unites these biblical scenes in the churches are not the ancient biblical stories depicted but the liturgical words of the Mass that were sung below, before the church altar. These mosaic illustrations in churches function as visual counterparts to the ongoing audial liturgical prayers (Gutmann 1973: 146–48; Gutmann 1984b: 1325–26), and this may be what we have found in the Dura synagogue.

The stylistic sources of the Dura paintings have been a matter of scholarly dispute. The frontality of the figures in the Dura synagogue paintings appears to have been a relatively new development in art. Both ancient Western Asian art and Greco-Roman art generally adhered to the profile view in narrative compositions. The figures simply interacted with each other in their own space within the narrative panels and demanded no interaction with the viewer.

In his book entitled *Orient oder Rom* (1901), Josef Strzygowski reviewed the argument among art historians about whether the sources for frontality in later Christian art should be sought in Western Asia, or whether they are a product of Hellenistic-Roman imagination.[2] Many scholars still debate whether the frontality found in Dura should be attributed to provincial Roman art—a pejorative term denoting inferior art that crudely and naively copied the major art characteristic of Rome, the imperial capital—or whether it was a development of Parthian art (Gutmann 1984b: 1331–33). There are too few Parthian art remains to give a conclusive answer, though it is apparent that areas under Parthian control knew several styles, none of which was all-embracing. Malcolm Colledge (1977: 143) aptly summarized this problem:

> The Parthians imposed no common language of art, and let diverse traditions flourish. . . . This lack of control by the Parthians reflects on social and political as much as on art history, in which the very term "Parthian" ought clearly to be dropped in favour of others more stylistically and chronologically accurate.

The schematic, rigid, and hieratic frontality of all figures seems to be an artistic mode that made its appearance in first-century C.E. Syria, especially Palmyra. It grew out of an artistic synchretism of Hellenistic-Roman, Parthian-Iranian, and native Arab-Syrian elements (Goldman 1985). Frontality appeared in isolated instances in both Western Asian and Hellenistic-Roman art. When so employed, it functioned as one of several possible postures that an artist could choose for rendering figures within a composition. Still, frontality as a conscious compositional scheme for all figures within a narrative scene was at home primarily in first-century C.E. Palmyra. This compositional technique required a different relationship and interaction on the part of its viewers. It demanded a spiritual confrontation and interaction of the figures on the wall with the worshipers viewing them. For instance, the large, staring eyes on the figures facing the spectator revealed "an inner life hidden in a charged cloud of flesh" (Brown 1971: 74). These figures were no longer detached from the viewer, as was the profile figure—the convention of narrative figural renderings in both Western Asian and Hellenistic-Roman art. Spiritual, cultural, and theological needs growing out of the new socioeconomic and political developments in that Western Asian desert region were the underpinnings of this novel artistic practice. J. H. Breasted called this mode of portrayal "Oriental Forerunners of Byzantine Painting" (1924), but whether the art of such Western Asian cities as Dura and Palmyra directly inspired the later Roman and Christian art, or whether both independently adopted it for similar spiritual reasons, remains to be explored.

The Dura paintings, both in the synagogue and in related Palmyrene shrines like the Temple of the Gadde, show a close stylistic and iconographic affinity to surviving Palmyrene art. Palmyra (then called Tadmor), in the middle of the Syrian desert, was one of the most important caravan cities of Syria—a crossroad for diverse peoples and cultures providing the Roman West with luxury goods from the East. Palmyrene soldiers served in the Roman army in such faraway places as Africa and Europe; its leaders showed loyalty to Rome for most of its brief existence (Drijvers 1976: 1–3). We know that Jews lived in Palmyra and must have been active there when Palmyra flourished and reached its economic height in the second and early third centuries C.E. (Teixidor 1979: IX). Close connections between Palmyra and neighboring Dura are borne out not only by the stylistic and iconographic parallels in the works of art but also by the direct procurement of sculptures from nearby Palmyra in order to enrich the Palmyrene shrines in Dura. B. Goldman (in press) concludes,

> Considering that the Palmyrenes brought their gods, their shrines, and their sacred images to Dura, it is reasonable to suspect that they also hired Palmyrene artists to come to the hinterlands and decorate the prosperous households and well-endowed sanctuaries.[3]

It should be noted that Palmyrene inscriptions at Dura reveal the influence of Syro-Palestinian traditions, and the Jewish legends portrayed in the Dura synagogue also show their Palestinian derivation. Furthermore, Palmyrene Jews were interred in the Palestinian tombs at Bêt Šĕʿārîm (Teixidor 1979: IX; Gutmann 1983: 100–4; Avigad 1971: 260–61). It is therefore not unreasonable to conjecture that it may have been a Jewish synagogue situated in Palmyra whose more sophisticated cycle of paintings, influenced by Palestinian Jewish liturgy, customs and legends, served as the model for the Dura synagogue (Kraeling 1979: 391).

Clark Hopkins (1979: 131) correctly emphasized that if scholars of ancient history, art, or religion were told about an ancient synagogue with figurative paintings they "would not have believed it. . . . The stern injunction in the Ten Commandments against the making of graven images would be sufficient to prove them right." Malcolm Colledge (1977: 120) also writes that the Dura synagogue was refurbished "in apparent defiance of the Second Commandment." Hopkins, Colledge, and other scholars failed to consider that the so-called Second Commandment cannot be viewed as an unchanging concept that never transcended its own original biblical context. It would be more accurate to speak of Second Commandment*s*, in the plural, for Judaism is not a static religion: its involvement with multiple civilizations, cultures, and societies constantly demands new interpretations and evaluations of the original biblical injunction. Thus, in the course of Jewish history multiple commandments have been formulated.

We need only look at the Bible itself to realize that within the book of Exodus is the clear mandate, "You shall not make for yourself a sculptured image or any likeness" (Exodus 20: 4–5) juxtaposed with the story of Bezalel who "was endowed with a divine spirit of skill, ability and knowledge in every kind of craft" (Exodus 31: 1–5) to fashion the very images condemned in the earlier section of Exodus. Similarly, first-century Palestinian Jewry is known to have violently objected to the placement of a statue of the Roman emperor Caligula in the Jerusalem Temple; the biblical Second Commandment was cited to undergird the grievance (Josephus, *Antiquities*, 18.8.2[264]). Third-century Babylonian Jewry, on the contrary, offered no objection to the placement of a royal statue in the synagogue of Něhardě'ā' (B Rôš Haššānâ 24b; B 'Aḅôdâ Zārâ 43b). Several recent studies have analyzed in great detail this much misunderstood problem (Gutmann 1971: 3–16; 1977: 5–25; Baumgarten 1975: 79–89).

The Dura synagogue paintings were made approximately 244–45 C.E. and were buried as a result of the Roman defense system against the feared Sasanian invasion which occurred about 256 C.E. During the eleven years of their public existence, the Dura paintings could hardly have influenced later Christian art. The putative synagogue of Palmyra would also not have exerted an influence on later Christian art, as Palmyra was sacked by Rome in 272 C.E., a disaster that helped precipitate its final downfall a year later. Although the Dura synagogue cycle of paintings lay buried, and those of other synagogues were destroyed, scholars hypothesize that illustrated Jewish manuscripts existed in antiquity and served as models of inspiration for these synagogues and for later Christian art. They base their conjecture on iconographic parallels between the Dura synagogue paintings and later Jewish and Christian art, the appearance of Jewish legends—extrabiblical stories—in later Jewish and Christian art, and the assumed existence of ancient illustrated classical literary manuscripts.

Certain considerations, however, tend to argue for other conclusions. First, the few iconographical details chosen for comparison are of such a general nature that neither the Dura synagogue paintings nor their models need have served as a source of inspiration. The costumes worn and the mode of representation in these later illustrations are so different that they make this premise questionable (Gutmann 1984b: 1334; Cutler 1981: 45 and following).

Second, it is a now generally accepted fact that aggadic elaborations, originally drawn from such works as Targums and midrashic books, exist in illustrated Christian manuscripts. The assumption, however, that behind these legendary depictions lie illustrated Jewish manuscripts is doubtful, as similar exegetical, legendary, and homiletical explanations are found in patristic literature (Gutmann 1983: 101–4). Hence, many scholars reject the hypothesis of the existence of illustrated Jewish manuscripts in antiquity. They feel that Christian literary works and/or oral teaching are more likely to have served as direct sources of inspiration for extrabiblical stories illustrated in Christian art. Thus the point of view (Schubert 1983: 1) that it is "heute schon fast eine *'communis opinio'* . . ., dass es sowohl jüdische Bildvorlagen in der Spätantike gegeben hat" is countered by Brenk (1975: 128), who writes:

> jüdisches Legendgut illustrieren, bedeutet nicht notwendigerweise, dass es eine malerische Vorlage jüdischen Ursprungs zu Rate gezogen ist. Jüdische Stoffen machen noch keine jüdische Kunst. Da jüdische Legenden von Christen gelesen wurden, ist es durchaus möglich, dass eine Illustration überhaupt erst durch Christen erfolgte.

David Wright (1980: 8) concluded, "I suspect some of the other biblical Jewish elements had crept in generally, mostly by literary transmission, perhaps even oral teaching."

Third, the existence of classical and Jewish illustrated literary manuscripts in antiquity has been accepted by Kurt Weitzmann and his followers (Gutmann 1984b: 1333). Wright (1980: 7) humorously comments:

> Visiting Princeton some twenty-five years ago, I was told that a biblical scholar had discovered a mistake in the accepted text of Genesis II.2: on the seventh day God did not rest, He created an illuminated manuscript, and that manuscript became the source of all pictorial iconography. It was the pious duty of the School of Princeton to reconstruct as much as possible of this ultimate *Urhandschrift.* . . . The fault lies not with Weitzmann, but some of his pupils, who have attempted to codify a doctrine and have baptized it with his name.

Many scholars have rejected this argumentum ex silentio. They assert that no such illustrated literary manuscripts are mentioned in surviving ancient sources. The few manuscript fragments that have come down to us reveal primarily sketches that served a didactic function in ancient natural science books. No continuous classical literary cycle of painted illustrations in manuscript scrolls has survived (Deichmann 1983: 355). These scholars also point out that it is not customary to expose precious manuscripts to dirty workshops, and they stress the unlikelihood of the Dura atelier possessing a library of biblical books ranging from Genesis to Maccabees. Furthermore, the Dura painting cycle does not reflect the style of the assumed Alexandrian Jewish manuscripts.

No lavishly illustrated classical manuscript securely antedates the late fourth or early fifth century C.E. and no illustrated Jewish manuscript is known prior to the late ninth century C.E. The earliest Christian cycles, whether on walls or in manuscripts, bespeak an indebtedness to Roman imperial narrative and epic art found, for instance, in such Roman imperial triumphal monuments as arches and columns and epic frescoes. Recent research has demonstrated that the stylistic and icono-graphic similarities of illustrated cycles, whether in late classical manuscripts of Virgil or Christian biblical manuscripts, probably derive from pictorial guides—pattern, model, or motif books—which may have been a fairly common Roman workshop accessory. These pictorial guides served as transmitters of similar iconographic and formal elements such as stereo-typed figures and architectural and landscape motifs—so-called pictorial *topoi*—from country to country, workshop to workshop, and from one artistic medium to another (Stevenson 1983: 109–10; Wright 1980: 7; Deichmann 1983: 357–58; Gutmann 1984b: 1334; Kitzinger 1975: 109–21; Toynbee 1972: 109–10; Mielsch 1981: 253–54; Colledge 1977: 136–37; Dunbabin 1982: 69–70).[4]

The Hellenistic-Roman attitude toward books radically differed from that which typified the Judeo-Christian world. No canonical book, such as the Bible, secured recognition as an authoritative moral guide in the Hellenistic and Roman cultures. No one book in the Greco-Roman world was considered so holy or was so celebrated as the Gospels or the Bible. The Greco-Roman book was not holy in itself; it was simply a utilitarian object, a vehicle of information, not a conveyor of God's sacred words. Depictions from Hellenistic and Roman societies never show the Hellenistic-Roman gods, such as Zeus-Jupiter, with a sacred book in their hands—a common attribute of Jesus, the Evangelists, and the prophetic figures in Christian art. Authors, philosophers, and pedagogues are usually depicted holding or reading scroll texts; they are never transcribing or writing holy words, as is the case in the Judeo-Christian world (Birt 1907: 69–71, 197–99; Elsen 1967: 87–89). The very transmission of the written sacred word is assigned to God at Mount Sinai in Judeo-Christian traditions, and the recording of God's holy words, considered an act of great religious merit, was assigned to people of high status, such as priests, scholar-scribes, or monks. In Hellenistic-Roman civilization, the inferior task of reading and writing was usually left to slaves, and even the transmission of the alphabet was attributed to a mortal Phoenician, Kadmos/Cadmus (Gärtner 1969: 42; Roberts and Skeat 1983: 12–14). In no classical text do we read anything comparable to the words of the book of John (1:1): "In the beginning was the Word, and the Word was with God, and the Word was God" (RSV). "Oral instruction and conversation, not reading and study" were stressed in the Hellenistic-Roman world (Kenyon 1932: 21). Books in the classical cultures "may be useful to refresh the memory, but are greatly inferior to the spoken word as a means of education" (Kenyon 1932: 21; Carcopino 1940: 114–21; Wilken 1983: 96–98).

There is no doubt that illuminated medieval Christian manuscripts influenced monumental church cycles in paint, mosaic, and stone. However, retrojecting and imposing a medieval Christian mentality, that held the illuminated book in the highest esteem and in a privileged position, into Hellenistic-Roman antiquity is not warranted. Fresco painting appears to be the preferred art carrier in the Roman world (Brendel 1979: 95). Only Christianity and Judaism and subsequently Islam declared the book sacred because it contained God's holy words. This phenomenon was simply not known in the Greco-Roman sphere.

Given this attitude, it seems unlikely that money and time would have been expended on the preparation of luxurious and precious illustrated, classical, literary manuscripts, as books in themselves were accorded little intrinsic sacred value or function.

The Dura Europos synagogue paintings have opened up hitherto unforeseen horizons in ancient religious art and history. While they have helped clarify some issues pertaining to stylistic, iconographic, and literary problems, they have also raised others that await solution.

I should like to express my gratitude to my good friend, Professor Stanley F. Chyet, for reading this paper and suggesting many improvements.

Notes

1 The following corrections and additions should be made to this article: page 93, note 6 should read: Joseph Gutmann, "The Sacrifice of Isaac: Variations on a Theme in Early Jewish and Christian Art," in: *Thiasos tōn Mousōn: Studien zu Antike und Christentum, Festschrift für Josef Fink zum 70. Geburtstag,* edited by D. Ahrens, Köln-Wien, 1984, 115–22. On page 99, note 20, line 7 insert: an Interpretation of a Panel. Page 102, note 26, lines 9–10 should read: (1976), 109 is not aware of the above cited traditions. On the claim that "the image of the Israelites as an army at the Red Sea is itself anachronistic," compare: page 103, note 28 (line 8 should read, *Pirkei Avot* 5:4) and page 104, note 30, line 3, *Wolfenbüttel.* Page 117, note 5, line 1 should read, *Targum Pseudo Jonathan* 22:14. Page 117, note 6 add, J. Swetman, *Jesus and Isaac* [Analecta Biblica, number 94, Rome, 1981]. Compare also S. P. Brock, "Genesis 22 in Syriac Tradition," *Mélanges Dominique Barthélemy,* Göttingen, 1981, 1–30. Page 120, note 13 add, J. A. Lerner, "Christian Seals of the Sasanian Period," *Nederlands Historisch-Archaeologisch Instituut te Istanbul,* 41 (1977). Pages 18–22 reveal a series of Western Asian seals with Sacrifice of Isaac depictions, dating perhaps from the fifth century C.E., that appear to follow the Dura synagogue prototype. Page 120, lines 13–15 should read: Nine terracotta tiles found near Hajeb-el-Aïoun, North Africa, in the Bardo Museum, Tunisia, which date to the second half of the sixth century. . . . I am grateful to Dr. Nejib Ben Lazreg for this information. In light of the securely dated terracotta tiles from North Africa, the mosaic at Bêt 'Alpā' should probably also be dated to the second half of the sixth century. Compare ibid., page 121, note 17.

2 I have avoided using such common terms as Near Eastern or Oriental art, since these designations are rooted in nineteenth-century imperialism. E. Said (1978: 95) has incisively shown that these terms are Western projections that support domination and control of that part of the world called "Orient." "The Orient that appears in Orientalism, then, is a system of representations framed by a whole set of forces that brought the Orient into Western learning, Western consciousness, and later, Western empire" (Said 1978: 202–3).

3 I am greatly indebted to my colleague, Professor Bernard Goldman, for making this unpublished paper available to me.

4 In a personal communication of September 11, 1984 Professor Dunbabin commented on my article (Gutmann, 1983), "An example like yours, so very remote in place and in two very different media, neither of them exactly 'high art,' seems to me a fairly conclusive argument . . . which nothing but circulating patterns or models can possibly explain."

Bibliography

Avi-Yonah, M.
  1973   Goodenough's Evaluation of Dura: A Critique. In *The Dura-Europos Synagogue: A Re-Evaluation (1932–1972)*, edited by J. Gutmann, pages 117–35. Missoula, Mont.: Scholars.

Avigad, N.
  1971   *Beth She'arim: Report on the Excavations during 1953–1958*, volume 3. New Brunswick, N.J.: Rutgers University Press.

Baumgarten, J. M.
  1975   Art in the Synagogue: Some Talmudic Views. In *The Synagogue: Studies in Origins, Archaeology and Architecture*, edited by J. Gutmann, pages 79–89. New York: Ktav.

Birt, T.
  1907   *Die Buchrolle in der Kunst: Archäologisch-Antiquarische Untersuchungen zum antiken Buchwesen*. Leipzig, W. Ger.: Teubner.

Bloch, P.
  1963   Nachwirkungen des Alten Bundes in der christlichen Kunst. In *Monumenta Judaica. 2000 Jahre Geschichte und Kultur der Juden am Rhein*, pages 735–81. Cologne, W. Ger.: Melzer Verlag.

Breasted, J. H.
  1924   *Oriental Forerunners of Byzantine Painting*. Chicago, Ill.: University of Chicago Press.

Brendel, O.
  1979   *Prolegomena to the Study of Roman Art*. New Haven, Conn.: Yale University Press.

Brenk, B.
  1975   *Die frühchristlichen Mosaiken in S. Maria Maggiore zu Rom*. Wiesbaden, W. Ger.: Franz Steiner.

Brown, P.
  1971   *The World of Late Antiquity AD 150–750*. London: Thames and Hudson.

Carcopino, J.
  1940   *Daily Life in Ancient Rome*. New Haven, Conn.: Yale University Press.

Colledge, M. A. R.
  1977   *Parthian Art*. Ithaca, N.Y.: Cornell University Press.

Cutler, A.
  1981   Misapprehensions and Misgivings: Byzantine Art and the West in the Twelfth and Thirteenth Centuries. *Mediaevalia* 7: 41–77.

Deichmann, F. W.
1983   *Einführung in die christliche Archäologie.* Darmstadt, W. Ger.: Wissenschaftliche Buchgesellschaft.
Drijvers, H. J. W.
1976   *The Religion of Palmyra.* Leiden, The Netherlands: Brill.
Dunbabin, K. M. D.
1982   The Victorious Charioteer on Mosaics and Related Monuments. *American Journal of Archaeology* 86: 69–89.
Elsen, A.
1967   *Purposes of Art: An Introduction to the History and Appreciation of Art.* New York: Holt, Rinehart, Winston.
Fischel, H.
1973   *Rabbinic Literature and Greco-Roman Philosophy: A Study of Epicurea and Rhetorica in Early Midrashic Writings.* Leiden, The Netherlands: Brill.
Foerster, G.
1981   Synagogue Inscriptions and Their Relations to Liturgical Versions. *Cathedra* 19: 11–40 (Hebrew).
Gärtner, H.
1969   Kadmos. In *Der kleine Pauly Lexikon der Antike,* volume 3, edited by K. Ziegler, W. Sontheimer, and H. Gärtner, columns 40–42. Stuttgart, W. Ger.: A Druckenmüller.
Goldman, B.
1985   A Dura-Europos Dipinto and Syrian Frontality. *Oriens Antiquus* 24.
in press   Foreigners at Dura-Europos: Pictorial Graffiti and History. *Le Muséon.*
Gruenwald, I.
1980   *Apocalyptic and Merkavah Mysticism.* Leiden, The Netherlands: Brill.
Gutmann, J.
1971   The "Second Commandment" and the Image in Judaism. In *No Graven Images: Studies in Art and the Hebrew Bible,* edited by J. Gutmann, pages xiii–xxx, 3–16. New York: Ktav.

1973   Programmatic Painting in the Dura Synagogue. In *The Dura-Europos Synagogue: A Re-Evaluation (1932–1972),* edited by J. Gutmann, pages 137–54. Missoula, Mont.: Scholars.

1977   Deuteronomy: Religious Reformation or Iconoclastic Revolution? In *The Image and the Word: Confrontations in Judaism, Christianity and Islam,* edited by J. Gutmann, pages 5–25. Missoula, Mont.: Scholars.

1983   The Illustrated Midrash in the Dura Synagogue Paintings: A New Dimension for the Study of Judaism. *American Academy of Jewish Research Proceedings* 50: 92–104.
1984a   *The Jewish Sanctuary.* Leiden, The Netherlands: Brill.
1984b   Early Synagogue and Jewish Catacomb Art and its Relation to Christian Art. In *Aufstieg und Niedergang der römischen Welt,* part 2, volume 21.2, edited by H. Temporini and W. Haase, pages 1313–42. Berlin: de Gruyter.
Hopkins, C.
1979   *The Discovery of Dura-Europos,* edited by B. Goldman. New Haven, Conn.: Yale University Press.
Kenyon, F. G.
1932   *Books and Readers in Ancient Greece and Rome.* Oxford: Oxford University Press.
Kitzinger, E.
1975   The Role of Miniature Painting in Mural Decoration. In *The Place of Book Illumination in Byzantine Art,* edited by K. Weitzmann, et al., pages 99–142. Princeton, N.J.: Princeton University Press.

Kraeling, C. H.
1979   *The Synagogue: Excavations at Dura-Europos, Final Report* VIII.1. New York: Ktav.
Lieberman, S.
1950   *Hellenism in Jewish Palestine: Studies in the Literary Transmission, Beliefs and Manners of Palestine in the I Century* B.C.E.–*IV Century* C.E. New York: Jewish Theological Seminary of America.
Mielsch, H.
1981   Funde und Forschungen zur Wandmalerei der Principatszeit von 1945 bis 1975, mit einem Nachtrag 1980. In *Aufstieg und Niedergang der römischen Welt*, part 2, volume 12.2, edited by H. Temporini, pages 157–264. Berlin: de Gruyter.
Revel–Neher, E.
1984   *L'arche d'alliance dans l'art juif et chrétien du second au dixième siècles.* Paris: Association des amis des études archéologiques Byzantino-Slaves et du Christianisme Oriental.
Roberts, C. H., and Skeat, T. C.
1983   *The Birth of the Codex.* London: Oxford University Press.
Said, E.
1978   *Orientalism.* New York: Vintage.
Scholem, G.
1973   *Sabbatai Ṣevi: The Mystical Messiah.* Princeton, N.J.: Princeton University Press.
Schubert, K.
1983   Die Illustrationen in der Wiener Genesis im Lichte der rabbinischen Tradition. *Kairos* 25: 1–17.
Smith, M.
1975   Goodenough's Jewish Symbols in Retrospect. In *The Synagogue: Studies in Origins, Archaeology and Architecture*, edited by J. Gutmann, pages 194–209. New York: Ktav.
Stevenson, T. B.
1983   *Miniature Decoration in the Vatican Virgil. A Study in Late Antique Iconography.* Tübingen, W. Ger.: E. Wasmuth.
Strzygowski, J.
1901   *Orient oder Rom.* Leipzig, W. Ger.: J. C. Hinrichs.
Teixidor, J.
1979   *The Pantheon of Palmyra.* Leiden, The Netherlands: Brill.
Toynbee, J. C. M. C.
1972   Some Problems of Romano-Parthian Sculpture at Hatra. *Journal of Roman Studies* 62: 106–10.
Wilken, R. L.
1983   *John Chrysostom and the Jews. Rhetoric and Reality in the Late 4th Century.* Berkeley, Calif.: University of California Press.
Wright, D. H.
1980   The School of Princeton and the Seventh Day of Creation. *University Publishing* Summer 7–8.
Yahalom, J.
1980   Synagogue Inscriptions in Palestine–A Stylistic Classification. *Immanuel* 10: 47–56.

5. The Šĕmaʿ and its Blessings: The Realization of God's Kingship

Reuven Kimelman

The liturgical rubric entitled *Šĕmaʿ* and its accompanying blessings is composed of a concatenation of three pentateuchal paragraphs (Deuteronomy 6:4–9, 11:13–21; Numbers 15:37–41) surrounded by three blessings, two before and one after. The three blessings are designated by their closing eulogy. These are respectively, "Creator of lights," "who loves His people Israel" or "who chooses His people Israel in love," and "redeemed Israel." The liturgy does not provide any explicit explanation of the meaning of the liturgical rubric nor of its origins. For historical information we are dependent upon extraliturgical sources. For its liturgical meaning we must rely on outside sources as well as on an analysis of the rubric itself.

Two sources report on the early history of the *Šĕmaʿ* and its blessings. According to the Mishna (Tāmîd 5:1) and Josephus (*Antiquities,* 4.8.13 [212–13]) the three paragraphs of the *Šĕmaʿ* were part of the Temple service; they were preceded by a blessing and the Decalogue, and followed by a blessing. Since there is no similar statement with regard to the non-Temple liturgy, scholars have disagreed on its composition. One position (Heinemann 1977: 230, notes 30–31) holds that it contained all three blessings and that the Temple service was an abbreviation thereof. Another (Finkelstein 1932: 15, note 4; 17) holds that the second blessing preceding the *Šĕmaʿ* superseded the Decalogue.

The excision of the Decalogue remains problematic. The most recent discussion of the whole subject is that of Urbach (1985). According to the Talmud (B Bĕrākôt 12a; J Bĕrākôt 1.8.3c), sectarian carping about the exclusive Sinaitic origin of the Decalogue led to its removal. It is hard to believe that this is an adequate explanation for the excision of something so central to the liturgy as the Decalogue. It is possible that the Decalogue was never part of the synagogue liturgy or that once the first two blessings were associated with the *Šěma*ʿ there was no longer any place for its recital within the new framework. The so-called Nash Papyrus does contain both the Decalogue and the *Šěma*ʿ, but, as Haberman (1954) and Yadin (1969) have shown, this, as well as Qumran evidence, relate to phylacteries of the Temple and not necessarily to non-Temple liturgy. Of course, it is always possible, as Dr. Meir Bar-Ilan mentioned to me, that the phylacteries served as a kind of portable prayerbook. At any rate, there has not yet been found any liturgical rubric of the period which contains the Decalogue and two blessings as a preface to the *Šěma*ʿ.

We are also not in a position to know whether the preliminary Temple blessing is to be identified with the first or the second blessing of the later synagogue. The third-century Palestinian, Rêš Laqîš (B Běrākôt 11a–b), and most modern scholars (Finkelstein 1932: 18–19) identify it with the first blessing, while the third-century Babylonian Mar Samuel (ibid.) and the Palestinian Talmud (J Běrākôt 1.8.3c) identify it with something similar to the second blessing. Nonetheless, even if it could be shown that semblances of these blessings circulated in Temple times, it would take additional evidence to show that they were part of a synagogal liturgy and even more to show that they were juxtaposed to each other. Baillet (1982: 111) tried to reconstruct a Qumran fragment to make it appear as if there were already a prayer about sunrise juxtaposed to one on the chosenness of Israel. However, from the photographed fragments at the back of his book (xxxvii) it is clear that the present state of the fragment does not allow for this reconstruction.

Mishna Běrākôt 1:4 knows already of a defined liturgical unit in which the *Šěma*ʿ is embedded in a framework of three blessings for both morning and evening. (The evening service has appended an additional blessing called *haškîbēnû* intended to allay normal nocturnal apprehensions, but it is not intrinsically related to the liturgical core.)

Mishna Běrākôt 2:2 contains an explicit statement on the purpose of the *Šěma*ʿ. The first paragraph of the *Šěma*ʿ reflects the "authority of God's kingship," and the second paragraph reflects the "authority of the commandments." The data provided by the Mishna allow for two lines of inquiry. First, to what degree do the three blessings of the framework correspond to the three core paragraphs of the *Šěma*ʿ? Second, to what degree does the central idea of realizing God's kingship supply the ideational context for the whole liturgical rubric? In order to discern the correspondence between the blessings and the *Šěma*ʿ we must first ascertain the motif of each blessing. Since the primary idea of each blessing is encapsulated in its conclusion (*ḥatîmâ*), it follows that when the three blessings were formulated, the themes were God as creator of lights (in the morning) and darkness (in the evening); God as lover of Israel; and, finally, God as redeemer of Israel.

Ultimately all the blessings assumed a common rhetorical structure. Each blessing promotes a specific theological dogma with regard to an event (creation, revelation, or redemption) that is not immediately available to experience. However, in order to enhance its plausibility, the dogma is grounded in an event that is available to experience. The first blessing of the morning service proclaims that God is the creator of the world. (It is clear from the early *piyyûṭîm* that either embellished the prayers or replaced them on special occasions that the theme of the first blessing is the creation of the world, not just that of the lights [Fleischer 1985: 85].) The worshiper's receptivity to this thesis is enhanced by being sensitized to the daily wonders of the universe as reflected in the natural transformations from light to darkness and back to light. Indeed, the third-century Palestinian amora, Rabbi Samuel bar Naḥman, argued that the response to such transformations accounts for thrice-daily prayer (Genesis Rabbâ 68, 9 in Theodor and Albeck 1965: 779).

The first blessing of the evening service contains several variations on the theme of the change from light to darkness and back to light. The redundancy serves to underscore the regularity and predictability of the heavenly changes at dusk to allay any fear of chaos in the face of rapidly approaching darkness. Indeed, the evening, as depicted by the blessing, evidences optimal divine control. The change of the evening guard presents, as it were, a cast of thousands. Every role is synchronized to produce a splendidly orchestrated evening spectacle.

The first blessing of the morning service, for its part, focuses upon the compassion and goodness of God in bringing daily light. Common to both is an appreciation of the intricate operation of the universe. Engendering amazement at the wonderful and wisely formed creation enhances receptivity to the theological agendum of the blessing and leads to the acclamation that God is creator and controller of the world. There is little theologically that needs be added to then affirm that God is one. The logic of the connection, albeit in reverse, is brought out in the midrashic statement, "Whoever declares God is one acknowledges that He created His world" (Midrash Leqaḥ Tôḇ, Genesis 1, 5 in Buber 1960: 5a).

The love of God for Israel forms the thesis of the second blessing. His everlasting love is attested to by the gift of the Torah, which is pointedly called "the statutes of life." Thus the Torah is a gift of love that provides guidance for living. Since God loves, he teaches. The exhortation is: study the Torah, heed its commandments, and you will experience it as an expression of God's love. In the end, you, too, will proclaim that "God loves His people, Israel." This blessing leads into both the second line of the *Šĕma*, which states, "You shall love the Lord your God," and the second paragraph, which admonishes heeding the commandments lest dire consequences ensue.

The case for God's love is made by the second blessing. Positioning it before the *Šĕma* makes the point that we are to love God, because He loved us first. We are aroused to love by becoming aware that we are loved. As both modern (Mirsky 1963: 324; Liebreich 1966: 154) and medieval commentators (Abudarham 1963: 75–76; Rabbenu Shlomoh 1971: 89) have noted, the biblical commandment to love God becomes liturgically the reciprocation of divine love. As a midrash observes, "Israel says: 'You shall love the Lord your God' [Deuteronomy 6:5]. And God says to them: 'With everlasting love have I loved you' [Jeremiah 31:3]" (Ginzberg 1969: volume 1, 118). (In contrast, Maimonides [Hilkôt Yĕsôdê Ha-Tôrâ 2:2] apparently views the data of the first blessing as an adequate *preparatio* for love. For him, the contemplation of divine wisdom as reflected in the wonders of creation evokes the love entreated in the second line of the *Šĕma*.) Moreover, perceiving the commandments as expressions of divine loving guidance helps arouse the desire to observe them, which is the aim of the second paragraph of the *Šĕma*. The assumption is that the love of God entails keeping His commandments. What the second paragraph of the *Šĕma* achieves through threats, the blessing before the *Šĕma* achieves through love.

The third blessing shares the thesis of the third paragraph of the *Šĕma*, namely, that God is the redeemer of Israel; it is a bit different from the preliminary blessings in that there is no tangible evidence, like the sunrise or the Torah's laws of life, to substantiate the thesis. The liturgist perforce falls back on the redemption from Egypt. However, the liturgy does not evoke the Exodus for historical reasons alone. On the contrary, the Exodus was a foreshadowing and paradigm of what was to come in the future. God's past conduct serves as a warranty for the future. Since this is so often the point, and, as Joseph Caro (*Kesep Mishna, Hīlkôt Qĕrî'at Šĕma* 1, 7, under the word "katāb") has noted, it need not always be spelled out; though, as Gĕnîzâ fragments attest, it sometimes was made explicit (Mann 1925: 307, 321; Ginzberg 1969: volume 2, 516).

In sum, as the first blessing serves as the liturgical prelude to the first line of the *Šĕma*, so the second blessing serves as the prelude to the second line and the second paragraph of the *Šĕma*. The third blessing, taking its cue from the third paragraph of the *Šĕma*, functions as the finale of the whole rubric. (The symmetry of the morning service led Heinemann [1981: 19, note 26] to see it as the model for the evening service.) The Hebrew diagram is as follows:

Blessing	Biblical Paragraph	Blessing	
	שמע . . . אחד	יוצר המאורות	1.
. . . והיה אם שמוע	ואהבת . . .	אוהב עמו ישראל	2.
גאל (גואל) ישראל	ויאמר. . .		3.

Still absent at this stage are the explicit references to the kingship of God that characterize the present liturgy. Once the Mishna propounded the idea that the purpose of the *Šĕmaʿ* was the acceptance of divine sovereignty, the liturgical rubric was reworked accordingly, thus granting an additional liturgical-theological coherence to the whole rubric. (This assumes that the elements of request and allusions to redemption in the first two blessings are later developments.)

The first explicit introduction of the kingship motif is the interpolation after the opening line of the *Šĕmaʿ*. It reads: "Blessed be the name of His sovereign glory for ever and ever." The insertion serves to underscore the point that by reciting the verse, "Hear, O Israel: The Lord our God, the Lord is One," God is being declared sovereign. The original context of the phrase was in response to the mention of the Tetragrammaton in the Temple. There, however, it read, "Blessed be His glorious Name forever." As Finkelstein noted (1942–43: 38), "The change of the form שם כבודו to שם כבוד מלכותו was doubtless intended to emphasize the Kingship of God." Henceforth, the recitation of the *Šĕmaʿ* could no longer be construed as merely a reading of the Torah. It became, as Finkelstein (1925: 177) has pointed out, a declaration of allegiance to the kingship of God.

In the course of time, the kingship motif became so associated with the *Šĕmaʿ* that all medieval rites (that is, *Seder Rav Amram, Siddur Rav Saadiah,* Maimonides, *Maḥzor Romi,* along with the Sefardic, Ashkenazic, and Yemenite rites) adopted it as the climactic verse of the *malkhiot* service in the High Holiday *musaf* liturgy. This is despite the fact that the *Šĕmaʿ* lacks the normal requirement for inclusion in this medley of verses, namely, an explicit reference to kingship. Immediately afterwards, the prayer asks God to make manifest his reign over all. In fact, a Genizah fragment (Mann 1925: 329) has the *Šĕmaʿ* verse worked into this request.

Once the goal of the *Šĕmaʿ* and its blessings became the recognition of God's sovereignty, the liturgy sought ways to acclaim God king and produced both a precedent and a model for this idea. The precedent is Israel's song of salvation intoned after crossing the Sea of Reeds. It culminates with the acclaim, "The Lord will reign for ever and ever" (Exodus 15:18; Leviticus Rabbâ 2, 4 in Margulies 1953–60: 42). The model is the acclamation of the angels, as recorded by Isaiah, who, upon seeing God enthroned on high, called out, "Holy, Holy, Holy is the Lord of Hosts, the whole earth is full of His glory" (Isaiah 6:3). The precedent of ancient Israel accepting God's sovereignty upon emerging from the Sea was inserted in the third blessing, which lauds God for having redeemed Israel.

The kingship motif became central to the third blessing quite early. Rabbi Judah Hanasi mandated its insertion there (following Ginzberg 1941: 208), while "others" required mentioning the tenth plague and the splitting of the Sea (T Běrākôt 2, 1; J Běrākôt 1.9.3d). The position of Rabbi Judah Hanasi is already reflected in T Běrākôt 1, 10, which argues for the primacy of the kingship motif over the Exodus one. One way of meeting both of the above requirements, as Fleischer (1985: 5) has noted, is by the insertion of verses from Moses' Song of the Sea. According to Heinemann (1981: 16), this phenomenon is already attested to in a prayer from the amoraic period. Apparently it is an abbreviated form of the third evening blessing. Following the position of Rabbi Joshua ben Levi, that all of the aforementioned elements be mentioned, it states: "We acknowledge You, O Lord our God, that you took us out of Egypt and redeemed us from the house of bondage, and performed for us miracles and mighty acts at the Sea and we sang to you" (B Běrākôt 14b). If Heinemann is correct, then the phrase, "we sang to you," points to the verses of the Song of the Sea which had been incorporated to meet the kingship motif requirement.

However, the version of this prayer that appears in the Palestinian Talmud (Běrākôt 1.9.3d) neither mentions the miracles at the Sea nor the singing. If these two represent the incorporation of the Sea-splitting and kingship motifs, as mandated by the Tôseptā', then the Babylonian Talmud represents a version which incorporated the two elements to conform to the rulings recorded in the Tôseptā'. In any event, by the period of the anonymous *piyyûṭîm* the practice of incorporating verses from the Song of the Sea was, according to Fleischer (1981: 49), almost universal.

These verses seek to engender an identification between the redeemed of the past and the not-yet-redeemed of the present. They are presented just as they were originally intoned. The worshipers join the chorus, acclaiming together the words of those redeemed. As the liturgy states, Moses and Israel sang (the Song of the Sea) antiphonally, that is, part by part responsively, but all together said, "Who is like You O Lord among the celestials? Who is like You glorious in holiness?" (Exodus 15:11).

(Dr. Meir Bar-Ilan has suggested to me the likelihood that this verse was sung antiphonally by Moses and Israel, each intoning one "who" part. This seems to be the case in the Persian version of the liturgy, as edited by Shlomoh Tàl [1980: 9, lines 1–2; 65, lines 10–11] for it repeats the word *'ānû* twice. According to Philo, the chorus of the Therapeutae, modeling itself after the chorus of the Song of the Sea, sang hymns to God "sometimes chanting together, sometimes taking up the harmony antiphonally" [*Contemplative Life* 88].)

By citing a verse acclaiming God's incomparability next to one proclaiming God's kingship, the liturgy links up again the themes of God's oneness/uniqueness with God's sovereignty. This connection is made explicit also in the first blessing where God alone is declared king and, of course, in the *Šěma'* where immediately after the statement that God is one/alone/unique, is inserted the idea that His kingship be blessed.

After citing Exodus 15:11, the blessing, in some rites, continues:

> Your children, beholding [testimony to] your sovereignty by your dividing the sea before Moses, responded saying, "This is my God."

This last response is a direct quotation from the response of Israel at the Sea. It corresponds with the position of Rabbi Nehemiah, that the Song of the Sea was intoned both antiphonally and consecutively. Israel neither repeated the words of Moses as youngsters who recite the Hallel in school (according to Rabbi 'Aqîbā'), nor did Israel only utter a refrain as worshipers do when responding to the precentor's recital of the Hallel in synagogues (as Rabbi Eleazar the son of Rabbi Yôsî Ha-Gělîlî says). Rather, Israel responded to each phrase of Moses with the subsequent phrase, just as the *sôfēr* who is "*pôrēs* the *Šěma'*" in the synagogue (T Sôṭâ 6, 2–3). "This is my God," may be, accordingly, as Jacob Friedman has pointed out to me, an allusion to Israel's response when it said, "This is my God and I will glorify Him" (Exodus 15: 2).

The role of this verse in proclaiming God king is highlighted in the following two midrashim:

> When the Holy One, blessed be He, revealed Himself at the Sea, not one of them had to ask: Which one is the king? On the contrary, as soon as they saw Him, they recognized Him, and all of them loudly proclaimed, "This is my God and I will glorify Him." (Měkîltā' in Horowitz and Rabin 1960: 127; Goldin 1971: 113)

> This nation first proclaimed Me king by the sea . . . and said, "This is my God and I will glorify Him." (Pěsîqtā' Rabbātî 10 in Friedman 1880: 39b)

Indeed, there are extant Gěnîzâ versions (Mann 1925: 307, 321; Fleischer 1985: 161, 361) of the third blessing which instead of reading, "This is my God," read, "The Lord is our King."

The reenactment of the choral response of the Song of the Sea continues in the morning service:

> The redeemed sang, at the seashore [this] new song to you [antiphonally], but all together acclaimed you king by saying, "The Lord is king for ever and ever." (Exodus 15:18)

The song climaxes with the acknowledgment of divine sovereignty. As the preface to the liturgical rendition of the song says explicitly, "They willingly accepted His sovereignty over them." In fact, the preface and the reenactment parallel each other. The following chart illustrates how the reenactment repeats in poetry what the preface states in prose.

Reenactment	Preface
1a. מלכותך ראו בניך בוקע ים לפני משה	1. וראו בניו גבורתו
2b. ״זה אלי״ ענו	2. שבחו והודו לשמו
3c. ואמרו ״ה׳ ימלך לעולם ועד״	3. ומלכותו ברצון קבלו עליהם

Rabbi Nehemiah held that the Song of the Sea was intoned just as the synagogal rendition of the *Šĕmaʿ*. What probably lies behind the controversy between Rabbi Nehemiah and his colleagues is the proper rendition of the song. According to Rabbi Nehemiah, the rendition of the song should be evocative of the public rendition of the *Šĕmaʿ*. Both, as Heinemann (1981: 98) underscored, are to be intoned antiphonally or responsorially. Since both are ways of realizing divine sovereignty, it was only natural that their public rendition follow the same pattern.

As the expression "the acceptance of divine sovereignty" links the third blessing with the *Šĕmaʿ*, so does it link the first blessing with the *Šĕmaʿ*. The first blessing prefaces the angelic *qĕdûšâ*—"Holy, Holy, Holy is the Lord of Hosts; the whole earth is full of His glory" (Isaiah 6:3)—with the expression "all [the angels] are accepting divine sovereignty." (We are not discussing here the origin of the use of the *sanctus*. It is attested to in early Christian literature [Werner 1984: 115–21] and alluded to in Qumran literature [Weinfeld 1983].) The portrayal of the angels in the act of accepting divine sovereignty is due to its position before the *Šĕmaʿ* and to the impact of conceiving the whole liturgical rubric as a way of inducing Israel to accept divine sovereignty.

Since the angelic *qĕdûšâ* is portrayed as a way of realizing divine sovereignty, it is not surprising that Fleischer (1969) showed that in the Palestinian rite the *qĕdûšâ* was limited to the Sabbath and various holidays. This was the result not so much of the mystic origins of the *qĕdûšâ* as of the fact pointed out by many scholars (Finkelstein 1978a: 645; Weinfeld 1981: 508–09; Liebreich 1952) that the Sabbath is conceived of in the liturgy as the day of divine sovereignty par excellence. The inclusion of the *qĕdûšâ* in the Sabbath liturgy highlights the relationship between the Sabbath and the ideas of kingship and holiness.

The *Šĕmaʿ* and its blessings may now be seen as a tapestry in which three strands of realizing God's kingship are interwoven. Developing an insight of Weinfeld (1974: 138–39, note 21), we may say that ancient Israel realized God's sovereignty by the Song of the Sea; the angels realized it by chanting the *qĕdûšâ*; and contemporary Israel does so by proclaiming the *Šĕmaʿ*.

How is Israel to proclaim God as king? There are three available models of acclaiming kingship. They are the Greco-Roman acclamations of kingship, the angelic *qĕdûšâ*, and the Song of the Sea. Fortunately, the *Šĕmaʿ* can take its cue from all three, since all of them were at times intoned antiphonally.

The pertinence of the Greco-Roman royal antiphonal acclamation to the *Šĕmaʿ* was pointed out recently by Knohl (1984: 2). According to the Talmud, the angelic *qĕdûšâ* was also intoned antiphonally. The Isaianic portrayal of the angels "calling out to each other" was understood to imply that there were three sets of angels calling out "Holy" seriatim. According to Rab, "One group of angels said, 'Holy,' another said, 'Holy,' while the third said, 'Holy is the Lord of Hosts'" (B Ḥûllîn 91b). Rab's position is not the only one recorded there, but it does represent the original position unfettered by nonexegetical considerations. The result is a single verse intoned antiphonally without any set of angels singing it all. Since one "Holy" responds to the other, there is no reason to assume that the verse, "Blessed be the glory of the Lord from His place" (Ezekiel 3:14) was originally the response. How and why it was interpolated will be dealt with in another study. The third model is the Song of the Sea whose antiphonal execution has already been discussed.

If both the *qĕdûšâ* of the first blessing and the selections of the Song of the Sea in the third blessing were sung antiphonally, we should look for a similar pattern for the *Šĕmaʿ*, namely, a single verse intoned antiphonally. The suggestion that the response is "Blessed be the name of His sovereign glory for ever and ever" fails to meet either criterion. It is neither a biblical verse nor is it divided in two. It is also not normally said aloud (Urbach 1979: 401).

The theory which comes closest to meeting both criteria is that of Elbogen (1906: 594; Heinemann 1972: 19, 387–88, note 24). He argues that the reader began with the words, "Hear, O Israel," and that the congregation responded by repeating those words and completing the verse with "The Lord our God, the Lord is One." Elbogen's analysis, however, is based on a misunderstanding of Rabbi Nehemiah's position. He apparently was misled by the explanation in B Sôṭâ 30b (כולהו בהדי הדדי) or by the language that T Sôṭâ 6, 3 employed in presenting Rabbi Nehemiah's position. In actuality, Elbogen's position is that of Rabbi Eleazar ben Taddai as recorded in both Mĕḵîltāʾôt (Horowitz and Rabin 1960: 119; Epstein and Melamed 1955: 72). Rabbi Eleazar ben Taddai's suggestion with regard to the Song of the Sea was that Moses began the verse and Israel repeated what Moses said and then finished the verse. This, as Lieberman (1962, volume 3: 10–11) has shown, was the didactic method for inducing schoolchildren to memorize biblical verses, not the synagogal practice for reciting the *Šěma*ʿ.

The examples cited in the aforementioned Tôseptā' to illustrate Rabbi Nehemiah's position all present the first half of the verse intoned by Moses, while the second half alone is intoned by Israel. Finkelstein (1941–42: 400) drew up a chart clearly illustrating this distinction. As Goldin (1971: 77) points out, it is precisely because Israel knew on their own how to complete the verse that Rabbi Nehemiah, in the Meḵîltā'ôt (Horowitz and Rabin 1960: 118; Epstein and Melamed 1955: 72), attributes it to the Holy Spirit.

From the examples in the Tôseptā', it follows that the opening verse of the *Šěma*ʿ itself was divided. The *pôrēs*, or precentor, said, "Hear, O Israel," and the congregation responded, "The Lord our God, the Lord is One." There was no more reason for one party to say the whole verse than there was for one party to utter the whole Song of the Sea, or for one set of angels to utter the whole *qědûšâ* verse.

If we understand *pôrēs 'et Šěma*ʿ as dividing the *Šěma*ʿ verse into two, we can understand its antonym, *kôrēḵ 'et Šěma*ʿ, wrapping or "sandwiching" the *Šěma*ʿ together. The explanation of the practice as it appears in T Pesāḥîm 2(3), 19 should be understood as follows:

> They (the people of Jericho) would say, "Hear, O Israel, the Lord our God, the Lord is One" without stopping [between "Hear, O Israel" and "the Lord our God, the Lord is One"]. R. Judah said: They did stop [between the two parts of the verse], but did not say, "Blessed be the name of His sovereign glory for ever and ever."

Such an understanding of *pôrēs 'et Šěma*ʿ is alluded to in another source. A midrash asks, what part of the *Šěma*ʿ is deemed "the sovereignty of God?" and answers, "The Lord our God, the Lord is One." It then asks:

> Whence did Israel learn to recite the *Šěma*ʿ? R. Pînḥas b. Hāmā' said: Israel learned how to recite the *Šěma*ʿ at the Revelation at Sinai. How is this so? You find that it was with this word [*Šěma*ʿ] that God first began at Sinai. He said to them: "Hear, O Israel, I am the Lord your God." They all responded, saying, "The Lord our God, the Lord is One." (Deuteronomy Rabbâ 2, 31)

This division of the *Šěma*ʿ is alluded to in yet another midrash. It plays off Psalm 50:7 (which itself alludes to the first line of the Decalogue) against "Hear, O Israel" and 2 Samuel 7:23 against "the Lord our God, the Lord is One" (attributed to Āḇôt dě-Rabbi Natān, by Israel Ibn Al-Nakawa [1930: volume 2, page 96]).

And, of course, the oft-cited midrash (Sifrê Deuteronomy 6 in Finkelstein 1969: 52–3, and note 14), which explains "Israel" in the *Šĕmaʿ* as referring to the Patriarch Jacob, also assumes such a division of the verse. Indeed, there is a tradition that the recitation of the *Šĕmaʿ* is the way the children of Israel throughout the generations reconfirm their commitment to Jacob, that "the Lord our God, the Lord is One" (Deuteronomy Rabbâ in Lieberman 1964: 67). Finkelstein (1978b: 114b) suggests this as its liturgical meaning.

In contrast, we are suggesting that the ancient synagogal division of the *Šĕmaʿ* is best understood in terms similar to that of Rabbi Pînḥas bar Ḥamāʾ. Thus, just as the liturgical rendition of the Song of the Sea reenacts Israel's realization of God's sovereignty at the Sea, and the liturgical rendition of the angelic *qĕdûšâ* reenacts the heavenly acclamation of God as king, the public recitation of the *Šĕmaʿ* reenacts Israel's original acceptance at Sinai of God as king.

This understanding of the *Šĕmaʿ* helps explain the absence of the Decalogue in the liturgy. Once the *Šĕmaʿ* was conceived of as the acceptance of divine sovereignty, the Decalogue became superfluous. The third-century Palestinian amora, Rabbi Levi, underscored this duplication when he explained that the first two paragraphs of the *Šĕmaʿ* are recited daily precisely because they contain the Decalogue. According to this explanation, "I am the Lord your God" is contained in "Hear, O Israel, the Lord our God," and "You shall have no other gods before Me" is contained in "The Lord is One" (J Bĕrākôt 1.8.3c; Deuteronomy Rabbâ in Lieberman 1964: 69).

If the *Šĕmaʿ* assumes the Decalogue implicitly there is no need for the liturgical recitation of both. One daily covenant renewal ceremony, in biblical parlance (Exodus 34: 28; Deuteronomy 4:13), or one ceremony of acceptance of divine sovereignty, to use the Mishnaic parlance, is enough. For just as the Mishna refers to the *Šĕmaʿ* as the acceptance of divine sovereignty, so the Mĕkîltāʾ (Horowitz and Rabin 1960: 219) sees the acceptance of the Decalogue as tantamount to acceptance of God as king. Indeed, according to a later midrash, when Israel recites the Decalogue, it "stands, as if before Mount Sinai, and receives the Torah" (Pĕsîqtāʾ dĕ-Rab Kahanāʾ in Mandelbaum 1962: 204). (The fact that the Decalogue was later inserted into various places in the service (Urbach 1985: 142) is not pertinent, since it was never reinserted into its old place.)

By the time of the Mishna, the *Šĕmaʿ* had eclipsed the Decalogue as the biblical passage for realizing divine sovereignty. The new central role of the *Šĕmaʿ* required a special ceremony, *pôrēs ʾet Šĕmaʿ*. Whether this ceremony entailed a splitting of the *Šĕmaʿ*, as we have argued, or whether it entailed promulgating it as a royal edict, as Finkelstein (1941–42: 392; 1978b: 12b) has repeatedly argued, the mode of execution was aimed at evoking a royal presence. Apparently, once the *Šěma'* was deemed the central liturgical expression for realizing divine sovereignty, it assumed a special ceremonial mode whose purpose was to reinforce the sense of divine sovereignty. This sense may have been retained, as Ginzberg (1941: 146–47) pointed out, in the Palestinian practice of standing for the *Šěma'*.

As the whole liturgical rubric of the *Šěma'* and its blessings became interwoven with strands intimating divine sovereignty, there was less and less reason to make of the *Šěma'* itself something special. In addition, the prefacing of the whole rubric with the antiphonal response of the *barěkû*—call to prayer (Finkelstein 1941–42: 394–95; Heinemann 1972: 13)—obviates any need for a distinctive royal ceremony for the *Šěma'* itself.

In conclusion, note the parallel development between the expansion of the theme of realizing God's kingship from the *Šěma'* to the whole liturgical rubric, and the change of the expression for the public recitation of the *Šěma'*. At first, the expression was *pôrēs 'et Šěma'*, which denoted only the *Šěma'* (Finkelstein 1941–42: 388; 1942–43: 29–36). Subsequently, the expression became *pôrēs 'al Šěma'*, which came to denote the whole liturgical rubric. In both cases a distinctive expression was coined for designating the public realization of God's kingship.

Thanks to the kindness of Drs. Shamma Friedman and Chaim Milikowsky of Neve Schechter, I was able to complete this study in Jerusalem.

Bibliography

Abudarham, D.
    1963   *Abudarham Ha-Šālēm*. Jerusalem: Usha.
Al-Nakawa, I. I.
    1930   *Menorat Ha-Maor*. Edited by H. G. Enelow. New York: Bloch (Hebrew).
Baillet, M.
    1982   *Discoveries in the Judean Desert, Volume VII: Qumrân Grotte 4, Part III*. Oxford: Clarendon.
Buber, S., editor
    1960   *Midrash Leqaḥ Ṭôḇ, Genesis*, volume 1. Reprint. Jerusalem: S. Monson.
Elbogen, I.
    1906   Studies in Jewish Liturgy. *Jewish Quarterly Review* (old series) 18: 587–99.
Epstein, J. N., and Melamed, E. Z., editors
    1955   *Mekhilta d'Rabbi Šim'on b. Jochai*. Jerusalem: Mekize Nirdamim.
Finkelstein, L.
    1925–26 The Development of the Amidah. *Jewish Quarterly Review* (new series) 16: 1–4, 127–70.
    1932   La Kedouscha et les bénédictions du Schema. *Revue des études juives* 92: 1–26.
    1941–42 The Meaning of the Word פרס in the Expressions בפרוס עצרת, פורס על שמע, פרום הפסח, and פרום החג. *Jewish Quarterly Review* (new series) 32: 387–406.

1942–43 The Meaning of the Word פרס in the Expressions בפרוס עצרת, פורס על שמע, פרוס הפסח, and פרוס החג. *Jewish Quarterly Review* 33: 29–48.

1969 Editor. *Sifre on Deuteronomy*. New York: Jewish Theological Seminary.

1978a The Origin and Development of the Qedusha. In *Perspectives on Jews and Judaism, Essays in Honor of Wolfe Kelman*, edited by A. Chiel, pages 61–78. New York: The Rabbinical Assembly.

1978b The Prayer of King David According to the Chronicles. *Eretz Israel* 14: 110–16 (Hebrew).

Fleischer, E.

1969 The Diffusion of the Qedushot of the ῾Amida and the Yoẓer in the Palestinian Jewish Ritual. *Tarbiz* 38: 255–84 (Hebrew).

1972 Towards a Clarification of the Expression "Poreis ῾Al Shema." *Tarbiz* 41: 132–44 (Hebrew).

1974 The Influence of Choral Elements on the Formation and Development of the Piyyuṭ Genres. *Yuḥal* 3: 18–48 (Hebrew).

1981 Studies in the Problems Relating to the Liturgical Function of the Types of Early Piyyuṭ. *Tarbiz* 50: 41–63 (Hebrew).

1985 *The Yoẓer—Its Emergence and Development*. Jerusalem: Magnes (Hebrew).

Friedman, M., editor

1880 *Pesikta Rabbati*. Vienna: Kaiser.

Ginzberg, L.

1941 *A Commentary on the Palestinian Talmud*, volume 1. New York: Jewish Theological Seminary (Hebrew).

1969 *Genizah Studies in Memory of Doctor Solomon Schechter*. 2 volumes. Reprint. New York: Hermon (Hebrew).

Goldin, J.

1971 *The Song at the Sea*. New Haven, Conn.: Yale University Press.

Haberman, A. M.

1954 The Phylacteries in Antiquity. *Eretz Israel* 3: 174–77 (Hebrew).

Heinemann, J.

1972 Hebrew edition and annotation of I. Elbogen, *Der jüdische Gottesdienst in seiner geschichtlichen Entwicklung*, 1931. Tel-Aviv: Dvir.

1977 *Prayer in the Talmud: Forms and Patterns*. Translated by R. Sarason, from Hebrew, 1966. New York: de Gruyter.

1981 *Studies in Jewish Liturgy*. Edited by A. Shinan. Jerusalem: Magnes (Hebrew).

Horowitz, H. S., and Rabin, I. A., editors

1960 *Mechilta d'Rabbi Ismael*. Jerusalem: Bamberger and Wahrman.

Kasher, M.

1980 *Sēfer Šěma῾ Yiśrā'ēl*. Jerusalem: Bêt Tôrâ Šělēmâ.

Kimelman, R.

1969 While Saying the Shema. *Conservative Judaism* 23/2: 37–43.

1981 While Saying the Shema. In *Shanah BeShanah*, edited by A. Pitchenik, pages 254–60. Jerusalem: Hêḵal Šělōmô (Hebrew).

Knohl, I.

1984 A Parasha Concerned with Accepting the Kingdom of Heaven. *Tarbiz* 53: 11–21 (Hebrew).

Lieberman, S., editor

1955–73 *Tosefta Ki-fshutah*. 8 volumes. New York: Jewish Theological Seminary.

1964 *Midrash Debarim Rabbah*. Jerusalem: Wahrmann.

Liebreich, L.

1952   The Sabbath in the Prayerbook. In *Do'ar Jubilee Volume in Honor of Its Thirtieth Anniversary*, edited by M. Ribolov, pages 255–62. New York: Ha-Histadrut Ha-Ivrit of America (Hebrew).

1966   The Benediction Immediately Preceding and the One Following the Recital of the Shema. *Revue des études juives* 125: 151–65.

Mandelbaum, B., editor

1962   *Pesikta de Rav Kahana*. 2 volumes. New York: Jewish Theological Seminary.

Mann, J.

1925   Genizah Fragments of the Palestinian Order of Service. *Hebrew Union College Annual* 2: 269–338.

Margolioth, M., editor

1966   *Sefer Ha-Razim*. Jerusalem: Yediot Achronot.

Margulies, M.

1953–60 *Midrash Wayyikra Rabbah*. 5 volumes. Jerusalem: American Academy of Jewish Research.

Mirsky, A.

1963   The Source of the Prayer "Yoṣer." In *Hanoch Albeck Jubilee Volume*, pages 324–30. Jerusalem: Mossad HaRav Kook (Hebrew).

Rabbenu Shlomoh

1971   *Siddur of R. Solomon ben Samson of Garmaise (Worms) Including the Siddur of the Haside Ashkenas*. Edited by M. Hershler. Jerusalem: Hemed (Hebrew).

Smith, M.

1982   Helios in Palestine. *Eretz Israel* 16: 199–214.

Tal, S.

1980   *The Persian Jewish Prayer Book*. Jerusalem: Ben-Zvi Institute (Hebrew).

Theodor, J., and Albeck, C., editors

1965   *Midrash Bereshit Rabba*. Jerusalem: Wahrmann.

Urbach, E.

1979   *The Sages: Their Concepts and Beliefs*. 2 volumes. Jerusalem: Magnes.

1985   The Status of the Decalogue in Worship and in Prayer. In *The Decalogue Through the Generations*, edited by B. Z. Segal, pages 173–91. Jerusalem: Magnes (Hebrew).

Weinfeld, M.

1974   Sumerian Literature and the Book of Psalms, Part 2. *Beth Ha-miqra* 7: 136–41.

1981   Sabbath, Temple and the Enthronement of the Lord–The Problem of the Sitz im Leben of Genesis 1: 1–23. In *Alter Orient und Altes Testament*, volume 212, pages 501–12. Kevelaer: Verlag Butzon and Bercker.

1983   The Heavenly Praise in Unison. In *Meqor Hajjim, Festschrift für Georg Molia zum 75. Geburtstag*, pages 427–33. Graz: Akademische Druck-u. Verlagsanstalt.

Werner, E.

1984   *The Sacred Bridge*, volume 2. New York: Ktav.

Yadin, Y.

1969   Tefillin (Phylacteries) from Qumran (XQ Phyl 1–4). *Eretz Israel* 9: 60–85.

6.   On the *Yôṣēr* and Related Texts

Morton Smith

As is well known, the *yôṣēr*, the so-called "benediction of the *šĕmaʿ*" in the evening prayer, and the two benedictions before and after the *pĕsûqê dĕ-zimrâ* are in content and style similar to each other, but distinct from the rest of the elements of the service in which they occur.

To study their peculiarities one must either make or choose a text. Here, as a matter of convenience, the *Seder R. Amram Gaon* (Hedegård 1951) has been chosen. No doubt it is far from perfect, but it can be accepted—as religious documents often are—with resignation rather than absolute faith. Since it differs in minor points from the texts commonly used, and since variants of familiar texts are hard to recall, I print it here, divided into cola, to show its rhythmic structure—"rhythmic," rather than "metrical," because even implicit statements about ancient Hebrew metrics are apt to entail elaborate arguments, whereas in this case it seems enough to say that both the poem's sense and sound units immediately justify most of the divisions made hereinafter. Often these divisions are also made clear by rhymes. Nevertheless, it must be admitted that in some instances the points where the breaks should be made are dubious. What follows is therefore sometimes tentative, and corrections are welcome.

Before *pĕsûqê dĕ-zimrâ*	After *pĕsûqê dĕ-zimrâ*

ישתבח שמך לעד מלכנו   ברוך שאמר והיה העולם
האל המלך   ברוך אומר ועושה
הגדול והקדוש   ברוך גוזר ומקיים
בשמים ובארץ   ברוך עושה בראשית
כי לך נאה   ברוך מרחם על הארץ
יי אלהינו   ברוך מרחם על הבריות
ואלהי אבותינו   ברוך משלם שכר טוב ליראיו
שיר ושבחה   ברוך אל חי לעד וקיים לנצח
הלל וזמרה   ברוך הוא וברוך שמו
עז וממשלה   ברוך אתה יי אלהינו
נצח וגבורה   מלך העולם
ותהלה ותפארת   האל המלך
קדושה ומלכות   המשובח המפואר והמתנשא
ברכות והודאות   בלשון כל חסידיו ועבדיו
לשמך הגדול   [ובשירי דוד עבדך
מעולם ועד עולם   יי אלהינו
אתה אל   בתשבחות ובזמירות
ברוך אתה יי   נהודך נגדלך ונרוממך
מלך גדול בתושבחות   ונעריצך ונמליכך ונזכיר שמך]†
אל ההודאות   מלכנו אלהינו
אדון הנפלאות   יחיד חי העולמים
אדון כל המעשים   משובח עדי עד
הבוחר בשירה זמרה   ברוך אתה יי
חי העולמים   מלך מהולל בתושבחות

---

† Manifest gloss, rhythmically ragged

The *Yôṣēr*

[ברוך יי המבורך
לעולם ועד]
ברוך אתה יי אלהנו
מלך העולם
יוצר אור ובורא חושך
עושה שלום ובורא[a] *את הכל*
המאיר לארץ ולדרים עליה ברחמים
וטובו מחדש בכל יום
תמיד מעשה בראשית
מה רבו מעשיך יי
כלם בחכמה עשית
מלאה הארץ קנינך[b]
המלך המרומם לבדו מאז
המשובח והמפואר והמתנשא
מימות עולם
אלהי עולם
ברחמיך הרבים
רחם עלינו
אדון עזנו
צור משגבנו
מגן ישענו
משגב בעדנו
אל ברוך גדול דעה
התקין ופעל זהרי חמה
טוב יצר כבוד לשמו
מאורות נתן סביבות עזו
פינות צבאיו קדושים
רוממי שדי תמיד
מספרים כבוד אל
וקדושתו
תתברך יי אלהינו
בשמים ממעל
ועל הארץ מתחת
תתברך צורנו מלכנו וגואלנו
בורא קדושים
ישתבח שמך לעד מלכנו

יוצר משרתים
ואשר משרתיו כלם
עומדים ברום עולם
ומשמיעים ביראה יחד בקול
דברי *אלהים חיים ומלך עולם*[c]
כלם אהובים
כלם ברורים
כלם גבורים
כלם עושים
באימה רצון קוניהם
כלם פותחים את פיהם
בקדושה ובטהורה
ומשבחין ומפארין ומקדישין
את שם המלך
הגדול הגבור והנורא
קדוש הוא
כלם מקבלים עליהם
עול מלכות שמים
זה מזה
ונותנים רשות
זה לזה
להקדיש ליוצרם
בנחת רוח
בשפה ברורה
ובנעימה קדושה
כלם כאחד
עונים באימה
ואומרים ביראה
קדוש קדוש קדוש
יי צבאות
מלוא כל הארץ כבודו[d]
והאופנים וחיות הקודש
ברעש גדול
מתנשאים לעומתם
משבחים ואומרים
ברוך כבוד יי ממקומו

---

[c] Jeremiah 10:10
[d] Isaiah 6:3

[a] Isaiah 45:7
[b] Psalms 104:24

לאל ברוך נעימות יתנו
למלך אל חי וקים
זמירות יאמרו ותושבחות ישמיעו
כי הוא לבדו פועל גבורות
עושה חדשות בעל מלחמות
זורע צדקות מצמיח ישועות
בורא רפואות נורא תהלות
אדון נפלאות
המחדש טובו בכל יום
תמיד מעשה בראשית
כאמור לעושה אורים גדולים
כי לעולם חסדו[e]
ברוך אתה יי
יוצר המאורות

---

[e] Psalms 136:7. A gloss.

Evening Prayer (ערבית)

ברוך יי המבורך
לעולם ועד
ברוך אתה יי אלהנו
מלך העולם
אשר
בדברו מעריב מערבים
בחכמה פותח שערים
ובתבונה משנה עתים
ומחליף את הזמנים
ומסדר את הכוכבים
במשמרותיהם
ברקיע כרצונו
בורא יומם ולילה
גולל אור מפני חשך
וחשך מפני אור
מעביר יום ומביא לילה
ומבדיל בין יום ובין לילה
יי צבאות שמו
חי וקיים תמיד
ימלוך עלינו לעולם ועד
ברוך אתה יי
המעביר ערבים

For the present discussion the important thing is the type of rhythmic structure, not the details. If the above divisions are *in the main* justified, we find, instead of the regular trimeters of most psalms, a surprising lot of lines that seem to have only two feet or less, but also quite a few that seem to have four. The rhythm seems to move freely from threefold to fourfold divisions, and back. Similarly, the many two-foot units make the average lines considerably shorter than those of the Qumran hymns, at least as analyzed by Kittel (1981). The irregularities, too, are less; very long lines are very few. These differences of style seem to me so apparent that they need not be argued.

Besides stylistic differences, there are others that make these "prayers" peculiar. First, they are not really prayers. The only precatory element is the probable gloss in the *yôṣēr*, *'elōhê 'ôlām, bĕraḥamêḵā harabbîm raḥēm 'ālênû*. All the rest is pure praise. By ordinary standards these are hymns, not prayers.

Second, neither the *yôṣēr* nor the *ma'arîḇ 'arāḇîm* has any connection with the *šĕma'*. Of course, to the theologian's eye everything is necessarily connected with everything else, so creation was a necessary preparation for the giving of the Law. It was also a necessary preparation for the giving of the Marx brothers. But these two hymns never hint at either of those great, far-off events. Also, neither hymn leads directly to the *šĕma'*; both are separated from it—the *yôṣēr* by *'ahaḇâ rabbâ* and the *ma'arîḇ* by *'ahaḇat 'ôlām*.

Finally, neither hymn is deuteronomic in terminology or concerns, though the *šĕma'* is the heart of Deuteronomy. The theology of the deuteronomists is well known: Yahweh loved Israel, chose it from all the peoples, delivered it from Egypt, gave it the Law, and will give it the promised land. Yet not one of these themes is expressed in any of these hymns. What they celebrate is a god who is creator and king of the world, praised, eternal, blessed, beautiful, living, holy, and unique, the giver of light, whose name is marvelous. This collection of epithets (which would admirably describe the Egyptian sun god) accounts for about 190 of the 260-odd attributes to be found in the poems. The rest are mostly commonplace—merciful, miracle-working, mighty, great, feared, glorious, etc.—none of which occurs more than half a dozen times. The words by which the god of these hymns is described are almost never found in Deuteronomy and, if they do occur there, are not used in the same way and not used of God. Specifically: (eternity) עד, (verb) סדר יצר גזר פאר יחיד הרים ר־מם, הלל שבח, תושבחות, התנשא never occur in Deuteronomy. Deuteronomy never uses, of God, מלך ברוך קדוש, and עושה. It has תפארת and ברא only once each, and the participle חי only twice. Of all the leading words and concepts in our hymns, the only ones common in Deuteronomy are אל, עולם, and שם. The two traditions are about as separate linguistically as any two bodies of Old Testament material can be.

This is the more remarkable because the deuteronomic style and rhetoric are predominant in the prayers throughout the later books of the Old Testament, the apocrypha and pseudepigrapha, most of the New Testament, and the Judaizing New Testament pseudepigrapha. They also predominate in the services of the *Maḥzôr.* Evidently the prayers under consideration are material from a tradition other than the one that prevailed in most Jewish material from the last days of the Second Temple. Where did it come from?

The answer given by Elbogen (1931: 18–19), in his comments on the *yôṣēr*, was, from the *merkabâ* mystics. They took over the *qĕdûšâ*, originally a Babylonian geonic creation used only on Sabbaths and festivals, and about 750 C.E., "*wahrscheinlich,*" they succeeded in appending its short, relatively innocuous basic text to the *yôṣēr*, which at that time consisted of little more than its initial blessing and *ḥatîmâ.* All the material between these, except for the *qĕdûšâ*, is either connective, or expansion of the primitive elements, and in either case secondary.

The proof of this is that the intervening material contains many rhymes and acrostics, and these must be late. But we have acrostic poems in Greek inscriptions of Hellenistic and Augustan times (*Supplementum Epigraphicum Graecum* 7.14; Kaibel 1965: 979, etc.), not to mention Proverbs (31: 10–31, *'ēšet ḥayîl*) and Psalms (9–10, 25, 34, 37, 111, 112, 119, 145). This poetic form goes back to Akkadian times (Sweet 1969: 459–60), hardly proving a "late" date for our compositions. As for rhyme, Plato, to make fun of its use by Athenian rhetoricians of his day, inserted a few rhymed couplets into the silly, though charming, speech of Agathon in the *Symposium* (197 D). Rhymes are also used occasionally in the Old Testament (Judges 16:23–24; Isaiah 27:3). Norden wrote a masterly history of rhyme in Appendix 1 to his *Antike Kunstprosa* (1909), demonstrating that in Greek and Latin, "as in every other speech," rhyme could be used but was rarely employed deliberately by writers of metrical verse in the early stage of the literature. With the development of rhythmical prose, which made large use of strings of short cola ending in words of the same grammatical form (and therefore rhyming—exactly what we find in our hymns), rhyme became customary, admired, and widely used. The rise of such prose, and consequently the beginning of the penetration of rhyme into verse, he illustrated, was mainly from early Christian literature, starting with Paul. Since his time, Professor Eric Werner (1959) has demonstrated the importance of early Christian liturgical texts as implicit evidence of what was being done in Jewish synagogal worship.

Someone of the Pauline school, if not Paul himself, had some connection with the Qumran literature. K. G. Kuhn (1961) proved this by pointing out that the pseudo-Pauline Epistle to the Ephesians, "with its 'hymnodic' style, long spun-out sentences, and plerophoric strings of synonymous genitives, corresponds to the style of the Qumran texts, and the relation is proved by many parallels" of details and ideas. Hence, we may reasonably look in the Qumran material for those words listed above (page 92) that we did not find in Deuteronomy.

We find them promptly. The Qumran usage agrees so closely with the usage of the *yôṣēr* group that I shall mention only the main differences:

התנשא is not used of God in the Qumran texts, but הנשא is.

There is no certain use of יחיד to describe God.

Neither גזר nor סדר is used with God as subject.

This list is based on Kuhn's concordance (1960) and its supplement (1963), the indices of the volumes of *Discoveries in the Judaean Desert* that have appeared since 1963 (Sanders 1965; Allegro 1968; Baillet 1982),[1] and the index of *The Temple Scroll* (Yadin 1983). Since so much of the material is still unpublished, and so much of what has been published is dispersed in unavailable and unindexed articles, it would be incautious to base any argument on these dubious discrepancies, any or all of which might be wiped out by one more report. If anything, the evidence strongly suggests that there is no substantial difference between the terminology of the *yôṣēr* group and that of the Qumran documents, or, better, of the Hôdāyôt, the War Scroll, and the Manual of Discipline, which provide most of the parallels. (There is even less excuse for taking the Dead Sea documents as a unit than there is for taking the prayer book so.)

What, then, becomes of the rhythmic and stylistic differences with which we began? They clearly pose a problem, but one with so many possible solutions — differences of author, school, background, date, external influences, etc. — and so little relevant evidence that it must be left open. What is sure is that by the first century C.E., if not before, the deuteronomic tradition of petitionary prayer in rhetorical prose — appealing to the god of the fathers for agricultural, economic, and political benefits, and supported by references to the people's history — had come to be flanked by a poetic literature of praise addressed to an eternal, cosmic god, with no clear ethnic affiliations — the radiant, beautiful, blessed king of the world, surrounded by his ministering angels, the unique, living holy one, whose great name is to be praised forever.

To what extent this new tradition is an outgrowth of earlier Israelite elements, especially those previously apparent in the Psalms and the wisdom literature, and to what extent it reflects outside influence, most likely Egyptian, are matters for future research. The presently known fact is that from the first century on there were two traditions available for synagogue worship. No doubt differences between individual synagogues were reflected by the different uses each made of these traditions.

Notes

1   It is reported that the remaining volumes will appear before the beginning of the twenty-second century.

Bibliography

Allegro, J. M., editor
 1968   *Qumrân Cave 4, Part I*. Volume 5 of *Discoveries in the Judaean Desert*. Oxford: Clarendon.
Baillet, M.
 1982   *Qumrân Grotte 4, Part III*. Volume 7 of *Discoveries in the Judaean Desert*. Oxford: Clarendon.
Elbogen, I.
 1931   *Der jüdische Gottesdienst in seiner geschichtlichen Entwicklung*. Third edition. Frankfurt/Main: J. Kaufmann.
Hedegård, D., editor
 1951   *Seder R. Amram Gaon*, Part 1. Lund: P. Lindstedt (Hebrew).
Kaibel, G.
 1965   *Epigrammata graeca*. Reprint. Hildesheim: G. Olms.
Kittel, B.
 1981   *The Hymns of Qumran*. Chico, Calif.: Scholars.
Kuhn, K.
 1960   *Konkordanz zu den Qumrantexten*. Göttingen: Vandenhoeck and Ruprecht.
 1961   Qumran 5e. In *Die Religion in Geschichte und Gegenwart*, third edition, volume 5, column 753. Tübingen: J. C. B. Mohr.
 1963   Nachträge zur "Konkordanz zu den Qumrantexten." *Revue de Qumran* 4: 163 and following.
Milik, J. T., editor
 1977   *Qumrân Grotte 4, Part II*. Volume 6 of *Discoveries in the Judaean Desert*. Oxford: Clarendon.
Norden, E.
 1909   *Die antike Kunstprosa*. 2 volumes. Leipzig: Teubner.
Sanders, J. A., editor
 1965   *The Psalms Scroll of Qumrân Cave 11*. Volume 4 of *Discoveries in the Judaean Desert*. Oxford: Clarendon.
Sweet, R.
 1969   A Pair of Double Acrostics in Akkadian. *Orientalia* (new series) 38: 459–60.
Werner, E.
 1959   *The Sacred Bridge*. New York: Schocken.
Yadin, Y.
 1983   *The Temple Scroll*. 3 volumes. Jerusalem: Israel Exploration Society, Hebrew University, and Shrine of the Book.

7. Sermons, Targums, and the Reading from Scriptures in the Ancient Synagogue

Avigdor Shinan

To comprehend the literary and spiritual activities carried out on the Sabbath days and festivals in the synagogues of 'Ereṣ-Yiśrā'ēl in the talmudic period—approximately between 200 and 600 C.E.—we should remind ourselves that in addition to praying[1] and reading from Scriptures, those attending were usually listening to a sermon and to the simultaneous translation of the reading into Aramaic.

The focus of all these activities was the reading from the Torah: from its inception, prayer was only the framework surrounding the Torah-reading,[2] the sermon usually dealt with its content, and the Targums sought to make it as intelligible and meaningful as possible. (Also the *piyyûṭ*—which in its very essence was a poetical substitute for the routine prayer [Fleischer 1970]—deals very often with the content of the biblical selection read on a certain day.) Those who participated in these synagogue activities—the *daršân*, preacher; *mĕtûrgĕmān*, translator;[3] and the *ḥazzān* or *payṭān*[4]—were to relate them to the biblical text being read, thus creating mutatis mutandis a network of relationships between them.

Any discussion of the literature of the synagogue should therefore open with the long-debated question of the division of the Torah into reading units in the so-called "triennial" cycle, preserved in 'Ereṣ-Yiśrā'ēl at least until the late geonic period and even later in remote communities.[5] This issue will be dealt with here from the selective point of view of the sermon and the Aramaic Targums.

There is universal agreement today that the reading of the Torah in the ancient synagogue took the form of flexible cycles that each spanned a period of approximately three years. These reading cycles are documented in explicit lists of *sĕdārîm*[6]—141, 154, and 167 in number[7]—as well as in the early midrashic collections, such as Midrash Leviticus Rabbâ,[8] and in the ancient *piyyût*, which tried to perpetuate the first verses of the Torah readings in a fixed manner (Fleischer 1975: 141). Nevertheless, views differ as to the actual number of cycles: were there only a few alternative cycles that were repeatedly used during specific periods, or were there an unlimited number of cycles reflecting a variety of local customs that enabled communities (or synagogues) to divide the Torah into different *sĕdārîm* each time they read it, according to the wishes or proclivities of the members, or perhaps to some other external factors?[9] There are, in fact, two questions: how many cycles existed at one time, and to what extent was each cycle fixed and used repeatedly? The most common answer to these two questions argues in favor of a limited number of cycles in existence at one time, each more or less in a fixed form. However, as I will show, this answer fails to take into consideration all of the available data. Taken together, the lists of *sĕdārîm*, the *piyyût*, and the divisions reflected in the midrashim only provide a partial picture. The lists that have come down to us could be coincidental; the division in the few midrashim may reflect only the local traditions known to their editors or compilers, and the works of *payṭānîm* who supposedly shared a literary tradition extended to only a few central synagogues. However, what was the situation in those hundreds of synagogues that were not fortunate enough to support a *payṭān* (at least on a regular basis) or whose customs were not recorded in the abovementioned lists or midrashic compilations?

The less popular view that a greater number of *sĕdārîm* existed becomes more tenable when we evaluate the wide range of texts at our disposal; both the Aramaic Targums and the rabbinic "sermons" elucidate this matter.

Consider first the pattern of the *pĕtîḥtā'*,[10] the Proem, a short literary unit, rich in rhetorical devices, which is believed to have been a sermon, at least in its initial stages. The *pĕtîḥtā'* was delivered in the synagogue and most likely served as an introduction to the scriptural reading. Midrashic literature contains almost two thousand *pĕtîḥtôt*—a fact that testifies to their popularity and longevity. It has been argued again and again that almost all the *pĕtîḥtôt* conclude with the first verse(s) that open that specific Torah reading. If this is true, then the *pĕtîḥtôt* are invaluable for ascertaining the various customs of Torah reading in antiquity. Let us examine one of the loveliest *pĕtîḥtôt*, from Leviticus Rabbâ 13:2 (Israelstam 1939: 164–65):[11]

R. Simeon b. Yoḥai opened [a discourse] with: *He rose and measured the earth* [Habakkuk 3:6]. The Holy One, blessed be He, measured all generations and he found no generation fitted to receive the Torah other than the generation of the wilderness; the Holy One, blessed be He, measured all mountains and found no mountain on which the Torah should be given other than Sinai; the Holy One, blessed be He, measured all cities, and found no city wherein the Temple might be built, other than Jerusalem; the Holy One, blessed be He, measured all lands, and found no land suitable to be given to Israel, other than the Land of Israel. This is indicated by what is written: *"He rose and measured the earth"—And He loosed nations* [ibid]. Rab said: He declared [the shedding of] the blood of heathens permitted, and He declared the [appropriation of the] property of heathens permitted. He declared [the shedding of] their blood permitted, as it is said, *Thou shalt save alive nothing that breatheth* [Deuteronomy 20:16]. He declared [the appropriation of] their property permitted, as it is said, *Thou shalt eat the spoil of thine enemies, which the Lord thy God giveth thee* [ibid.:14]. R. Huna said: *"And he loosed nations"* means He loosened their girdle, as it is written, *He looseth the bond of kings* [Job 12:18]. 'Ulla Bira'ah in the name of R. Simeon b. Yohai said: This may be compared to the case of a man who went to a threshing-floor, taking his dog and ass with him. He loaded five *se'ah* on his ass, and two *se'ah* on his dog. The ass walked along, but the dog panted, so the man took one *se'ah* and put it on the ass. The dog, nevertheless, kept on panting. Said the man to the dog: "When you are laden you pant, when you are not laden you also pant." [Even so was it with the non-Israelite nations]; they were unable to endure even the seven precepts accepted by the descendants of Noah, so God took these off them and put them on Israel. R. Tanhum b. Hanilai said: This may be compared with the case of a physician who went to visit two sick persons, one who [he judged] would live, and another who would [certainly] die. To the one who [he judged] would live, he said: "This you may eat, that you may not eat." But as for the one who was to die, he said: "Give him whatever he asks." Thus of the heathen who are not destined for the life of the World to Come, it is written, *Every moving thing that liveth shall be for food for you; as the green herb have I given you all* [Genesis 9:3]. But to Israel, who are destined for the life of the World to Come, [He said], *These are the living things which ye may eat*, etc. [Leviticus 11:2 and following].

The *pĕtiḥtā'* usually begins with a verse that, at first glance, lacks any connection to its closing verse. By establishing a contextual relationship between two remote verses—and, in the above example, the verse from the prophesy of Habbâqûq to Leviticus 11:2—the *daršân* achieves his goal, in our case, to introduce the problematic list of animals that are not to be consumed, by delivering a lively, didactic sermon that even contains a touch of eschatological promises.

Leviticus 11:2 (or 11:1 which precedes it) is the final verse in two more *pĕtîḥtôt* in Leviticus Rabbâ, as well as two other *pĕtîḥtôt* in the two editions of Midrash Tanḥûmāʾ. Therefore, the fact that we possess at least five *pĕtîḥtôt* on this verse alone is enough to claim that it probably served as the opening verse of one of the *sĕdārîm*. This is supported by the lists of *sĕdārîm*.

Recent contributions to the study of the *pĕtîḥtāʾ* (especially Bregman 1981: 47–51 and Sarason 1982) clearly prove that not all *pĕtîḥtôt* were actually performed before a live audience, and that at least some of them were literary creations. However, there can be little question that the last verse of the *pĕtîḥtāʾ* was used at times as the opening verse of a *sēder*. Needless to say, the list of verses found at the end of *pĕtîḥtôt* is larger than the list of *sĕdārîm* known to us from all other sources.

A caveat is appropriate here. Some *pĕtîḥtôt* should not be considered as testimony to the existence of *sĕdārîm* since they were created by the editors of the midrashic literature for the purpose of dividing their compilations into sections called *pārāšôt* (Heinemann 1972). Each *pārāšâ* was to open with at least one *pĕtîḥtāʾ*; new *pĕtîḥtôt* had to be written wherever there was no correlation between the *sĕdārîm* and the *pārāšôt*. This kind of a *pĕtîḥtāʾ* is easily recognized by its very short form or undeveloped discussion of its topic, as well as by the fact that it is the only *pĕtîḥtāʾ* in rabbinic literature that ends with this particular verse.

The first part of Midrash Exodus Rabbâ[12] illustrates this point. In its fourteen *pārāšôt* there are twenty-four *pĕtîḥtôt*. Eight of the fourteen verses found at the end of them (a little more than fifty percent) are known from other sources as opening a *sēder*. The other six verses are not recorded elsewhere, but in at least two cases—Exodus Rabbâ 3:1, 2 (on Exodus 3:6, see also Mann 1971: 368, 406) and Exodus Rabbâ 7:1, 2 (on Exodus 6:13, see Mann 1971: 406)—more than one *pĕtîḥtāʾ* appear in the Midrash, and they are perfectly built and complete both from the literary and thematic viewpoints. This supports our claim that the compiler of this Midrash has preserved here a custom, or customs, not found in other sources.

It is therefore a reasonable assumption, that the existence of more than one good and vivid *pĕtîḥtāʾ* built on a certain verse provides the basis for a claim that this particular verse marked the beginning of a *sēder* in one of the existing traditions. Many new *sĕdārîm* will be revealed to us if this assumption is accepted. Moreover, it would significantly influence our understanding of the structure of the midrashic compilations and allow us a fuller and more accurate description of liturgical rites. Thus we would avoid a hasty and inaccurate description of ancient Judaism, one that suggests unity and uniformity instead of diversity and disunity.

Another *pĕtîḥtā'* from Midrash Exodus Rabbâ 1:8[13] sheds additional light on our discussion:

> Our Rabbis commenced this Pārāšâ with the verse: *They have dealt treacherously against the Lord, for they have begotten strange children; now shall the new moon devour them with their portions* [Hosea 5:7]. This teaches that when Joseph died, they abolished the covenant of circumcision, saying: "Let us become like the Egyptians." You can infer this from the fact that Moses had to circumcise them on their departure from Egypt. As soon as they had done so, God converted the love with which the Egyptians loved them into hatred, as it is written: *He turned their heart to hate His people, to deal craftily with His servants* [Psalms 105:25], to fulfill that which is said: *"Now shall the new moon devour them with their portions."* Therefore it is written: *There arose up a new king* [Exodus 1:8].

The formula "פתחי לה פתחא להאי פרשתא," "commenced this *parāšâ* with this verse," is clear proof that Exodus 1:8 served as the beginning of a *sēder*, although there is no other proof in any other source to support this. "Our Rabbis" (רבותינו) opened their *pĕtîḥtā'* on Exodus 1:8 with a verse from Hosea, creating a wordplay between "moon" (*ḥōdeš*) and "new (king)" (*ḥādāš*) to explain their understanding of the reasons behind the decrees against the children of Israel.

But if we accept the passage's claim at face value and see Exodus 1:8 as a verse that at least once served as the opening of a *sēder*, we encounter yet another, more complicated problem. How can the eighth verse of Exodus be the beginning of a *sēder*? Were they not conforming to the ancient halakha[14] which required that at least twenty-one verses be read on each occasion? Alternatively, is it possible that the first verse of Exodus did not serve as the beginning of a *sēder*? Or is it possible that Exodus 1:8 began a scriptural reading on an occasion other than the Sabbath (such as a holiday)? Perhaps, in ancient times they did not take pains to resume the weekly reading from the exact point at which they had stopped the previous week.[15] Each of these possibilities leads to interesting and constructive, or perhaps destructive, conclusions. One may suggest that ancient halakha was not as normative as some believe it to have been, or that many customs of Torah reading on the festivals and on other special occasions were simply forgotten. My own interpretation of the above *pĕtîḥtā'* is that in antiquity the age-old division of the Torah into five books did not always affect the reading from the Scriptures. It was possible, then, to read the last chapter of Genesis and the first verses of Exodus on one occasion, without marking the beginning of a new book as an important liturgical event. It can further be proved that the midrashic literature records *pĕtîḥtôt* to verses from other books of the Torah that are located far less than twenty-one verses from the beginnings of those books.[16] It seems to me that the much later custom of reading the end of the Torah together with its beginning on the last day of the Feast of Tabernacles,[17] or our custom to read on Sabbath afternoon the beginning of the next Sabbath reading, reflects a similar trend: the avoidance of a break in biblical continuity. The Torah, as the liturgical year, is a neverending cycle.

Be it as it may, assuming that the *pĕtîḥtôt* indeed attest to otherwise unknown *sĕdārîm*—a theory accepted in all its dimensions only by Jacob Mann (1966, 1971)[18]—we are indeed on the right path towards describing the activities in the ancient synagogue. I am fully aware that this claim portrays a chaotic state of affairs, but I do not believe that the modern scholarly trend of arranging, classifying, and drawing rigid frameworks should be imposed on actual life, which is always much more complex and diverse than we imagine. This claim brings to mind the famous story in Leviticus Rabbâ 3:6 (Israelstam 1939: 42) about Rabbi Ḥananyâ bar Rabbi Aḥā' who happened to arrive at a certain place, only to find that he was to speak on a verse he had not expected to be the beginning of a *sēder*. Being an excellent *daršān*, preacher, he managed to find a way out of this predicament. This incident provides a vivid illustration of the diverse customs that prevailed in talmudic times.

Are the *pĕtîḥtôt* recorded in our midrashim the actual sermons as they were delivered before the congregation in the ancient synagogue? We have no sure answer to this question, since in the process of committing these *pĕtîḥtôt* to writing and transmitting them from generation to generation in written form, some of their oral features were undoubtedly removed.[19] Even if the copyists had preserved the text in its original form, there is no guarantee that it reflects an accurate transcript of the sermon. Furthermore, recent works on the *pĕtîḥtā'* (especially Bregman 1981: 47–51 and Sarason 1982) tend to stress its non-oral features and try to prove that it was from its very inception (at least in some cases) a literary composition. One can cite innumerable sources attesting to the fact that sermons were indeed delivered in the ancient synagogues of 'Ereṣ Yiśrā'ēl (Zunz 1947: 163–75; Heinemann and Petuchowski 1975: 107–12), but how many texts do we have that clearly and unequivocally record such sermons? We possess only fragments of such homilies.

If the *pĕtîḥtā'* is not to be considered—at least not without proof—an actual live sermon, are there any other texts that preserve, as close as possible to the original, those sermons given in the rabbinic period? The most recent work in this field—Heinemann's collection of public sermons from the talmudic period (Heinemann and Petuchowski 1975: 105–99)— includes seventeen literary units; thirteen of them originated in 'Ereṣ-Yiśrā'ēl, seven of which are *pĕtîḥtôt*. Therefore only six non-*pĕtîḥtāʾ* units from the vast literature were defined by him as publicly delivered sermons, but even this assumption is based more on intuition than on solid facts.[20]

In order to solve the question of rabbinic sermons, we have yet to mention those *pĕtîḥtôt* which open with an halakhic question. This pattern of *pĕtîḥtāʾ* has been preserved in relatively small numbers (about 150) and differs from the common *pĕtîḥtāʾ* only in its preface. See, for example, Deuteronomy Rabbâ 6:1 (Rabbinowitz 1939: 120–21):[21]

> *Halakha*: Is it obligatory to circumcise an infant who has been born without a prepuce? The Sages have taught thus: In the case of an infant born without a prepuce it is necessary to cause a few drops of the blood of the Covenant to flow from him, on account of the Covenant of Abraham. And whence do you learn this? From the Torah, as it is written, *He that is born in thy house, and he that is bought with thy money, must needs be circumcised* [Genesis 17:13].
>
> Another explanation: *"Must needs be circumcised."* By the duplicate expression [*himmol yimmol*] two operations of circumcision are implied, namely, circumcision and uncovering. R. Levi said: Scripture says, *"himmol yimmol"*; from this repetition of the word is to be inferred that he who performs the circumcision must himself be a circumcised person, for it is written, *"himmol yimmol."*
>
> R. Judan b. Pazzi said: Of Zipporah, the wife of Moses, Scripture records, *Then she said: A bridegroom of blood in regard of the circumcision—* la-muloth [Exodus 4:26]. Scripture does not say, la-milah, but *"la-muloth,"* that is to say, two operations of circumcision, viz. circumcision and uncovering. And why is an infant circumcised on the eighth day? Because God had compassion upon him in delaying the circumcision until he should have gained strength. And just as God shows mercy to man, so too has He shown mercy to cattle. Whence this? For it is said, *But from the eighth day and thenceforth it* [namely, the animal] *may be accepted for an offering,* etc. [Leviticus 22:27]. And what is more, God commands, *Ye shall not kill it and its young both in one day* [Leviticus 22:28]. And in the same way that God had compassion upon the cattle, so too was God filled with mercy for the birds, as it is said, *If a bird's nest chance before thee . . . thou shalt not take the dam with the young* [Deuteronomy 22:6].

After answering the simple question with a quotation from an authoritative source (for example, J Šabbāt 19.2.17a), the *daršān* goes on to develop the subject, and then concludes with a biblical verse that marked the beginning of the *sēder*.

What we don't know from this kind of *pĕtîḥtāʾ* is who asked the halakhic question.[22] Was it the *daršān* himself? Or was someone in the audience instructed by him to ask the question? Perhaps, as I am inclined to believe, a member of the community simply rose and gave the *daršān* a starting point for his sermon. This last possibility would account for the formula ילמדנו רבנו, let our teacher teach us, which sometimes precedes the halakhic question, and for the simple nature of the questions asked (as is the case in almost all *pětîḥtôt* of this kind). This explanation also provides these *pětîḥtôt* with a literary and psychological force: only by assuming the question could not have been foreseen by the *daršān*—and his audience was, of course, aware of it—could this kind of *pětîḥtā'* achieve dynamic dimensions. The listeners knew the *daršān* was to lead up to the beginning of the *sēder*, yet they were intrigued by how he would improvise a sermon that would tie in the biblical verse with the remote halakhic problem just raised. Nevertheless, we cannot rule out the possibility that a *daršān* might have "invited" certain halakhic questions or that the question might have been put forward by the *daršān* himself.

If the common *pětîḥtā'* cannot readily be considered a live sermon, can we regard the other kind of *pětîḥtôt* as real and actual presentations of a sermon?[23] Rabbi Levi ben Sisi (Genesis Rabbâ 81:2 in Freedman 1939: 746) was once asked questions in public that in some versions are prefaced by ילמדנו רבנו (Urbach 1978: 21). He was so overwhelmed by the awesome occasion, being seated on a high pulpit facing many people, that he could not answer those questions and returned ashamed and disappointed.

I would therefore suggest that a collection of all halakhic *pětîḥtôt* would supply us with a corpus of ancient sermons written in a way that would record, to some extent, their actual *Sitz im Leben* and performance. Such a collection, as far as I know, is still a desideratum. One by-product of such a collection would be, of course, a list of *sědārîm*, some of them unknown from other sources.[24]

Our survey will not be complete unless we deal with another literary corpus that can shed light on the complicated issue of the division of the Torah into reading units: the Palestinian Aramaic translations to the Pentateuch, the Targums. Surprisingly enough, although much research has been done on the Targums in the last centuries (Grossfeld 1972–1977), there has been no serious attempt to use the "Palestinian" Targums for studying the cycles of Torah reading in 'Ereṣ-Yiśrā'ēl.[25]

These Targums are a well-defined group of texts which represents the old custom of a verse-by-verse translation of the scriptural reading into Aramaic in the synagogues. Rabbinic literature provides quite a few references (Shinan 1979: 1–29; York 1979) to the Targum and to the *mětûrgěmān* (who translated and delivered the Targum). It is clear from these sources that the *mětûrgěmān* held a professional position and was the bearer of traditions that served, among other things, as a means of transmitting the teachings of the Rabbis to the common people. His audience comprised simple folk who had no great erudition of Torah and whose ability to absorb such learning was quite limited. The Rabbis, for their part, did not overly esteem the *mĕtûrgĕmān*, and his remarks were subject to their supervision. Nevertheless, they could not ignore the *mĕtûrgĕmān*'s central role to serve as a kind of popular extension of the scholarly world, who was to mediate between the spiritual leadership and the people (Shinan 1982).

There are several factors that must be taken into account when describing the *Sitz im Leben* of the Targums: the Targum was delivered only in the synagogue on the Sabbath and holidays (Shinan 1979: 1–29; York 1979); the Targum—important as it may have been—was inferior to the biblical text; the *mĕtûrgĕmān* had to function by memory only, since it was prohibited to use written texts for translating the Torah in public (Doubles 1975; Shinan 1979: 178–79); and the *mĕtûrgĕmān*, as all oral narrators, had developed a number of devices, such as the rhetorical speech, to capture the attention of his audience (Shinan 1979: 185–92).

Bearing all this in mind, let us look at the literary form of the Palestinian Targums.[26] When examined as a group—and disregarding for the moment the differences between them—a clear pattern emerges. Most of the verses are translated verbatim, or close to that, with a limited number of short additions, while others contain lengthy expansions overflowing with rhetorical features, sometimes longer than the verse itself and sometimes preceding the translated verse. Their themes are general in nature, more general than those of the biblical verses. One wonders why these verses and not others were chosen to be expanded in such a manner. Let us examine an Aramaic targum to Genesis 50:1–12 (Ms Neofiti 1 in Diez Macho 1970–78):

1 And Joseph fell upon the face of his father and wept over him and kissed him. And Joseph laid his father on a bed of ivory, overlaid with gold and set with pearls, and strengthened with precious stone, byssus and purple. And there were poured out there wines and perfumes; there were burnt there precious aromas. There stood there kingdoms and rulers from the sons of Ishmael; there stood there rulers from the sons of Esau; there stood there rulers from the sons of Keturah; there stood Judah, the lion; men of his brothers. Judah answered and said to his brothers: Come, let us plant for our father a tall cedar, its top reaching unto the heavens and its roots reaching unto the generations of the world, because from him there have gone forth the twelve tribes of the sons of Israel, because from him have gone forth priests with their trumpets and Levites with their harps. Then Joseph bent down over the neck of his father and Joseph wept over him and kissed him.

2   And Joseph commanded his servants the physicians to embalm his father, and the physicians embalmed Israel.

3   And forty days were completed for him, for thus are completed the days of embalming. And the Egyptians wept for him seventy days.

4   And the days of weeping passed and Joseph spoke with the men of the house of Pharaoh, saying: If I have found grace and favour in your sight, speak, I pray, in the hearing of Pharaoh saying:

5   My father made me swear saying: Behold I am dying. In my grave that I dug for myself in the land of Canaan, there you will bury me. And now, I will go up, I pray, to bury my father and return.

6   And Pharaoh said: Go up and bury your father as he has made you swear.

7   And Joseph went up to bury his father and there went up with him all the administrators of the land of Egypt,

8   and all the men of the house of Joseph, his brothers and the house of his father; only their little ones and their sheep and their oxen they left in the land of Goshen.

9   And there went up with him both chariots and horsemen and the host was very great.

10   And they arrived at the threshing-place of Atadah, which is beyond the Jordan and he made there a very big and bitter lamentation and they observed for their father a mourning of seven days.

11   And the inhabitants of the land of Canaan saw the mourning in the threshing-place of Atadah and they said: This is a bitter mourning for the Egyptians. Because of this its name was called Ebel Misraim which is beyond the Jordan.

12   And his sons did for him according as he had commanded them.

While the translation to verses 2–12 generally follows the biblical text, the translation to the first verse is to be considered as one of the abovementioned expansions: It is general in content, rich in rhetorical devices, and precedes the translation of the verse itself (from "Then Joseph bent . . ." onward).

This phenomenon of expanded targumic units occurs eight times in the Aramaic Targums to Genesis;[27] six of them correlate with the beginnings of *sĕdārîm* known from other sources, such as "And the Lord appeared unto him in the plains of Mamrē" (Genesis 18:1) or "And Jacob went out from Beer-sheba and went toward Haran" (Genesis 28:10) which mark a new *sēder* even in our late tradition; or "And God remembered Rachel and God harkened to her . . ." (Genesis 30:22) or "And God appeared unto Jacob again when he came out of Padan-Aram and blessed him" (Genesis 35:9)— verses that opened a new *sēder* in some of the old customs. In two instances these targumic expansions correlate with verses that bear no direct evidence for their use as a beginning of a *sēder*—Genesis 50:1, as cited above, and "And they said, should he deal with our sister as with a harlot" (Genesis 34:31). I would suggest that the Targums might also indicate the existence of *sēdārîm* in some customs, as, for example, in the case of these two expansions.[28] Since six of the eight expansions are located in verses that were without doubt the beginning of a *sēder*, it is more than reasonable to assume that the two other expansions could mark new *sēdārîm* as well—in which case, the Targums would testify to a *sēder* in Genesis 50:1.

What, then, can be said about the expansion of Genesis 34:31, the last verse of the story of Dinah in Šĕ̱kem? Here we should add one further element to our theory: sometimes an expansion might be found in the last verse of the Torah portion, and the following verse should, therefore, open the next *sēder*. It seems to me that Genesis 35:1 (which follows 34:31) served in one ancient custom as the beginning of a *sēder*. The fact that there are some *pĕtîḥtôt* in both Genesis Rabbâ and the Tanḥûmā' on this very verse further strengthens this assumption.[29]

It appears that the *mĕtûrgĕmān* enlarged upon his usual translation of the Torah portion by expanding upon the opening or closing verse of the *sēder*. This was done, on occasion, for literary-rhetorical reasons.[30]

Thus, we have seen that both the Targums and the *pĕtîḥtôt* may be used to illustrate the ancient Torah-reading customs in the synagogue. By enlarging the number of *sēdārîm*, and by declaring them to be of irregular form, a much more complex world is created but, as is true today, reality was then much more erratic and unpredictable than its descriptions.[31]

I have tried to shed light on the division of the Torah into *sēdārîm* by presenting to the reader *all* relevant texts together, as a group. The study of the synagogue in the rabbinic period and its literature (Targum, sermons and prayer, and the *piyyûṭ*) still awaits a comprehensive synthetical analysis.

Notes

1   For basic information on prayer in talmudic times, see Heinemann 1977 and Heinemann and Petuchowski 1975.
2   Compare Elbogen 1972: 171–85. The issue of prayer that accompanied the sacrificial cult at the Temple should not be confused with the issue under discussion.
3   For a fuller description of this liturgical function, see Shinan 1979: 1–29 and York 1979.
4   On this liturgical functionary, see Lieberman 1939: 222–23.
5   A vast literature is concerned with this issue. See, for example, Guilding 1960: 242–65; Heinemann 1968a; and Wacholder's preface to Mann 1971: lii–lxvii. For a recent discussion, see Fleischer 1980: 25–28.
6   The term *sēder/sēdārîm* is used here to describe the unit(s) of Torah reading in 'Ereṣ-Yiśrā'ēl (as opposed to the Babylonian unit, the *pārāšâ*).

7   For the complete lists, see Yoel 1968: 130–32.

8   Compare Heinemann 1971 and Heinemann 1968b.

9   Such as lack of time owing to other celebrations that took place on that Sabbath (a circumcision rite, for example), or the knowledge of each person who came to read from the Scriptures.

10   For a recently published bibliography on this issue, see Sarason 1982: 557–58, especially notes 2 and 3.

11   The text is corrected by me in a few instances. A full commentary on this literary unit could not be provided here.

12   Published from manuscripts by Shinan 1984. The first fourteen units (= *pārāšôt*) in this compilation of rabbinic material can be treated independently of the remaining units.

13   As translated by Lehrman (1939: 10) with slight emendations.

14   Mishna Měgîllâ 4:4: "One who reads the Torah may not read fewer than three verses"; Mishna Měgîllâ 4:2: "On the Sabbath—seven (people read from the Torah)."

15   As suggested by Heinemann 1964: 368. See also Sonne in Mann 1966: xxvi.

16   This is the case with Leviticus Rabbâ 3: 1, 2, 3 (on Leviticus 2:1, which is the eighteenth verse in that book) and Deuteronomy Rabbâ 1:10 (on Deuteronomy 1:11—compare Lieberman 1964: 10–13). See also Genesis Rabbâ 3: 1, 2, 3 (on Genesis 1:3), but in light of Heinemann (1972) a final decision on this point cannot be made.

17   Yaari (1964: 37–54) traces the roots of this custom to the geonic period.

18   See also the prolegomenon by Sonne in Mann 1966: xxi–xxxii and Wacholder's prolegomenon in Mann 1971: xxxvi–xxxvii.

19   On this aspect of rabbinic literature, see the bibliography cited by Shinan 1981: 50–56.

20   For example, the unit on "The sin of Moses and the sin of David" (Heinemann and Petuchowski 1975: 119–23) is identified as a sermon, yet there is no proof to support this. The same remark applies to the unit entitled, "The bones of Joseph" (Heinemann and Petuchowski 1975: 135–41).

21   Compare with Leviticus Rabbâ 13:2 as translated by me. See above, note 11.

22   For the various opinions, see Stein 1935 and Heinemann and Petuchowski 1975: 110–11.

23   This type of *pětîhtā'* also underwent changes made by copyists and editors.

24   In Deuteronomy Rabbâ (Rabbinowitz 1939), for example, one can find halakhic *pětîhtôt* to Deuteronomy 1:11, 4:7, 11:26, 24:9, and more—verses which are not recorded in Yoel 1962 as beginning a new *sēder*.

25   The term *Palestinian Targums* (which is not too accurate) is used in the scholarly world to describe a group of Aramaic texts: Targum Pseudo Jonathan (Rieder 1974), the text in Ms Neofiti 1 (Diez Macho 1970–78), the Fragment Targums (Klein 1980), and various fragments (for instance, Kahle 1930).

26   These are listed above in note 25.

27   For a different type of expansion in the Aramaic Targums, see Shinan 1979: 86–108.

28   The same picture emerges from the Aramaic Targums to the rest of the Pentateuch.

29   On this question, see above, pages 98–102.

30   But compare Shinan 1979: 86–108.

31   In the oral presentation of this paper I added a few remarks regarding the relationship between targumic literature and liturgy as an example of the need to study them together, as an integral part of synagogue literature.

Bibliography

Bregman, M.

1981   Circular Proems and Proems Beginning with the Formula *"Zo hi shene'emra beruah haq-qodesh.*" In *Studies in Aggadah, Targum and Jewish Liturgy in Memory of Joseph Heinemann,* edited by J. J. Petuchowski and E. Fleischer, pages 34–41. Jerusalem: Magnes and Hebrew Union College (Hebrew).

Diez Macho, A., editor
 1970–78 *Neofiti 1.* 5 volumes. Madrid and Barcelona, Spain: Consejo Superior de Investigaciones Científicas.

Doubles, M. C.
 1975 The Targum as Oral Literature: Some Methodological Considerations. *Abstracts of the 1975 Annual Meeting of the Society of Biblical Literature.* Chicago, Ill.: Scholars.

Elbogen, I.
 1972 *Der jüdische Gottesdienst in seiner geschichtlichen Entwicklung.* Tel-Aviv, Israel: Dvir (Hebrew).

Fleischer, E.
 1970 Studies in the Problems Relating to the Liturgical Function of the Types of Early Piyyût. *Tarbiz* 40: 41–63 (Hebrew).
 1975 *Hebrew Liturgical Poetry in the Middle Ages.* Jerusalem: Keter (Hebrew).
 1980 Remarks Concerning Early Palestinian Uses in the Reading of the Law and the Prophets. *Sěfûnôt* (new series) 16: 25–47 (Hebrew).

Freedman, H., translator
 1939 *Midrash Rabbah: Genesis.* London and New York: Soncino.

Guilding, A.
 1960 *The Fourth Gospel and Jewish Worship.* Oxford: Clarendon.

Grossfeld, B.
 1972–77 *A Bibliography of Targum Literature.* 2 volumes. Cincinnati, Ohio: Hebrew Union College.

Heinemann, J.
 1964 The "Triennial" Cycle and the Calendar. *Tarbiz* 33: 362–82 (Hebrew).
 1968a The Triennial Lectionary Cycle. *Journal of Jewish Studies* 19: 41–48.
 1968b Chapters of Doubtful Authenticity in Leviticus Rabbâ. *Tarbiz* 37: 339–45 (Hebrew).
 1971 Profile of a Midrash: The Art of Composition in Leviticus Rabba. *Journal of the American Academy of Religion* 39: 141–50.
 1972 The Structure and Division of Genesis Rabbâ. *Bar Ilan* 9: 279–89 (Hebrew).
 1977 *Prayer in the Talmud: Forms and Patterns.* Berlin and New York: de Gruyter.

Heinemann, J., and Petuchowski, J. J.
 1975 *Literature of the Synagogue.* New York: Behrman.

Israelstam, J., translator
 1939 *Midrash Rabbah: Leviticus.* London and New York: Soncino.

Kahle, P.
 1930 *Masoreten des Westens,* volume 2. Stuttgart, W. Ger.: W. Kohlhammer.

Klein, M. L., editor
 1980 *The Fragment Targum of the Pentateuch.* Rome: Biblical Institute.

Lehrman, S. M., translator
 1939 *Midrash Rabbah: Exodus.* London and New York: Soncino.

Lieberman, S.
 1939 Hazzanût Yannai. *Sinai* 4: 221–40 (Hebrew).
 1964 Editor. *Midrash Debarim Rabbah.* Jerusalem: Wahrmann (Hebrew).

Mann, J.
 1966 *The Bible as Read and Preached in the Old Synagogue,* volume 2. New York: Ktav.
 1971 *The Bible as Read and Preached in the Old Synagogue,* volume 1. New York: Ktav.

Rabbinowitz, J., translator
1939   *Midrash Rabbah: Deuteronomy*. London and New York: Soncino.
Rieder, D., editor
1974   *Targum Jonathan ben Uziel on the Pentateuch*. Jerusalem: Rieder (Hebrew).
Sarason, R. S.
1982   The Petiḥtot in Leviticus Rabba: "Oral Homilies" or Redactional Constructions? *Journal of Jewish Studies* 33: 557–67.
Shinan, A.
1979   *The 'Aggādâ in the Aramaic Targums to the Pentateuch*. Jerusalem: Makor (Hebrew).
1981   The 'Aggādic Literature: Written Tradition and Transmission. *Jerusalem Studies in Jewish Folklore* 1: 44–60 (Hebrew).
1982   On the Question of Beliefs and Concepts in the Targums. *Jerusalem Studies in Jewish Thought* 2: 7–32 (Hebrew).
1984   Editor. *Midrash Shemot Rabbah, Chapters 1–14*. Jerusalem and Tel-Aviv: Dvir (Hebrew).
Stein, M.
1935   Lĕhēqer Midrĕšê Yĕlammdēnû. In *Studies in Memory of Professor Dr. Moses Schorr*. Warsaw: Judaica Distribution Co. in Poland (Hebrew).
Urbach, E. E., editor
1978   *Sēfer Pitrôn Tôrah*. Jerusalem: Magnes (Hebrew).
Yaari, A.
1964   *Toldot Ḥag Simchat Tôrah*. Jerusalem: Mosad Harav Kook (Hebrew).
Yoel, I.
1968   A Bible Manuscript Written in 1260, *Kiryat Sefer* 38: 122–32 (Hebrew).
York, A. D.
1979   The Targum in the Synagogue and in the School. *Journal of the Study of Judaism* 10: 75–86.
Zunz, L.
1947   *Die gottesdienstlichen Vorträge der Juden*. Jerusalem: Mosad Bialik (Hebrew).

J. Yahalom

It is well known that the word פייטן (*payṭān*), liturgical poet, is the Hebrew form of the Greek ποιήτης, meaning maker or creator, and that the word *piyyûṭ* is derived from the same Greek root as the English words *poet* and *poem*. Although the word *piyyûṭ* originally was synonymous with *poetry*, one may ask whether, by western standards, this ancient type of liturgical composition is real poetry or belles lettres.

Prior to an examination of the significance of *piyyûṭ*, we should bear in mind two factors that inevitably prejudice our evaluation: the historical gap between ourselves and a literary work written over a thousand years ago, and the cultural background of a literature composed in the East, where a Semitic vernacular was still in full vigor and, more important, where a different set of aesthetic values prevailed. The function of *piyyûṭ* as liturgy and its preoccupation with previously established texts is also problematic. There is, in any case, at least one aesthetic value which was valid in ancient times and is esteemed even more nowadays, that is, innovation.

Traditional Jewish liturgy, as it has come down to us, consists of not only the standard prayers ordained in the ritual codes but also liturgical poems, including the aforementioned *piyyûṭîm*. Originally the realm of *piyyûṭ* represented a rebellion against standardized fixed prayer. *Piyyûṭîm* were actually more elaborate versions of prayers at a time when fixed prayer-texts did not yet exist, and a devotional impetus played a great role in the creation of these texts (Fleischer 1971: 573).

The hymn or prayer was a well-established genre in Jewish tradition. The biblical book of Psalms consists of no less than 150 chapters, which are actually the lyrical prayers of individuals standing singly before the Lord, imploring the Almighty to listen and understand. This genre has left its imprint on the postbiblical apocryphal psalms; for instance, the *Hôdāyôt*—Thanksgiving Psalms—discovered in Qumran imitate the style of the biblical Psalms in their personal tone.

In Judaism the domain of prayer and divine service is an essential sphere that has retained its Jewishness throughout the ages, one in which Jews presumably had no need to adopt foreign models. However, it is not inconceivable that certain features of Jewish liturgical poetry may have been borrowed from other cultures. Nevertheless we may ask, how did it come about that the descendants of King David, the Psalmist, developed the kind of poetry known as *piyyûṭ*?

It would undoubtedly be helpful to be able to find the missing links between the simple and beautiful biblical and postbiblical poetry, and the artificial and bizarre *Qôṣeṣ* style of the Byzantine *payṭān* Qāllîr. Where have these presumably lost texts been preserved? Many hymns must have disappeared long ago, and yet there should be at least some fragmentary evidence of the simple postbiblical prayer. We shall begin by unveiling some of these hidden poems found outside of the well-known official prayerbooks. Besides the Ashkenazi Maḥzôr we would include in this category the less well-known Yemenite Maḥzôr, prayerbooks of lost Jewish tribes, and the fragmentary oriental prayerbooks preserved in the Cairo Gĕnîzâ, the largest and oldest repository of medieval manuscripts, about a third of which consists of poetry. Another important source for postbiblical poetic writing is the ecstatic hymns preserved in the literature of ancient Jewish mystics known as יורדי מרכבה, those who seek access to the heavenly chariot.

Yet another source is Pereq Šîrâ, a short anonymous tract containing a collection of hymns put into the mouths of earthly creatures praising their Creator (Baer 1868: 547–52). Taken together, these hymns comprise a kind of cosmic song of praise. Most of the hymns are, in fact, biblical verses, the larger part containing citations from Psalms. A close relationship exists between Pereq Šîrâ and the Hēkālôt literature that includes the Merkābâ mysticism with its characteristic hymnal style and mystical tenor. Unlike the Hēkālôt literature, the texts of these hymns—which are not original compositions but biblical adaptations—seem to reflect an early date of composition and were based on prior homiletical support without explicitly stating so (Beit-Arié 1966, volume 1: 72). The book begins with a beautiful midrash on David and the frog:

אמרו עליו על דוד מלך ישראל ע״ה כי בשעה שסיים ספר
תלים זחה דעתו עליו, אמ׳ לפניו רבון העולמים כלום יש
בריה בעולם שיאמר שירה יותר ממני?

באותה שעה נזדמנה לו צפרדע אחת ואמרה לו: דוד אל תזיח
דעתך עליך שאנכי אומרת שירה יותר ממך . . .

ואיזו היא שירה שאני אומרת: קוה אל ה׳ חזק ויאמץ לבך
וקוה אל ה׳ (תהלים כז, יד) (Beit-Arié 1966, volume 2: 22–25)

It is told of David the king, may he rest in peace, that when he finished
the Book of Psalms he became overly happy, and he spoke to the Almighty,
saying, "Is there a creature in the whole universe that sings better songs
than I do?"

At that time a frog appeared before him and said, "David, do not rejoice
because I sing more poetry than you. . ." And what poetry do I sing?

"Wait [the Hebrew is onomatopaeic "qawwe"] for the Lord, Be strong,
and let your heart take courage, Wait for the Lord." (Psalms 27:14)

Another song preserved in two versions, in the Hēḵālôt literature and the
Babylonian Talmud, has cows praising the Almighty. A passage from ʿAḇôḏâ
Zārâ (24b) deals with the meaning of וישרנה הפרות בדרך על דרך בית שמש,
"And the kine took the straightest route to Bêt Šemeš" (1 Samuel 6:12),
drawing the cart upon which the Ark of the Lord had been placed by the
frightened Philistines. In this passage, several talmudic sages explain the
Hebrew וישרנה הפרות by means of a wordplay connecting the word וישרנה
to the root שיר, to sing, and not to the actual root ישר, straight. In answer to
the question, "What was the song they sang?" Rabbi Mēʾîr identifies the
song with Šîrat Ha-yām (אשירה לה׳ כי גאה גאה) which is, in fact, the song
that is put into the mouth of the ox in Pereq Šîrâ when he praises the Lord.
This may be so because the ox was considered one of the Holy Animals
(חיות הקדש) that carry the throne of glory (כסא הכבוד). Other rabbis
identify the song of the kine with some well-known psalms. Rabbi Yiṣḥaq
Naphâ, however, a Palestinian amora of the third century, ascribes to the
kine an otherwise unknown song, in which the kine are said to be addressing
the Ark with a majestic hymn:

רני רני השיטה
התנופפי ברב הדרך
המחושקת ברקמי זהב
המהללה בדביר ארמון
המפארה בעדי עדיים

Sing, oh sing, shrine of acacia wood,
Tower in all your splendor;
You, who are decked with golden embroidery,

Praised in the innermost sanctuary,
Resplendent with the finest adornment

A striking parallel song in the Greater Hēkālôt is recited daily by the Holy
Animals who serve the Lord. They carry and exalt His throne by singing,
much as the kine did:

רנן רנן מושב עליון
הריע הריע כלי חמדה
שנעשה בהפלא ופלא

Sing, sing for joy, seat of the Most High,
Exult, exult, O precious vessel,
so marvelously fashioned

The introductory repetition in the two poems reflects an ecstatic mood.
This mood is typical of the Hēkālôt literature, which describes the ecstatic
ascent to heaven of the יורדי מרכבה mystics. The hymns of these devotees
describe in solemn phrases—very much as the song of Rabbi Yiṣḥaq Napḥâ
does—the spirit of majesty and awesomeness that permeates the heavenly
realm in which God's *šĕkînâ* dwells (Scholem 1965: 24–27).

The famous עלינו לשבח stands in a close relation to these hymns. It is
ascribed already in the Jerusalem Talmud (Rôš Haššānâ 1.3.57a) to the
school of Rab (first generation amora) and originally served as a prayer for
the New Year service called תקיעתא דבי רב (Shofar-blowings of the school
of Rab). It includes the famous passage

ומושב יקרו/בשמים ממעל// ושכינת עזו/ בגבהי מרומים

His throne of glory is in the heavens above,
His abode of majesty is in the lofty heights

Typical of this text is its use of biblical parallelism. But here, as opposed to
the Bible, form strongly influences structure. In these hymns every passage
is divided into two symmetrical couplets which themselves consist of two
units, each having two stressed words (Mirsky 1977: 48–49). Our poetry is
based not only on the inner symmetry of ideas, but rather on the much
more restricted formal principle of four-part rhythm, which affects the
structure of every verse:

עלינו לשבח/ לאדון הכל// לתת גדולה/ ליוצר בראשית
שלא עשאנו/ כגויי הארצות// ולא שמנו/ כמשפחות האדמה
שלא שם/ חלקנו כהם// ולא גורלנו/ ככל המונם

It is our duty to praise/ the Master of all,
to exalt/ the Creator of the universe
who has not formed us/ like the nations of the world
and has not placed us/ like the families of the earth
who has not determined/ our destiny to be like theirs
nor our lot/ like that of all their multitude

Similar poems are quite common in our prayerbooks. One of these ancient hymns, ישמח משה, part of the fourth benediction of the Morning Service ʿAmîdâ for the Sabbath, was not recognized as such till recently (Mirsky 1965). This benediction does not begin as the regular fourth benediction for the ʿAmîdâ on festivals does with אתה בחרתנו, You chose us, or as the Sabbath ʿAmîdâ does with אתה קדשת, You have sanctified, but curiously enough with a third person future verbal form, ישמח. It then goes on to deal, in a very metaphorical way, with Moses, who was pleased with a gift of a glorious crown that was bestowed upon him and placed on his head as he stood on Mount Sinai. To say the least, this is not the anticipated content of the קדושת היום benediction, which should deal with the sanctification of the seventh day. A close textual examination of the form reveals immediately that we are dealing with a poem of three couplets, each consisting of four small units.

ישמח משה/ במתנת חלקו// כי עבד נאמן/ קראת לו
כליל תפארת/ בראשו נתת// בעמדו לפניך/ על הר סיני
לוחות אבנים/ הוריד בידו// וכתוב בהם/ שמירת שבת

Moses was pleased/ with the gift bestowed on him
for you called him/ a faithful servant.
A glorious crown/ did you place on his head
as he stood before you/ on Mount Sinai.
The two tablets of stone/ He brought down in his hand
and upon them it was engraved/ that the Sabbath be observed

Furthermore, as is appropriate for a *piyyûṭ*, every couplet starts with an alphabetical acrostic, the first with *yod* (ישמח), the second with *kap* (כליל), and the third with *lamed* (לוחות)—instead of שני לוחות, which is the original version found in Gĕnîzâ manuscripts. If we take into account that once there must have existed three other poems for the first three benedictions of the ʿAmîdâ, each of which contained three symmetrical couplets beginning with three consecutive letters of the alphabet, we soon realize that it is not by mere chance that our poem in the fourth benediction starts with the letter *yod*. Now it becomes even more clear why Raší, according to the Manhîg (Raphael 1978: 150), rejected ישמח משה and said instead

אתה בחרתנו . . . ותתן לנו ה׳ אלהינו את יום המנוחה
לשבת בו ולנוח בו ולשמרו וכן כתוב בתורתך ושמרו
בני ישראל את השבת

The objections and arguments of the Pôsqîm are all in the realm of content; they have nothing to do with form and structure. According to the Manhîg, Rašî could find no relevance between the Sabbath and the story of Moses bringing down the tablets of the Law. The ʾÔr Zārūaʿ, who quotes his teacher, Rabbi Elîezer of Worms (Hārokēaḥ), implies that ישמח משה has nothing to do with prayer since it includes neither praise nor request (Wieder 1981: 82–85). The expression of praise or request is actually a good definition of one of the main features of prayer, as opposed to *piyyûṭ*. ישמח משה is therefore a later poetical work that supplanted the ancient prayer. The prayer אתה בחרתנו concludes smoothly with ושמרו (Exodus 31:16) in contrast to today's wording וכתוב בהם שמירת שבת, a phrase which should have introduced the fourth commandment שמור את יום השבת לקדשו (Deuteronomy 5:12).

There is no doubt that poetic compositions existed in Palestine of which no trace has reached us. The few pieces that have survived are hidden in current prayerbooks, and it is our task to reconstruct and restore them.

One of the most beautiful poems, which forms part of the Sabbath morning benediction יוצר המאורות, Creator of the lights, and is still sung in synagogues today, contains ten couplets arranged in five strophes of two couplets each. The first two stanzas are written in an elevated style, with many pairs of synonyms that imply there is no expression comprehensive enough to grasp and encompass the essence of the Holy and Merciful. Note the tautological ברוך ומבורך, blessed and praised; גדלו וטובו, His greatness and goodness; דעת ותבונה, knowledge and wisdom; זכות ומישור, purity and justice; חסד ורחמים, kindness and mercy; and so on:

אל אדון/ על כל המעשים// ברוך ומבורך/ בפי כל נשמה
גדלו וטובו/ מלא עולם// דעת ותבונה/ סובבים אותו

המתגאה על/ חיות הקודש// ונהדר בכבוד/ על המרכבה
זכות ומישור/ לפני כסאו// חסד ורחמים/ לפני כבודו

God is the Lord/ of all creation
Blessed and praised/ is He by every soul
With His greatness and goodness/ is filled the universe
Knowledge and wisdom/ surround him.

He is exalted above/ the celestial beings
And adorned in glory/ above the chariot
Purity and justice/ stand before his throne
Kindness and mercy/ are in his glorious presence

Whereas אל אדון is quite an obvious piece of poetical work, there are many *piyyûṭîm* that are more successfully disguised and more difficult to identify. Among these are poems that are recited only once a year as part of the long form of the benediction (מטבע ארוך של ברכה). Such is the אשר הניא, which is recited on the eve of Purim after reading the *Mĕgîllâ*. Typical of these texts is their alphabetical order and the relative pronoun אשר at their beginning, which has no meaning unless the fixed preamble to the bene-diction is added to it (Yaari 1960):

ברוך אתה ה׳ אלהינו מלך העולם

אשר הניא/ עצת גויים// ויפר/ מחשבות ערומים

> Blessed be the Lord, king of the universe
> Who wrecked/ the counsel of the heathens
> And frustrated/ the plans of the crafty

The text goes on to tell us the story of the *Mĕgîllâ* and is suffixed by:

ברוך אתה ה׳ הנפרע לעמו ישראל מכל צריהם האל המושיע

> Blessed are You, O Lord, who metes out punishment to the
> oppressors of Israel, Your people, O redeeming God.

Worthy of mention is one stanza of this poem, comprising the letters *mem* and *nun* of the acrostic. The first verse, having brought the story of persecu-tion to its climax, poses a dramatic question:

מי זה יעמוד/ לכפר שגגה// ולמחול חטאת/ עון אבותינו

> Who would rise/ to atone for errors
> To gain pardon/ for our fathers' sins?

The second verse gives the answer in an artistic way, introducing for the first time the myrtle (הדסה-אסתר):

ניץ פרח/ מן לולב// הן הדסה עמדה/ לעורר ישנים

> A shoot blossomed forth/ from a palm branch
> Hadassâ [the myrtle] rose/ to stir those who were asleep

The anonymous poet goes on to describe Esther's share in the salvation of the Jewish nation.

The use of the rhetorical question was further developed in the poetry of the most ancient *payṭān* known by name, Yôsê ben Yôsê; his works are still recited in many synagogues on the second day of Rôš Haššānâ as part of the Mûsāf service known as מלכיות (Malḵûyôt). Yôsê ben Yôsê's מלכיות start very majestically with the long forms of the future verb אהללה, I will praise; אשירה, I will sing; אספרה, I will tell; and אאפדנו, I will adorn.

Already in the second stanza the poet switches very quickly to rhetorical questions. The lofty questions of the poet have only one answer:

אהללה אלהי/ אשירה עוזו// אספרה כבודו/ אאפדנו מלוכה . . .
בקהל אבשר/ ברוב עם אהלל// למי שאת ויתר עוז/ ולמי המלוכה

I will praise my Lord/ I will sing praise to his strength
I will declare his glory/ I will adorn his kingship. . .
In public I will announce/ I will praise him in a multitude of people
Who is most august and who abounds in power?
Who is deserving of Kingship?

(Mirsky 1977: 8–14)

Yôsê ben Yôsê is the first exponent of the *payṭānic* style to be known by name. Literary research has come to regard him as a representative of the period preceding the introduction of rhyme in our poetry because this artifice was lacking in his preserved poems. His poetry is distinguished by its simplicity. He and his anonymous colleagues lived in Palestine when the Hebrew language was still very vigorous, at least insofar as poetry was concerned. Jews living in small villages still cultivated the soil, and the pure spirit of fishermen living on the banks of Lake Kinneret is reflected through verses like:

בשריצת דגים/ במעמד דייגים/ יעלוז לבנו

(MS Bodleian 2851/4)

> by the swarming of fish
> in the presence of fishermen
> our heart rejoices

In addition to reflecting reality, the poets must have imbibed the spirit of the prevailing culture. In this respect the poems represent a kind of parallel to midrashic literature. They appear at the same time and develop in a parallel fashion; both are manifestations of the same spirit and attitude. It is true that early *piyyûṭ* had not yet absorbed much material from the midrash, but even in the early period there is something in the *piyyûṭ* that reminds us immediately of the midrashic style and spirit. Characteristically rhetorical techniques, with theses and antitheses common in midrash, are found in the *piyyûṭ* (Mirsky 1958: 456–57).

One of the most famous rhetorical devices found in midrash is the מידה כנגד מידה, measure for measure. It relies on different kinds of repetition between two unrelated topics, with regard either to sound and wording or to meaning. In the long run, this kind of repetition furthered the development of the couplet into a rhyming unit. Synonyms and homonyms, paranomasia and alliteration all seem suitable to this end. Ultimately this led to the emergence of end-rhyme based on sound parallelism, but it must have taken a long time for this to evolve. In a later period, this poetic element spread through the Aramaic liturgy of the Syriac Christian Church, via Latin, to the vernacular languages of Europe (Hrushovski 1971: 738). Yannai is the first poet to have systematically employed end-rhyme in his poetry. In spite of his central position as a Palestinian poet, and as the alleged teacher of the famous Qāllîr, his poems were unknown until the Gĕnîzâ fragments were examined, making hundreds of his poems available today. Although he did not have to discover or invent rhyme, he must have elevated it to the prominent position it acquired later on, when rhyme was considered an essential element in medieval poetry. Yannai played an important role in the development of ancient Jewish poetry. He must have been popular in his community, since he was expected to appear in the synagogue on each and every Sabbath with new material. His poetry was closely related to the portions of the Torah that were read in the triennial cycle practiced in ancient Palestine. Thus, each of his compositions was recited only once every three and a half years. Yannai's creativity may be compared to that of Johann Sebastian Bach, who, during a relatively short period as cantor in Leipzig, was obliged to write a new cantata for every Sunday. Once performed, many of these cantatas were never repeated in the liturgical year and, as a result, many of his compositions have been lost (Emery 1980: 795). In the case of Yannai, however, things turned out differently. As a result of the great esteem in which his poems were held, Yannai became famous, and his compositions were still being recited more than five hundred years after his death. Together with the disappearance of the Palestinian communities towards the end of the first millennium, his impressive contributions to Jewish cultural life in the Homeland likewise sank into oblivion.

The process that led to the emergence of rhyme—which later dominated Yannai's poetry—is illuminating. One of the most important milestones in the development of rhyme is a lamentation for the Ninth of Ab, which is still recited by Ashkenazi communities on the eve of that day. In this dirge the whole universe participates in Israel's agony over the destruction of the Temple. The tribes of Jacob weep bitterly, and even the planets shed tears:

אז בחטאינו/ חרב מקדש// ובעוונותינו/ נשרף היכל

בעיר שחוברה לה/ קשרו מספד// וצבא השמים/ נשאו קינה . . .

טלה ראשון/ בכה במר נפש// על כי כבשיו/ לטבח הובלו

יללה השמיע/ שור במרומים// על כן בכור שור/ שחו קרניו

> Because of our sins/ the Temple was destroyed,
> because of our crimes/ the Sanctuary was burnt.

> In the city that once was bound firmly together/
> lamentations were heard,
> And the host of heaven/ sounded a dirge. . .
> Aries [the ram] first of all [the constellations]/ wept bitterly
> for his sheep/ were being led to slaughter.
> Taurus [the bull]/ howled on high
> for the horns of the firstling bull/ were brought low

The poem goes on to name the constellations of the zodiac one by one, each with its special relation to earthly events. Some of the interesting links are based on metaphorical connections: the ram (Aries) laments the loss of his sheep, which represent the people of Israel. Others are based on repetitious sounds: the bull (Taurus) sheds tears over the firstling bullock. Regarding their *sitz im leben*, we may conjecture that these poems, based on lists of the signs of the zodiac, were recited while the community was gathered on the floor around a zodiac mosaic, a common feature in ancient Palestinian synagogues (Hübner 1983: 23). The reciter may even have improvised on the theme of the constellations and their connections to the catastrophes of the Children of Israel. In fact, two different major traditions concerning the version of this *piyyût* have been preserved; apart from the well-known Ashkenazi version, a second one has been preserved, almost to our own day, by the ancient Jewish community of Rome in its famous מחזור רומא, Roman cycle.

Although the poet here aptly expresses his sympathy for those in peril, one should guard against the assumption that this liturgical poetry is the Romantic type found in western poetry. A parallel poem, heretofore unpublished, in which the planets comprise the principal chain of motifs, has been preserved in some Gĕnîzâ manuscripts, which are, evidently, remnants of ancient eastern prayerbooks. This poem lacks the emotional element that we are accustomed to encounter in poetry, and yet can nonetheless be regarded as poetry. It is designed for the happy occasion of the successful return of the High Priest from the Holy of Holies on the Day of Atonement, and begins with אז בצאת כהן מבית קדש, developing much the same as the dirge but with a different mood and feeling:

לצאתו ישמח/ טלה הראשון//בעת הגישו/ כבש התמיד
מעת הזה/ דם פר בקודש//העטה ששון/ לבכור שור . . .
שבח וזמרה/ יתן גדי// בשורו עזאזל// משתבר . . .

(Cambridge University Library T-S H6.24)

> When he [the high priest] emerges/ the Ram [Aries] the first
> will be happy/ since he has sacrificed/ a male lamb.
> Having sprinkled/ the blood of the bull on the Holy of Holies
> he showered the firstling Bull [of the constellations] with joy. . .

Praise and song/ will the Capricorn utter
when he sees that the scapegoat/ has been broken to pieces

This poem, although parallel in many respects to the previous one, does not reflect the human values we appreciate in poetry. Nevertheless, we sense here the poetic rhetoric that is so familiar in *'aggādâ* and midrash. The poet as well as the homilist tries to bridge apparently unrelated topics and to discover hidden links between words that would be unrelated otherwise. An imaginative diction that draws words from unconnected semantic fields into one circle is typical of the colorful poetics of *piyyûṭ* and midrash alike, with one important difference: In *piyyûṭ* this device prescribes rigid poetic structures in which the tautological elements are placed most conspicuously at the very end of the verse. However, in the early stage of the development of this poetry, rhymes of different kinds were interspersed everywhere: at the beginning, at the end, or throughout a verse, evoking an effect similar to that produced by English and German alliteration. In the zodiac *piyyûṭîm* rhyme was based mainly on words of similar meaning but not of similar sound, using connected pairs like ram and lamb (טלה/כבש), bull and ox (פר/שור), and so on. At the same time, rhyme relied also on the repetition of whole words throughout the strophe, which generally turned out to be the key words in the strophes (Yahalom 1971: 765).

To demonstrate the development and status rhyme achieved, we will concentrate on the simple word אבן, stone, which may assume different nuances and subtle meanings in eastern environments. We find it used as a rhyme-word in an ancient dirge attributed to Yôsê ben Yôsê. In one of his verses he complains helplessly:

טורי אבן/ פסו ממלואת אבן// ואיך נסיר לב אבן/ וידו בנו אבן

(Mirsky 1977: 209)

Rows of stone/ vanished from the [breastplate] setting of stone
and how could we remove our stony heart/ since they cast on us stones

Yannai uses "stone" in his composition for the biblical *sēder* beginning ויהי כל הארץ שפה אחת . . . ותהי להם הלבנה לאבן, And the whole earth had one language . . . and they had brick for stone (Genesis 11:1–3):

כבד לבם כאבן/ ולבינה היתה להם לאבן// לכן ניפצם כאבן/
אל אשר דברו מפוצץ אבן

(Zulay 1938: 13; Rabinovitz 1985: 114)

They had a heart heavy as stone/ and they had brick for stone
Therefore they were shattered like stone/ by God whose word penetrates stone

The employment of such stylistic devices must have been widespread among poets in Palestine and its vicinity, and it had its manifestations not only in Hebrew but in foreign languages and among non-Jews as well.

The greatest of all Byzantine poets, and a near contemporary of Yannai, is Romanos the Melodist, whose writings are considered masterpieces of world literature. It is likely that he was born in Syria to a Jewish family and was christened only as an adult. According to legend, he was miraculously endowed with the gift of writing and is said to have composed about a thousand metrical sermons known as *kontakia* (Trypanis 1981: 420–24). It is interesting to find in his poetry verses built upon similar stylistic principles as the ones observed in the *piyyûṭ* (Schirmann 1953–54: 158–59). In his composition for the resurrection, he forms one of his strophes on the words λίθος and πέτρα, stone and rock:

> λίθος ἦν ἐπὶ τοῦ μνήματος
> πέτρα δὲ ἔνδον τοῦ μνήματος
> γέγοναν λίθοι οἱ τηροῦντες
> θεωροῦνθες τὸν ἄγγελον λίθῳ καθήμενον

(Maas and Trypanis 1963: 182)

> There was a *stone* against the tomb,
> of *rock* was the interior of the tomb.
> *Stones* became the guards
> When they beheld the angel seated on the *stone*
> (Refrain: saying to the women: The Lord is risen)

Comparison between Yannai and Romanos reveals that both poets used, except for the word-motif *stone*, the same device to adorn the last line of their strophes, an epithet for God and for the angel respectively. Yannai concludes with אל אשר דברו מפוצץ אבן, God whose word penetrates stone, whereas Romanos employs the ending ἄγγελον λίθῳ καθήμενον, the angel seated on the stone. In both cases the last lines are longer than the preceding ones.

Similar rhetorical devices even had a practical function in admonishing the community. In a pattern known as improperia, a sentence expressing God's favor to Israel during the Exodus and the entry into the Promised Land is contrasted with one containing reproaches against the Jews who tortured and crucified Jesus. In Christian sources the list is adduced to prove Israel's wickedness in rejecting Jesus, whereas in Jewish sources the list is utilized to prove Israel's ungratefulness to God and to Moses (Flusser 1974: 51–52). This juxtaposition of God's grace and Israel's sins is, in any event, centered around key words.

The Jewish improperia were recited on the Ninth of Ab, the day of destruction, whereas the Christian improperia were prescribed for Good Friday, the day of the passion. In some instances, the different sources even use the same key words or related pairs, such as water and vinegar and the rivers of Babylon and the Jordan River.

The Midrash Êkâ Rabbâ (7:8) mainly expounds pairs of biblical passages: הים ראה וינום הירדן יסוב לאחור, The *sea* saw and fled; the *Jordan* turned back (Psalms 114:3) describing the Exodus, as opposed to על נהרות בבל שם ישבנו גם בכינו, by the *rivers* of Babylon we sat and wept (Psalms 137:1) describing the Exile (Lerner 1981: 85). Yannai's lament, on the other hand, uses word-motifs as sound rhymes and employs fixed poetic structures (Mirsky 1967–68: 129–36):

בימי משה הֻבקעו מי תהומות

ובימי ירמיהו הֻבקעה עיר חומות

בימי משה וֻעל הים נמו אז ישיר [Exodus 15:1]

ובימי ירמיהו וֻעל נהרות נמו איך נשיר [Psalms 137:4]

(Zulay 1938: 295)

> In the days of Moses the waters of the abyss divided
> In the days of Jeremiah the city and the walls divided
> In the days of Moses they said: Then he sang on the *sea*
> In the days of Jeremiah they said: How could we sing on the *rivers*

The poet weaves his poem around an alphabetical list of couplets, which represents in its fixed order the inner coherence of the Exodus, the crossing of the Red Sea, the trials in the desert, and the entry into the Promised Land in contrast to the disruptive effects of the destruction of the Temple, the Exile, the Diaspora, and so on.

The most developed strophic pattern known among the anonymous Byzantine hymns is a poem composed of twenty-four strophes connected to each other by an alphabetical acrostic, known as Ἄρχοντες Ἑβραίων. This fifth-century text was written for Good Friday (Grosdidier de Matons 1977: 23–25); it systematically develops the contrast between the favorable deeds of the Savior and the sinfulness of his persecutors, the Jews. One of his most convincing strophes includes the following accusation:

> Ὄξος ἐν τῇ σπόγγῳ
> καὶ χολήν σε ἐπότισαν
> τὸν ἐν γῇ ἀνύδρῳ
> ποταμοὺς ἀναβλύσαντα (Pitra 1876: 483)

> With a sponge they made you drink vinegar and bitterness,
> You who have caused rivers to flow on dry land

Aside from the historical roots, such as the ancient tradition of related pairs embedded in the biblical *parallelismus membrorum* (Avishur 1977: 51), there must have been common contemporary factors in the eastern prayer house and its rhetorical and cultural background that led to common—Jewish and Christian—developments in its poetry (Schirmann 1953–54: 125).

A poem by Yannai, in which the rhyme is based mainly on a repetition of pairs of opposites derived from the roots אהב and שנא, love and hate, is illuminating. The poem is based on the biblical *sēder* beginning וירא ה' כי שנואה לאה, And the Lord saw that Lēâ was hated (Genesis 29:30), which includes the story of the "dull-eyed" Lēâ, who was unloved by Jacob, envied by her sister Rachel, and, according to a midrash, hated for her deceitfulness by seafarers and land travelers. It is from this starting point that the poet develops the intricate relations of Israel, the nations, and God.

Our eyes are weak with longing for your love,	כלו עינינו לאהבתך,
O loving one,	אוהב
for we are hated by the hating enemy.	נשנאים משנאת אויב
Look how afflicted we are from within,	ראה נא בעינינו מבית
See how hated we are from without—	ושור שנאתנו מבחוץ
as You looked on Lēâ's affliction	כלאה אשר ראיתה בעניה
and saw her tormented by hate.	ושרת בשנאת ענויה
Within the house she was hated	מבית היו לה שונאים
and from without detested.	ובחוץ היו לה משניאים
But not every loved one is loved	ולא כל אהוב אהוב
nor every hated one hated:	ולא כל שנוי שנוי
there are some who are hated below	יש שנואים במטה
and yet beloved above.	ואהובים במעלה
Those whom You hate are hated;	שנואיך שנואים
those whom You love are loved.	ואהוביך אהובים
The hatred against us is because	שנאתנו כי אהבנוך,
we love You, O Holy one!	קדוש

(Carmi 1981: 215)   (Zulay 1938: 399; Rabinovitz 1985: 173–174)

This poem was published as late as 1939 in Nazi Berlin (Spitzer 1938–39: 6–7); the German translation interpreted the opening line with a creative misunderstanding, typical for those dark times:

> Nach Deiner Liebe vergehn uns die Augen,
> Der die vom Feindhass Gehassten Du liebst.

This interpretation, of course, upsets the balance achieved in the first couplet and ignores the rhetoric of the connected pair אויב/אוהב, but it must have best suited the feelings of German Jewry on the eve of the Kristallnacht and other bitter events.

The ancient poet, on his part, gradually develops the idea that it is God's love that matters and that it even may be strengthened when contrasted with earthly misfortunes. The *pointe* is nevertheless hidden in the last and shortest couplet, where the poet states that not only is God's love aroused by earthly hatred, but earthly animosity itself is enhanced by the heavenly affection of Israel. This course of ideas brings the poem to full circle, leading it from a tone of prayer at the beginning to a contemplative statement at the very end.

Bibliography

Avishur, Y.
  1977   *The Construct State of Synonyms in Biblical Rhetoric.* Jerusalem: Kiryat Sepher (Hebrew).
Baer, S.
  1868   *Sēder ʿAḇôdat Israel.* Roedelheim, W. Ger.: I. Lehrberger (Hebrew).
Beit-Arié, M.
  1966   *Perek Shira–Introductions and Critical Edition.* Ph.D. dissertation. Jerusalem: Hebrew University (Hebrew).
Carmi, T.
  1981   *The Penguin Book of Hebrew Verse.* New York: Penguin.
Emery, W.
  1980   Johann Sebastian Bach. In *The New Grove Dictionary of Music and Musicians*, volume 1, columns 793–95. London: Macmillan.
Fleischer, E.
  1971   Piyyuṭ. In *Encyclopaedia Judaica*, volume 13, columns 573–602. Jerusalem: Keter.
Flusser, D.
  1974   Hebrew Improperia. *Immanuel* 4: 51–54.
Grosdidier de Matons, J.
  1977   *Romanos le Mélode et les origines de la poésie religieuse à Byzance.* Paris: Beauchesne.
Hrushovski, B.
  1971   The Major Systems of Hebrew Rhyme from the Piyyuṭ to the Present Day (500 A.D.–1970): An Essay on Basic Concepts. *Hasifrut* 2/4: 721–49 (Hebrew).
Hübner, W.
  1983   *Zodiacus Christianus—Jüdisch-christliche Adaptationen des Tierkreises von der Antike bis zur Gegenwart.* Königstein/Ts.: A. Haim.
Lerner, M. B.
  1981   New Homilies for the Ninth of Aḇ. In *Samuel Belkin Memorial Volume*, edited by M. Karmeli and H. Lif, pages 84–107. New York: Yeshiva University (Hebrew).
Maas, P., and Trypanis, C. A.
  1963   *Sancti Romani Melodi Cantica–Cantica Genuina.* Oxford: Clarendon.
Mirsky, A.
  1958   History of Rhyme. *Moznaim* 6: 450–58 (Hebrew).
  1965   Yěsôd Qěrôḇâ. *Sinây* 57: 127–32 (Hebrew).
  1967–68 From Midrash to Piyyûṭ to Jewish Poetry. *Lěšonénu* 32: 129–39 (Hebrew).
  1977   *Yosse ben Yosse Poems.* Jerusalem: Bialik (Hebrew).
Pitra, J. B.
  1876   *Analecta Sacra Spicilegio Solesmensi Parata*, volume 1. Paris: Typis Tusculanis.

Rabinovitz, Z. M.
　　1985　*The Liturgical Poems of Rabbi Yannai*. Jerusalem: Bialik (Hebrew).
Raphael, Y.
　　1978　*Sefer Hamanhig–Rulings and Customs, R. Abraham ben Nathan of Lunel*. Jerusalem:
　　　　　Mosad Harav Kook.
Schirmann, J.
　　1953–54　Hebrew Liturgical Poetry and Christian Hymnology. *Jewish Quarterly Review* 44:
　　　　　123–61.
Scholem, G.
　　1965　*Jewish Gnosticism, Merkabah Mysticism, and Talmudic Tradition*. New York: Jewish
　　　　　Theological Seminary of America.
Spitzer, M.
　　1938–39　*Almanach des Schocken Verlags auf das jahr 5699* (תרצ״ט). Berlin: Schocken.
Trypanis, C. A.
　　1981　*Greek Poetry—From Homer to Seferis*. London: Faber and Faber.
Wieder, N.
　　1981　The Controversy about the Liturgical Composition "Yismaḥ Moshe"–Opposition
　　　　　and Defence. In *Studies in Aggadah, Targum and Jewish Liturgy in Memory of Joseph
　　　　　Heinemann*, edited by J. J. Petuchowsky and E. Fleischer, pages 75–99. Jerusalem:
　　　　　Magnes (Hebrew).
Yaari, A.
　　1960　Hanôqēm et Niqmātēnû. *Maḥanayîm* 43: 27–31 (Hebrew).
Yahalom, J.
　　1971　Rhyme in the Early Piyyuṭ. *Hasifrut* 2/4: 762–66 (Hebrew).
Zulay, M.
　　1938　*Piyyutē Yannai*. Berlin: Schocken.

9. The Current State of Galilean Synagogue Studies

Eric M. Meyers

Despite the rather obvious fact that the ancient synagogue is universally regarded as one of the most stunning achievements of Jewish antiquity, and also that recent years have witnessed a spate of new publications on the subject, there is, in my opinion, a sense in which either only well-controlled and well-planned new excavations or carefully planned publication of previously excavated or discovered material can break the scholarly stalemate that seems to dominate the field today. Some admirable publications that give much cause for optimism are the two-volume synagogue catalogue of Hüttenmeister and Reeg published by the Tübingen Atlas Project; Marilyn Chiat's *Handbook of Synagogue Architecture*, Brown Judaic Studies Number 29; *Ancient Synagogues Revealed*, edited by Lee I. Levine and published by the Israel Exploration Society; and Joseph Naveh's *On Stone and Mosaic*, a catalogue of Aramaic and Hebrew synagogue inscriptions published by Maariv, unfortunately available only in Hebrew.

These publications, especially when complemented by articles, excavation reports, and occasional short monographs such as Z. Ma'oz's Golan survey of Jewish settlements and synagogues (1983), leave the general impression that the field of study is alive and well. In many ways this is true, but the lack of scholarly consensus on many key issues, particularly chronology and typology, leaves the field betwixt and between in Israel. And for some unknown reason the field remains uninteresting to or understudied by most Americans and Europeans. The tragedy is, moreover, that most sites in the Galilee and Golan beg both excavation and restoration, and very little is being done. At times excavation is made difficult by ultra-orthodox extrem-

ists who protest liberal and Christian "pollution" of their sites; Hîrbet
Šemaʿ, fully restored by the American team that A. T. Kraabel and I led,
lies in ruins owing to profanation by these pious vandals and the inability of
the Israel Department of Antiquities to cope with this vandalism. The last
season at Nabratein was marred by midnight attacks of these ultra-orthodox
vandals stealing supplies, knocking down columns, and destroying balks
—the sina qua non of all archaeological discourse. It was volunteers from
the Nature Preserve who, in 1981, stopped the vandalism.

Turning more to the scholarly side of things, I would like to address the
state of the field in a more traditional manner. Recent excavations in Galilee have demonstrated that the synagogue emerged in that region with a
diversity of types. Heretofore it was believed that specific types of synagogue
structures developed within specific time frames. According to this older
theory the ancient synagogue emerged in Galilee as a basilical structure in
the second to third centuries, developed in the fourth century into a
broadhouse transitional phase with a fixed repository for the Torah, and
culminated with the evolution of the apsidal type in the Byzantine period.
Over the course of time, decoration that once adorned the exterior was
transferred to the interior, as relations with the imperial power and Christian world worsened (Meyers 1980). Today, however, newly discovered diversity may be demonstrated by the early second-century C.E. broadhouse
synagogue identified at Nabratein in 1981 (E. Meyers and C. Meyers 1981:
34), the third-century basilicas with *bîmâ* excavated in 1977–78 at Gûš
Ḥālāb (Meyers 1981) and Nabratein, and the third-century broadhouse at
Ḥîrbet Šemaʿ excavated in 1971–72 (Meyers, Kraabel, and Strange
1976)—all of which conflict with the old theory of Galilean synagogue
development.

We may assess the current state of the field by focusing our discussion on
the basilical synagogue, with some additional examples of the broadhouse
type. I hope to show that recent work demonstrates the old consensus can
no longer be maintained. Indeed, by focusing on the basilica we may observe
the coexistence until the early medieval period of apsidal buildings along-
side those without apses.

The Basilica

In the basilica, as in the various forms of the ancient synagogue, the
major architectural, if not theological, feature is the wall of orientation facing Jerusalem. It is generally assumed that this most salient
and telling feature of the synagogue is derived from the biblical practice
of praying towards Jerusalem (1 Kings 8:44, parallel 2 Chronicles 6:34;
1 Kings 8:48, parallel 2 Chronicles 6:38; Daniel 6:11). This custom

achieves legal force in the rabbinic period when it is translated into law (J Běrākôt 4, 8b–c), but the same principle also seems to have been operative in the first-century buildings at Masada and Herodium (Foerster 1973).

The principle of sacred orientation may be observed in the basilical structure uncovered in the American excavations at ancient Mêrôn (E. Meyers, Strange, and C. Meyers 1978), where the triple facade faces south towards Jerusalem. Most scholars agree that this example dates to a time when the ark was not yet a permanent fixture in the synagogue but was a portable structure brought into the main sanctuary during worship. The precentor, or reader of Scripture, would stand before it facing Jerusalem (though compare the example of the Nabratein broadhouse, where one might have faced the opposite direction, towards the congregation—E. Meyers and C. Meyers 1981). Possible representations of a portable ark may be observed in sculpture at Capernaum and in mosaic elsewhere (Hachlili 1976: 43–53). In our view, the portable ark of the synagogue harks back to Nathan's rebuke of David (2 Samuel 7:4 and following), when the prophet argues poignantly, in theological terms, for a movable shrine.

Both the orientation of the basilica and the suggested location of the ark require the so-called "awkward about-face" of the worshiper. If the Jerusalem-oriented entrances were both functional and the focus of worship, the worshiper would have had to turn around immediately upon entering the building from the south. The lack of an entrance on the northern, or opposite, side would have necessitated such a turnaround. At Mêrôn, and at most other basilical sites, no convincing proof of entrances either on the north, east, or west has been found. The Nabratein basilicas, however, are the exceptions to this rule.

All of this presupposes the existence of some kind of Torah Shrine (either portable or permanent) on the interior southern (Jerusalem-oriented) wall, even though none has been found in situ; the evidence at both Mêrôn and Capernaum supports such a theory (Strange 1976: 140–41). A novel arrangement was found in the basilica-like synagogue excavated at Bêt Šěʿārîm: a raised *bîmâ*, or podium, for the reading of the scrolls is situated in the back wall of the nave opposite the three monumental doorways, which face Jerusalem. The building dates from the second quarter of the third century to the middle of the fourth century (Avigad and Mazar 1976: 233–34). If the Torah Shrine was portable and brought out during services, we would not expect to find any trace of it today (Kraabel 1974: 438). The excavators at Bêt Šěʿārîm noted significantly, however, that a Torah Shrine was relocated on the Jerusalem wall during the last phase of the building's history. The excavator of the ʿÊn-Gedî synagogue also observed this change

(Avi-Yonah 1973a: 341). Both instances tend to suggest a major theological development some time in the late third or early fourth century C.E., when public reading of Scripture in a worship setting reached a high point. Whether such a transformation can be related to external circumstances affecting the Jewish community, such as the Christianization of the empire or the reading of Scripture by sectarians, is a matter that deserves further study. Saul Lieberman felt this was a matter of Jewish self-definition vis-à-vis Christians and Jewish-Christians, indicating that Jews venerated a specific canonical form of Torah (personal communication).

The origin of the basilica is generally conceded to be the typical Greco-Roman basilica, possibly mediated to Palestine through builders employed by Herod the Great, one of the most notable patrons of Roman building in the eastern Mediterranean world. Still others suggest that the basilica is mediated through Syro-Roman and Nabatean prototypes. In any case, the synagogue qua basilica is still innovative in that it has adapted a public structure, whether sacred or profane, that emphasizes the exterior and has modified it to suit its own unique religious purposes.

New discoveries indicate a much higher degree of flexibility in dating all types of synagogues than previously and attest to the simultaneous existence of more than one type. For example, the basilica at Capernaum is widely regarded as late or Byzantine, whereas the broadhouse at Ḥîrbet Šemāʿ is dated much earlier. It is our contention that the only certain way of dating any ancient building is through scientific excavation and scholarly evaluation of the data that emanate from such excavation. With respect to the general categories of synagogue buildings, present excavations indicate even more anomalies than the variation in ground plan and internal furnishing already mentioned, so that even the concept of a standard basilica can be maintained no longer.

The Case of Gûš Ḥālāb

The 1977–78 American excavations at the ancient site of Gûš Ḥālāb (Giscala), just a few kilometers north of Mêrôn (Meyers 1977: 253–54; see figure 9.1), reinforce the opinion that only careful excavation can provide the answers to important questions of dating and typology. In the jargon of field archaeologists, this site provides a classic example of the axiom "the answers always lie below." Heinrich Kohl and Carl Watzinger, who excavated at Gûš Ḥālāb during their survey in the early part of this century, clearly did not go far enough in their work; their published plan of Gûš Ḥālāb (see figure 9.2) indicates they erroneously identified what now are clearly storage areas as the closing, or interior, wall of a very large square basilica (1916: plate 15). Our work at Gûš Ḥālāb points out the errors in the German typological assumptions and reinforces the notion that variety exists even within the broadly defined category of "basilical synagogues."

The founding of the Gûš Ḥālāb synagogue surely can be dated to the third century C.E. However, the southern wall, which faces Jerusalem, has only one entrance, the one with the down-facing eagle incised on the underside of its lintel stone (see figure 9.3). If a gallery for additional seating had existed, it would have been on the northern side, where the only other certain entrance to the building was found (see figure 9.4). What is "basilical" about this building is its two rows of four columns running north-south. It is rectangular only if we define its newly discovered, interior, load-bearing walls as the interior space of the building. Indeed, what is interesting about this building is that these interior walls, on the west, north, and east, demarcate the interior space of the building and internally transform a roughly square structure—originally thought by the Germans to be the synagogue interior—into a rectangular basilica with a large corridor on the western side, a gallery on the north, and a series of rooms along the east. This is a unique arrangement in this kind of building.

Also of major interest is the *bîmâ* along the southern wall, which happens to be the only ashlar wall among all the exterior walls. This *bîmâ* dates to the fourth century, or second phase of the building's use, and is off-center in the building, just to the west of the entrance. Among the debris were found smaller pieces of architectural fragments that suggest an *aedicula*, or Torah Shrine, in conjunction with this *bîmâ*, possibly built atop it, or perhaps in another, still earlier phase during the third century. The discovery of the *bîmâ* at Gûš Ḥālāb represents the first of its kind in the general category of buildings we call basilical, except for the anomalous findings at Bêt Šĕʿārîm and ʿÊn-Gedî. The Gûš Ḥālāb basilica with this plan existed into the sixth century, when, shaken by the earthquake of 502 C.E., it was destroyed or damaged beyond repair in 551 C.E.

New data from recent excavations are bringing fresh insights. While the material from Gûš Ḥālāb alters somewhat the old views, it underscores the capacity of an individual religious community for limited originality. The overall architectural forms, however influenced by the surrounding Greco-Roman provincial world, reflect a freedom from rigidity that is refreshing to the student of Roman provincial art (see figures 9.5 and 9.6).

The Case of Nabratein

The 1980–81 excavations at Nabratein, just north of Safed, provide additional unexpected information on the basilical-type synagogue (see figure 9.7). First, the third-century building with six columns, destroyed in a

306 C.E. earthquake, housed a fixed Torah Shrine, good portions of which were preserved intact. It also had unexpected entrances on the north and east, though as a result of erosion neither one is completely clear. Although the Byzantine basilica, which was dedicated in the time of Justinian (562 C.E.) and survived into the mid-seventh century, had no preserved fixed repository for the scrolls, it apparently housed a wooden ark (see figure 9.8) and had no *bîmâ*. Depictions of the possible ark were found on pieces of black ceramic and, hence, its existence seems reasonable (E. Meyers and C. Meyers 1982).

More surprising was the discovery of an early broadhouse phase at Nabratein dating to the second century (see figure 9.9). If Ḥirbet Šemaʿ called into question ideas about the development of the Galilean synagogue, then this building provides the new theorists' coup de grace. Although there is no fixed shrine, twin *bîmâ*s flank the Jerusalem-oriented wall, and a break in the cement in the center of the floor suggests that a table there was used for reading and possibly translating the Torah. Was the *dĕrāšâ* given on the *bîmâ* or at floor level?

A single new excavation could completely shatter the old theories and prove conclusively that a fixed shrine, the *ʾārôn haqqōdeš*, existed in an early Galilean structure. This, then, would indicate that later mosaics and other artistic depictions do, in fact, portray the actual accouterments that existed in the earlier Galilean synagogue.

The Significance of Stratigraphic Archaeological Findings

Many other examples could be marshalled to further illustrate that several different types of synagogues existed simultaneously from the second century C.E. onwards. However, I will conclude by commenting on the hesitancy of some scholars to accept the data I have discussed, and by suggesting the significance of such diversity.

It seems to me that a good deal of scholarly skepticism derives from a refusal to accept data that has been uncovered by methods that are not universally accepted. By and large the balk-debris methodology instituted by the British (Wheeler and Kenyon) and further developed by the Americans (Albright, Wright, Dever, and Meyers) has not had enough impact on Israeli Classical-period archaeological expeditions. Instead of relying solely on well-dated archaeological deposits, dating by this method is fixed on the basis of art-historical and architectural developments—a technique which in America informs the disciplines of art history and Classical studies more than those of Near Eastern history or archaeology.

A lack of attention to serious stratigraphic archaeology in many late, Classical-period sites is illustrated by the recent publication of *Hammath Tiberias: Early Synagogues* (Dothan 1983). So many new discoveries have been made in the Galilee and Golan that a decade or more could now easily be devoted to making this material accessible and acceptable to modern scientific scholars. Such careful publication and preparation of material should be accompanied by critical presentation of rabbinic materials relevant to the study of the ancient synagogue, for most of these sources remain inaccessible to American and Israeli archaeologists.

If stratigraphic archaeology has helped dispel the old theory of the development of fixed synagogue types in Galilee, then attention to regionalism has enabled scholars to distinguish between features of different areas (Meyers 1976b). Indeed, it is now clear that clusters of settlements close to the Rift Valley, or merely close to major or even minor roadways, adhered more liberally to the Second Commandment. Remote areas that specialized mainly in cultivating local agricultural products are less likely to have engaged in ornate decorative practices, such as the use of colored decorated mosaics. Also, areas geographically or commercially "close" to Greek cities had a greater familiarity with the Greek language. Further attention to regions and subregions like these may help to illuminate not only the development of the synagogue but also the variegation within Jewish communal life as a whole (Meyers 1985).

Such diversity is an important feature of Judaism in late antiquity. Accept for a moment that different synagogue types coexisted from the second century onwards and that decorative practices differed between the Rift Valley areas and the remotest areas of the Upper Galilee or the Golan. Also observe that Greek is spoken in the urbanized cosmopolitan areas of Galilee more frequently than in the rural areas. In addition, suppose that both Jews and Jewish-Christians had their own places of worship, as well as places of study or public gathering, as is evidenced at Capernaum, where the synagogue and the octagonal church are said to represent separate religious identities. Similarly, at Gûš Ḥālāb, where two synagogues have been found, it is possible that one represents the worship facility of the new Christians. Is it not reasonable to suppose also that this diversity in synagogues possibly reflects the social stratification of Judaism in Roman Palestine?

In addition to great diversity, even discontinuity, between Upper and Lower Galilee, north and south, there is also diversity in synagogue types within a single region, as we have noted at Ḥîrbet Šemāʿ, Mêrôn, Gûš Ḥālāb, and Nabratein. Such diversity within a region reflects man's continual need to differentiate himself even from his closest neighbor. What it indicates beyond this is not yet clear.

Loosening the fetters of a rigid typological understanding of the synagogue can open up new ways of understanding the Judaism of Roman and Byzantine Palestine. Considering blocks of material remains regionally enables us to understand the rich diversity associated with a rabbinic Judaism once assumed "normative" or "monochromatic." Similar studies should now be undertaken to determine the place of ministry or origin of rabbis known to us from rabbinic literature. Relevant epigraphic evidence should also be collected by region and related to areas known to be popular among the sages. In addition to shedding light on the matter of pluralism, the material remains of Galilee indicate a surprisingly high level of culture at the end of the Roman period and beginning of the Byzantine period (third to fifth centuries C.E.). It is perhaps significant to point out that a cultural peak in the third century corresponds with the rescensional activity associated with the codification of the Mishna. Another peak in the fourth and fifth centuries corresponds to the time when the Palestinian Talmud was given its final form. Still another parallel literary achievement may be observed in the fourth to sixth centuries C.E., when the *piyyût*, sermon, and targum were utilized and further developed in the synagogue liturgy. Any suggestion that Palestinian Jewry was eclipsed or in decline in late antiquity is contradicted by the amount of material culture that has been uncovered and by an extremely varied and developed literary repertoire whose forms survive in present-day Jewish liturgy. My view that many Jews moved into the Golan area at that time may be explained in part by the Gallus Revolt (352 C.E.), but archaeological and literary evidence also seems to place special importance on the Lake region, the Kinneret and Tiberias in particular (Meyers, Strange, and Groh 1978).

While the relative calm in the Eastern empire was broken briefly by the Gallus Revolt, a measure of prosperity in Palestine reigned until the accession of the emperor Justinian in 527 C.E., when a period of repression began (Avi-Yonah 1976: 246–51). Such prosperity is evidenced by the extent of synagogue- and church-building that took place despite the hostilities between Jews and Christians reported in the patristic literature (Wilkinson 1977: 179–81). The intense building activity and relative prosperity may be the result also of the new status—Holy Land—conferred on Palestine by masses of pilgrims who brought their wealth into the country from a newly Christianized empire (Groh 1977).

Thus, new archaeological data force us to rethink the generally accepted opinion of previous generations, that Palestinian Jewry was in decline after Constantine. For still unknown reasons, the Palestinian version of the Talmud, compiled around 400 C.E., does not signify the end of Jewish creativity in the Holy Land but rather a high point in the material and literary culture of the Jewish people, a culture that takes on a significant and lasting new form in the synagogue.

The Byzantine period also marks a high point in the history of Christianity, as it witnesses unprecedented church-building in the Holy Land. This building activity could not have been entirely the result of imperial efforts during and following the reign of Constantine. It is also a testimony to the tenacity of the Jewish-Christian church in Palestine.

Such is the current state of Galilean synagogue studies. Future synagogue studies must approach the subject with a much broader framework that includes art and architecture, stratigraphy, full material culture, social and regional setting, and literary sources. Such an approach will allow the mute stones of antiquity to transmit their message. Thereby, one of the most important areas of Western religious history will be illuminated, for it is upon the ground of the ancient synagogue that the Christian church and Muslim mosque spring forth into full bloom in late antiquity; and it is upon this ground that Jewish history rests and from which Judaism spread to many other lands. Diversity and flexibility have always been the hallmarks of Judaism in Eretz Israel and in the Diaspora; Galilean synagogue studies reflect these qualities.

Bibliography

Avigad, N., and Mazar, B.
   1975   Beth She'arim. In *Encyclopedia of Archaeological Excavations in the Holy Land*, volume 1, pages 229–47. Jerusalem: Massada.
Avi-Yonah, M.
   1973a   Ancient Synagogues. *Ariel* 32: 29–43 (Hebrew).
   1973b   Editor's Note. *Israel Exploration Journal* 23: 43–45.
   1976   *The Jews of Palestine*. New York: Schocken Books.
   1977   *The Holy Land*. Grand Rapids, Mich.: Baker Book House.
Chiat, M. J. S.
   1982   *Handbook of Synagogue Architecture*. Series: Brown Judaic Studies 29. Chico, Calif.: Scholars.
Dothan, M.
   1983   *Hammath Tiberias: Early Synagogues*. Jerusalem: Israel Exploration Society.
Foerster, G.
   1973   The Synagogues at Masada and Herodium. *Eretz Israel* 11: 224–28.
Groh, D. E.
   1977   Galilee and the Eastern Roman Empire in Late Antiquity. *Explor* 3: 78–93.
Hachlili, R.
   1976   The Niche and the Ark in Ancient Synagogues. *Bulletin of the American Schools of Oriental Research* 223: 43–53.
Hüttenmeister, F., and Reeg, G.
   1977   *Die antiken Synagogen in Israel*. Series: Beihefte zum Tübinger Atlas des Vorderen Orients No. 12/1. Wiesbaden, W. Ger.: Reichert.
Kohl, H., and Watzinger, C.
   1916   *Antike Synagogen in Galilaea*. Leipzig, W. Ger.: Wissenschaftliche Veröffentlichung der deutschen Orient-Gesellschaft.
Kraabel, A. T.
   1974   Ancient Synagogues. In *New Catholic Encyclopedia*, supplemental volume 16, pages 436–39. Palatine, Ill.: J. Heraty.

Levine, L., editor
  1981   *Ancient Synagogues Revealed*. Jerusalem: Israel Exploration Society.
Loffreda, S.
  1973   The Late Chronology of the Synagogue of Capernaum. *Israel Exploration Journal* 23: 37–42.
Ma'oz, Z.
  1983   *The Jewish Community and Synagogues of the Golan*. Qaytsrein, Israel: Nature Preserve Society (Hebrew).
May, H. G.
  1944   Synagogues in Palestine. *The Biblical Archaeologist* 7: 1–20.
Meyers, E. M.
  1976a   Synagogue Architecture. In *The Interpreter's Dictionary of the Bible*, supplementary volume, edited by K. Crim, pages 842–44. Nashville, Tenn.: Abingdon.
  1976b   Galilean Regionalism as a Factor in Historical Reconstruction. *Bulletin of the American Schools of Oriental Research* 221: 93–101.
  1977   Gush Halav 1977. Notes and News. *Israel Exploration Journal* 27: 253–54.
  1980   Ancient Synagogues in Galilee: Their Religious and Cultural Setting. *Biblical Archeologist* 43: 97–108.
  1981   Ancient Gush Halav (Giscala), Palestinian Synagogues, and the Eastern Diaspora. In *Ancient Synagogues: The State of Research*, edited by J. Gutmann. Series: Brown Judaic Studies 22. Chico, Calif.: Scholars.
  1985   Galilean Regionalism: A Reappraisal. In *Approaches to the Study of Ancient Judaism*, edited by W. S. Green. Series: Brown Judaic Studies 32. Chico, Calif.: Scholars.
Meyers, E. M.; Kraabel, A. T.; and Strange, J. F.
  1976   *Ancient Synagogue Excavations at Khirbet Shema'—Upper Galilee, Israel 1970–1972*. Series: Annual of the American Schools of Oriental Research 42. Durham, N.C.: Duke University Press.
Meyers, E. M., and Meyers, C. L.
  1981   Remains of an Ancient Synagogue Ark in Galilee. *Biblical Archaeology Review* 6: 24–40.
  1982   The Ark in Art: A Ceramic Rendering of the Torah Shrine from Nabratein. *Eretz Israel* 16: 176–85.
Meyers, E. M., and Strange, J. F.
  1977   Survey in Galilee: 1976. *Explor* 3: 7–18.
Meyers, E. M.; Strange, J. F.; and Groh, D. E.
  1978   The Meiron Excavation Project: Archeological Survey in Galilee and Golan, 1976. *Bulletin of the American Schools of Oriental Research* 230: 1–24.
Meyers, E. M.; Strange, J. F.; and Meyers, C. L.
  1978   In *Second Preliminary Report on the Excavations at Ancient Meiron*, pages 73–103. Series: Annual of the American Schools of Oriental Research 43. Durham, N.C.: Duke University Press.
Safrai, S.
  1963   Was There a Women's Gallery in the Synagogue? *Tarbiz* 32: 329–38 (Hebrew).
Saller, S. J.
  1972   *Second Revised Catalogue of the Ancient Synagogues of the Holy Land*. Jerusalem: Franciscan.
Saunders, E. W.
  1977   Christian Synagogues and Jewish Christianity in Galilee. *Explor* 3: 70–78.

Strange, J. F.
1976   Capernaum. In *The Interpreter's Dictionary of the Bible*, supplementary volume, edited by K. Crim, pages 140–41. Nashville, Tenn.: Abingdon.
1977   The Capernaum and Herodian Publications. *Bulletin of the American Schools of Oriental Research* 226: 65–73.

Sukenik, E. L.
1934   *Ancient Synagogues in Palestine and Greece*. London: Oxford University Press.

Wilkinson, J.
1976   Christian Pilgrims in Jerusalem during the Byzantine Period. *Palestine Exploration Quarterly* 108: 75–101.
1977   *Jerusalem Pilgrims before the Crusades*. Warminster, Eng.: Aris and Phillips.

10. The Art and Architecture of the Synagogue in its Late Roman Setting in Palestine

Gideon Foerster

"If he [saw an idolatrous shrine and] thought it to be a synagogue, and bowed down to it—surely his heart was directed to heaven!" (B Šabbāt 72b and elsewhere). Although this statement is brought in a strictly halakhic context regarding idolatry, it nevertheless has a direct bearing on our subject. There exists an overall resemblance between the external appearance of the synagogues of the late Roman period (second to third centuries) and that of pagan temples or other secular buildings in the eastern Roman Empire. The date of this quotation corresponds well to the late Roman setting under discussion.

The remains of some thirty monumental synagogues scattered over the Galilee and Golan demonstrate an apparent uniformity in plan and style (Foerster 1983: 231–56).[1] The recently excavated synagogue at Ḥôrbat Sûmaq on Mount Carmel provides another example (Dar 1984). All the synagogal remains of this type were found in rural areas; unfortunately none was discovered in urban centers such as Tiberias or Sepphoris, and the remains at Bêt Šĕʿārîm are neither well preserved enough nor sufficiently documented to affect our deliberations. The lack of evidence from urban centers, however, does not detract from the general picture that emerges from the series of monumental synagogues, which in their plans, elevations, and decorations are clearly related to and dependent upon classical and contemporary traditions.

The overall architectural concept of the synagogues may be compared to the plan of assembly places, audience halls, and religious buildings in the Greco-Roman world (odea, basilicae, and bouleuteria) as well as to some assembly places (the so-called *salles aux gradins*) in the temples at Dura Europos or in southern Syria's Nabatean temples (the תיאטרא)—Foerster 1972: 56–80; 1981.

In these last-mentioned pagan places of assembly, the worshipers watched and participated in the rituals. The plan of these places was adopted already, we believe, by the architects of the synagogues in the Second Temple period at Masada, Herodium, Gamla, and elsewhere. These early buildings, however, were without any of the decorations typical of the late Roman synagogues (Foerster 1977). The architects of the late Roman synagogues utilized the architecture of contemporary pagan temples and audience halls, thus creating a building plan that answered the requirements of the community and its liturgy.

The synagogue of the late Roman period featured a monumental and richly decorated facade generally oriented towards Jerusalem and clearly intended to be the focal point of the building. The facade was dominated by the main entrance, some windows, and a gable crowning the whole. The main entrance and any side ones that existed were richly adorned. Fine ashlar masonry of either limestone or basalt was characteristic of these buildings—at least on the facade (figure 10.1). The interior of these generally rectangular buildings was simple and arranged in a traditional Classical style, with two or three colonnades dividing the hall into a central nave and two or three aisles (figures 10.2 and 10.3). Apart from the columns, bases, pedestals, and capitals, there was the usual Greco-Roman entablature. The walls of the interior were sometimes decorated with a separate order consisting of pilasters and a rich frieze. Moulded stucco and the remains of painted plaster attest to further decoration.

In some late Roman synagogues galleries were created by another, second order on a smaller scale. Seats for the worshipers were built along the walls, and floors were generally laid with stone tiles and occasionally with mosaics.

Jewish liturgical requirements in the synagogue were simple and did not involve the rich and complicated processions and ceremonies that characterize Christian liturgy. Thus, the main features of the prayer hall are one or two aedicula-shaped shrines, intended to house the Torah scrolls, installed on both sides of the main entrance facing Jerusalem (Foerster 1983: 234–35).[2] The reading of the Law must have taken place not too far from this spot.

The main elements of the style known as Roman Baroque, found on monumental and richly decorated temple facades, generally facing east, were adopted by the synagogue planners, although the orientation had to be changed since the direction of prayer was towards Jerusalem. The planning, character, and style of the synagogue facades derive from and are related to those of Roman temples in Syria and Asia Minor (Foerster 1972: 80–92), as is evidenced by the symmetrical and rhythmic division of the facade by entrances and windows, at times crowned with a gable in either the "Syrian" or Classical manner (figure 10.4). The transformation of temple aediculae (where statues were set) into windows (since the synagogue obviously did not contain statues) is a significant adaptation. Note, too, that many windows were needed to light the dark interior, as the liturgy took place inside the synagogue and not in front of it.

The entrances were framed by well-cut and finely carved and decorated doorjambs and lintels in Attic or Ionic style, as prescribed by Vitruvius, as well as by simple pilasters (Foerster 1972: 92–94). The richly decorated lintels in some of the synagogues were not always found in such a variety and frequency in pagan temples of the Roman period. Their inclusion stresses the significance attached to the facade facing Jerusalem. Apart from the formal architectural decorations, one of the most common ornaments on the lintels is the wreath-stephanos, or corona, found on a wide range of monuments in the Roman world and particularly in religious contexts (altars and funerary art). The wreaths or garlands, carried by eagles, victories, and cupids on some lintels, also are clearly borrowed from similar adornments on triumphal arches, lintels of Roman temples, various other architectural structures, and funerary art (figure 10.5). Of particular historical and chronological interest is the by now well-known lintel from the synagogue at Dabbura in the Golan. Ornamented with a wreath supported by a pair of eagles, it carries the Hebrew inscription, "This is the bêt ha-midrāš of Rabbi Eliʻezār Ha-qappār." This lintel supplies us with valuable evidence for the use of such motifs, the identity of the building and the leading person associated with it, as well as its general historical setting (Foerster 1972: 98–103). The frequent use of pairs of eagles or victories carrying or supporting the wreath on lintels indicates a similar dating for all of these buildings and possibly a relatively small group of artisans involved in the building of the Galilean synagogues.

Another common motif on the lintels, as on friezes and in funerary art, also derived from Greek and Roman art (though its roots lie in ancient Near Eastern art) is pairs of lions in an antithetic posture flanking an amphora or bull's head. These motifs are used rather formally, as they frequently are in Roman iconography, but this does not negate possible symbolic value (Foerster 1972: 109–12).

One dominant group of lintels divided into three panels framed by a guilloche and cymatium and decorated with a wreath in the central panel seems to have no clear parallel in Roman art. One such lintel found in Horbat Qazion most probably dates this group to the end of the second century c.e. (Foerster 1972: 113).

In the character, style, and content of decorated synagogue lintels we can see direct and indirect influences of contemporary Roman art and architecture, particularly of the second and third centuries C.E., as well as other characteristics that the synagogue architects and builders created independently. These features point to a certain laxity in Roman architectural formulas, particularly in the rich ornamentation of the lintels, which at times were the outstanding decorated parts of the synagogues. This was the case at both Kěfar Barʿām and Gûš Ḥālāb (figure 10.6).

The influence of Roman iconography and architecture of the second and third centuries can be seen in the pulvinated friezes decorating the exteriors and interiors of some synagogues, particularly those at Capernaum, Kôrāzîn, and Ḥôrbat Dakka. The friezes were adorned with floral (including rosettes and other vegetal designs) and "peopled" (human and animal representations) acanthus scrolls, as well as vine scrolls, some of which depicted Dionysic representations (figures 10.7 – 10.12). Mythological representations of Helios or a Medusa head appear on some friezes. In many cases the friezes are so badly mutilated that their content can only be surmised. The friezes have many parallels, in both shape and content, to contemporary Roman art and architecture. There are, however, clear indications of originality on friezes adorned with wreaths and geometric carvings of five- and six-pointed stars, popularly known as "Solomon's Seal" and "David's Shield," which are not found on friezes in Roman art (see figures 10.8 – 10.10). Furthermore, representations alluding to the Torah Shrine, and perhaps to the Temple, were added to the formal architectural decoration of the synagogues at Capernaum and Kôrāzîn. The pomegranates, vine and grapes, barley, and olive fruits represented on some of the acanthus scrolls at Capernaum are most likely part of the formal embellishment found in Roman iconography in Syria and other provinces, and are not necessarily connected with the seven species of the Holy Land, as many scholars assume (Foerster 1972: 125–39) (see figure 10.7).

The architraves of the ancient synagogue were carved in the customary Greco-Roman fashion, lacking ornamentation except for the usual mouldings (Foerster 1972: 124–25). The carved cornices bore intricate details at Capernaum and Kôrāzîn, but at other synagogues only the profiles had been carved (Foerster 1972: 139–43). Here again the efforts of the synagogue architects and builders to observe the Classical formulas were limited by the availability of skilled craftsmen and the raw materials at their disposal. The limited use of intricate Corinthian capitals, which were widely employed in Roman architecture, and the widespread use of simple, so-called Tuscan (Roman-Doric) capitals also may be explained by this lack of resources. This, probably, is also the reason for the bossed condition of most Ionic capitals at the synagogues of Ḥôrḇat 'Ammûdîm, Ḵôrāzîn, and Gûš Ḥālāḇ (Foerster 1972: 117–24).

Analysis and study of the style and quality of late Roman synagogue art have been limited mainly to Capernaum and Ḵôrāzîn, but they are substantiated by ornamentation found at other synagogues, and particularly by lintel decorations found elsewhere. Since most figural representations have been defaced, the study of quality and style is difficult. However, in the few cases where these representations have been preserved—such as the eagles and capricornus carved on a cornice at Capernaum or the eagle carved on the soffit of a lintel at Gûš Ḥālāḇ—the carving, though in a flat relief and lacking plasticity, was executed by skilled sculptors (see figures 10.6 and 10.13). The stylized and very inferior representations of Dionysian subjects at the Ḵôrāzîn synagogue, partially a result of the hard basalt in which they were carved, exhibit similar low relief and rigidity (see figure 10.12). These qualities and style of figurative stone-carving are typical of Roman art in the eastern empire and are even more apparent in floral decorations. Acanthus and vine scrolls were carved in a low and stylized relief lacking almost any plasticity, and the sculptors and masons tried to conceal this inferior craftsmanship by carving sharp angular leaves at different relief levels to produce contrasting light and shade effects. This style is reminiscent of not only Jewish art in the Second Temple period, and, particularly, of the carving on ossuaries, but also of the forerunners of this art form in first-century Palmyra and second- and third-century Roman art in the East as a whole. Corinthian capitals found in some synagogues were recently reexamined and dated to the third century C.E. (Fisher 1984). These were cut in a style and technique similar to contemporary Roman art, though they exhibit variations even in the same building as a result of the craftsmens' skills and the quality of stone available. Different periods of construction, however, cannot be ruled out. Similar diversity in the quality and style of stone-carving may be found in the entablature in a single building.

Thus, the acanthus scrolls at the Capernaum synagogue show two clearly divergent types, one relatively naturalistic type that exhibits softness and roundness in the leaves, the other stylized and lifeless (see figures 10.7 and 10.8). At Ḵôrāzîn the hard basalt stone contributed to a rather inferior, stylized, flat, and frozen stone-carving. There was, nevertheless, a strenuous effort by the synagogue builders to mimic the intricate details of the mouldings of Roman architecture. Ovolo, cymatium, astragal, dentiles, and other formal details were carved and moulded, though not always successfully. The general decline in the quality of the carvings and the execution of details characterizes not only the Galilean synagogue but also third-century Roman art in general. It should be stressed again that the inferior quality of the stone-carving is not necessarily a chronological indicator but rather is in some cases an indication of provincial art styles or of the skills of local masons and sculptors and occasionally is the result of unsuitable stone.

Studying the art and architecture of the Galilean synagogues leads one to conclude that these synagogues are a local, original, and eclectic Jewish creation. The singularity of these buildings is expressed in the original building plans as well as in ornamental and formal architectural elements that, though usually related to contemporary Roman art and architecture, sometimes illustrate non-Roman iconography—this notwithstanding the sporadic incorporation of strictly Jewish symbols into the formal decorations originating from Roman art.

The dating of the Galilean synagogues is based on art-historical and architectural considerations. The connections to and parallels with Roman art and architecture begin during or later than the second half of the second century, and the style and quality of carving and sculpture point to the third century as the main construction period of these synagogues. This date is corroborated by a dedicatory inscription from the Jewish community to Septimus Severus and his family (197–198 C.E.) on the monumental building at Qazion that has clear affinities to the Galilean synagogues. Yet in order to establish a reliable chronology for the foundation of these synagogues, we should consider methodical archaeological explorations and excavations as well as the art-historical and architectural information.

Capernaum was the first site where a Galilean synagogue was thoroughly excavated. The Franciscan fathers Virgilio Corbo and Stanislao Loffreda have been excavating the synagogue and the ancient settlement surrounding it since 1968. Their surprising late fifth-century C.E. date for the synagogue has incited heated argument with those supporting the traditional third-century date.[3] The controversy has prompted further excavations in other sites across the Galilee and Golan. Eric Meyers and his colleagues have excavated Ḥôrbat Šemā‘, Mêrôn, Ḥôrbat Něbôrayâ, and Gûš Ḥālāb; Kôrāzîn has been studied by Z. Yeivin; Ḥôrbat ‘Ammûdîm was partially excavated by Lee I. Levine;[4] and some sites in the Golan were excavated by Z. Ma‘oz (1980). All of these Galilean sites were founded, according to the excavators, during the third century C.E., confirming the chronology earlier suggested by Heinrich Kohl and Carl Watzinger. It should be noted, however, that a cultural conservatism in the fourth and fifth centuries would in some cases permit a later dating than would seem immediately apparent. After all, synagogues in the Golan that exhibit changes in planning and architectural style and are dated to the fifth and sixth centuries retain some Galilean synagogue traditions.

Certainly we can document a sudden burst of building activity, carried out in a relatively short period of time, and probably motivated by economic and spiritual prosperity. Dedicatory inscriptions in Hebrew, Aramaic, and Greek enable us to identify some of the individual members and communities who created these impressive monuments in the spirit of the ancient world, and in so doing honored and glorified themselves and perpetuated the House of God—"the small sanctuary," as it was called after the destruction of the Jerusalem Temple.

Notes

1   Note also the prompt publication of the work of synagogue excavations since 1977 at Gûš Ḥalāb, Mêrôn, and Ḥôrbat Nĕbôrayâ (E. M. Meyers, Strange, and C. L. Meyers 1979, 1981a, 1981b, 1982a); Capernaum (Corbo 1975, 1976, 1977, 1982; Loffreda 1979); Kôrāzîn (Yeivin 1973); and Ḥôrbat 'Ammûdîm (Levine 1982).

2   Capernaum (Strange 1977: 70); Ḥôrbat Nĕbôrayâ, en-Nabratein, (E. M. Meyers, Strange, and C. L. Meyers 1982b: 37, 43); Gûš Ḥalāb (E. M. Meyers, Strange, and C. L. Meyers 1979: 42, figure 2).

3   The excavators themselves have largely modified their view, even though not fully stated, as evidenced by an article in which Loffreda (1979: 220) says, "The construction of the famous synagogue of Capharnaum was completed in the third quarter of the fifth century A.D." This implies that building could have commenced earlier and that its completion was delayed, which was not uncommon in projects of this kind in antiquity. This allows for the discrepancy between the style and character of some parts of the building and the late date suggested by its excavators.

4   Most of the excavation reports mentioned in note 1 include careful and detailed studies of the stratigraphy and finds from the sites excavated but completely skirt any attempt to study the art-historical implications of the buildings in light of their results. One wonders if this is a reaction to earlier work, particularly of Heinrich Kohl and Carl Watzinger, or if it is just a lack of training in the classics.

Bibliography

Corbo, V.
   1975   *Cafarnao I. Gli edifici della Città*. Jerusalem: Franciscan Printing.
   1976   Edifici antichi sotto la sinagoga di Cafarnao. *Studia Hierosolymitana* 1: 158–76.
   1977   Sotto la sinagoga di Cafarnao un'insula della città. *Liber Annuus* 27: 156–72.
   1982   Resti della sinagoga del primo secolo a Cafarnao. *Studia Hierosolymitana* 3: 313–57.
Dar, S.
   1984   Notes and News. H. Sumaq. *Israel Exploration Journal* 34: 270–71.
Fisher, M.
   1984   The Corinthian Capitals of the Capernaum Synagogue—A Late Roman Architectural Feature in Eretz-Israel. *Eretz Israel* 17: 305–11.
Foerster, G.
   1972   *Galilean Synagogues and Their Relation to Hellenistic and Roman Art and Architecture*, part I. Ph.D. dissertation. Jerusalem: Hebrew University (Hebrew).
   1977   The Synagogues at Masada and Herodion. *Journal of Jewish Art* 3–4: 6–11.

1981   Architectural Models of the Greco-Roman Period and the Origin of the "Galilean" Synagogue. In *Ancient Synagogues Revealed*, edited by L. I. Levine, pages 45–48. Jerusalem: Israel Exploration Society.

1983   The Synagogues in Galilee. In *The Lands of Galilee*, volume 1, edited by A. Shmueli, A. Sofer, and N. Kliot, pages 231–56. Jerusalem: Defense Ministry (Hebrew).

Hüttenmeister, F., and Reeg, G.

1977   *Die jüdischen Synagogen, Lehrhäuser und Gerichtshöfe.* Volume 1 of *Die antiken Synagogen in Israel.* Wiesbaden, W. Ger.: Ludwig Reichert.

Kohl, H., and Watzinger, C.

1916   *Antike Synagogen in Galilaea.* Leipzig, W. Ger.: Hinrichs.

Levine, L. I.

1982   Excavations at the Synagogue of Horvat ʿAmmudim. *Israel Exploration Journal* 32: 1–12.

Loffreda, S.

1974   *Cafarnao II. La Ceramica.* Jerusalem: Franciscan Printing.

1979   Pot Sherds from a Sealed Level of the Synagogue at Capharnaum. *Liber Annuus* 29: 215–20.

Maʿoz, Z.

1980   *Jewish Settlements and Synagogues in the Golan.* Second Edition. Jerusalem: Society for the Preservation of Nature.

Meyers, E. M.; Kraabel, A. T.; and Strange, J. F.

1976   *Ancient Synagogue Excavations at Khirbet Shemaʿ, Upper Galilee, Israel 1970–1972.* Series: Annual of the American Schools of Oriental Research 42. Durham, N.C.: Duke University Press.

Meyers, E. M.; Strange, J. F.; and Meyers, C. L.

1979   Preliminary Report on the 1977 and 1978 Seasons at Gush Halav (el-Jish). *Bulletin of the American Schools of Oriental Research* 233: 33–58.

1981a   The Ark of Nabratein–A First Glance. *Biblical Archeologist* 44: 237–43.

1981b   *Excavations at Ancient Meiron, Upper Galilee, Israel, 1971–72, 1974–75, 1977.* Cambridge, Mass.: American Schools of Oriental Research.

1982a   Preliminary Report on the 1980 Excavations at en-Nabratein, Israel. *Bulletin of the American Schools of Oriental Research* 244: 1–25.

1982b   Second Preliminary Report on the 1981 Excavations at en-Nabratein, Israel. *Bulletin of the American Schools of Oriental Research* 246: 35–54.

Strange, J. F.

1977   The Capernaum and Herodium Publications. *Bulletin of the American Schools of Oriental Research* 226: 65–73.

Yeivin, Z.

1973   Excavations at Khorazin. *Eretz Israel* 11: 144–57 (Hebrew).

11. The Byzantine Setting and its Influence on Ancient Synagogues

Yoram Tsafrir

This article discusses Byzantine influence on the ancient synagogues in *Palaestina*.[1] The starting point of our discussion is the common agreement that the creation and design of synagogues cannot be explained as a self-contained process within Judaism. There are many clear ties and close interrelations between the synagogue and its general cultural environment that can be recognized in liturgy, architecture, and art.

What was the character of the Jewish interchange with its Byzantine surroundings? What was the general setting in which this dialogue occurred (through Jewish architects)? Was there any paradigm of architectural concepts and manners to which they related, and what was the role of originality and innovation in Jewish cultural creations? These questions raise yet another issue: when synagogal remains cannot be dated by means of historical documents, inscriptions, coins, or ceramic evidence, can a synagogue be dated to the Roman or Byzantine periods by means of its architecture alone? This question has become a well-known point of controversy among archaeologists in the discussion of the date of the Galilean synagogues.

The possibility of architectural archaisms, the long process of cultural transformation, and the importance of regional characteristics that are now known to be stronger than previously thought (see, for example, Kloner 1981: 11–19) complicate the problem. Nevertheless, after these qualifications are carefully considered, I believe that in most cases it is indeed possible to date the synagogues on the basis of their architecture.[2]

For many years now scholars have classified the architecture of ancient synagogues in Israel under three headings: the "early type," the "transitional type," and the "later type" (see, for example, Avi-Yonah 1959: 220–36; 1961: 157–90; 1973: 32–33, reprinted in Avi-Yonah 1981: 272–73). Of these, the latter two fall within the purview of the Byzantine period, and it is the architecture of these buildings and especially of the "later" type that is the substance of our discussion—namely, the influence of the general Byzantine matrix on the synagogues of that period in Israel.

The Byzantine period began officially with Constantine's takeover of Palestine and the East in 324 C.E., but indeed the entire fourth century C.E. was a transitional phase (Tsafrir 1984: 221–23). It is therefore not surprising that in the realm of synagogues, too, most of the structures that can be classified as the "transitional" type fall (according to most scholars) within the span of this century. Our particular interest focuses upon those synagogues that are decidedly of the Byzantine period, among them Bêt 'Alpā', Na'arān, the northern (Samaritan?) synagogue at Bêt Šě'ān, Nîrîm, and Gaza.

For a better understanding of the manner of development of the later synagogues of the Byzantine period, we must return to the earlier, late Roman period. The early Galilean synagogues have been described frequently, and therefore we need only emphasize here that these synagogues reflect a great innovation in the ancient synagogue and in religious architecture in general; they introduced the common body of worshipers into the inner space of the building. Even so, they did not deviate from the accepted conventions of the Hellenistic-Roman world that emphasized external ornamentation of religious buildings. This derived from the concept of the temple as the house of the god, with the worshipers located within the temenos opposite its facade. Hence, the facade became the most ornamented and imposing part of its edifice. The Jews used their buildings in an entirely different manner, yet they did not deviate from the general architectural concept prevalent in the Roman world and even were inspired by contemporary pagan temples.

Recent excavations have provided no evidence for the construction of even one synagogue during the second century C.E.[3] It is, of course, expected that such evidence will be found in the future, but it seems rather unpromising to depend on future discoveries to explain the absence of second-century classical synagogues. It is probable that the common prayer houses of the second and even early third centuries had the shape of simple residences, albeit large and rich ones, with one large room where liturgy was performed and perhaps other rooms for additional functions. Such buildings would have been analogous to the later Christian "domus ecclesiae"[4] (figure 11.1).

The immediate conclusion is that the "earlier" Galilean synagogues are a result of an early third-century C.E. Jewish invention. Thus they are not necessarily connected with or derived from the synagogues of the Second Temple period—like those at Masada, Herodium, Gamla, and other buildings of that period (as suggested by Avigad 1981: 42–44; Netzer 1981: 49–51).

The location of the Jewish prayer house in a special building, of a type unknown before, was not an imitation or adaptation of well-known precedents; instead it represented a new tendency. The Christians, for their part, waited several more decades before they replaced their modest "domus ecclesia" with a new type of basilical church.

In the third century, Roman sacral architecture flourished. The gentile part of the Galilee, the Hauran, southern Syria, and Arabia were dotted with temples. Today no one denies Heinrich Kohl's and Carl Watzinger's conclusion that the Galilean synagogues belong to this architectural world, at least in their general design and stone moulding.[5]

The Jewish architects accepted a new challenge to design a synagogue that would house its worshipers within its precincts rather than in front of the temple, as had been the case in pagan temples and also in the Temple of Jerusalem. Some oriental religions, like Mithraism, held their services indoors, but those communities were small and intimate; their prayer halls were also small and usually located underground to express the mystical character of the cult.

Classical temples that served as the "House of God" were admired by worshipers who stood in the temenos in front of the main facade. Therefore the temples were "extroverted": their outer faces were decorated more richly than their interiors, a feature that became normative for all—including Jewish—religious architecture. When the builders of the synagogues changed the main function of the building by bringing the congregation indoors, they didn't even consider erecting a structure with an exterior less impressive than its interior and whose facade was not its focal point. It thus became mandatory to build the facade facing Jerusalem. The blatant deficiency in the interior arrangement of the synagogue—which necessitated entering from the facade and having to make an about-face once within in order to pray—and the lack of a suitable installation for the Holy Ark were thus not an error of judgement but an expression of tenacity to the principles of Roman sacral architecture.

Only after architectural values had changed could the basic synagogue plan be modified. This redirection of values was the result of the change in religious architecture throughout Europe and the East that occurred when the church superseded the temple. The Christian basilica, which became prevalent (particularly in the Holy Land) beginning in the reign of Constantine in the first third of the fourth century C.E., developed out of the basilica of Roman civic architecture. These later buildings were inherently "introverted," for they were intended to house their numerous visitors, and thus were admirably suited to the Christians who, in competition with paganism, chose to divorce themselves from architectural forms associated with pagan cults.[6]

The Christian modification of the basilical plan was not extensive but, nevertheless, had a significant influence on the character of the building (Zevi 1957: 78–88). The Roman basilica was basically a central space surrounded on four sides by aisles, set off by a row (or rows) of columns. The Christian architects eliminated the two rows of columns parallel to the shorter walls of the structure, leaving only the two longitudinal rows. They also deepened the tribunal and apse at one of the shorter ends (generally the one to the east) and fixed the entrance at the opposite end. In this manner, the central space was transformed from a static expanse—the Roman nave contained within four rows of columns—into a long space having a sort of flow, directing the eyes of the worshiper from the entrance of the church down the nave and toward the apse and the altar (figure 11.2).

Constantine encouraged the officials of the church to embellish their "temples" and their ritual, so that they would be just as splendid as those of the pagans. This was a significant trend in the struggle for the allegiance of the masses, who were faced with a choice between the new religion and loyalty to traditional worship. The church officials chose to attract the potential convert with spiritual substance and regal splendor. The interior of the church was ornamented in a most impressive manner, with carved columns, mosaics, wall-paintings, golden lamps, and precious building materials. The dimness within, the splendor of the priests, the burning candles, and the incense all complemented the mystical atmosphere that was the very essence of early Christian worship.

The exterior of the church, however, though pleasing to the eye, did not by any means exhibit the splendor of the interior. The rather modest exterior better suited the Christian tradition of austerity. This decided contrast between modest exterior and rich interior was representative and indicative of the introversion sought by Christian architects, and this, in turn, suited the Christian claim to introspection. Eventually, the Christian basilicas were found in every town and village. Though only a few of them succeeded in attaining the dimensions and opulence of the principal churches and central cathedrals of the Empire, even the modest churches maintained the basic principles of plan and design of inner space, the embellishment of the interior, and the contrasting simplicity of external ornamentation.

These Christian values suited the needs of the Jews as well. Under the influence of Christian architecture, the synagogue structure became introverted, and its external aspect, though not neglected, became secondary.

This transformation of architectural values began in the fourth century C.E. and reached its peak from the fifth century C.E. on.

As a result of this transformation of values, it was possible to make do with lower-quality construction of the outer walls and facade, and to use less-expensive materials, such as partly dressed fieldstones bonded in mortar and then plastered over. This is in contrast to the previous period when only well-dressed ashlars were used, with much stone-carving on the exterior. This "practical carelessness" was, of course, one of the prominent features of construction in the Byzantine period in general (Tsafrir 1984: 301, 317–18). The builders saved themselves the trouble of precise planning and the bother of exact symmetry by whitewashing the poor-quality finish with mortar and plaster. This practice undoubtedly reduced the cost of construction of synagogues as well, and it may be assumed that it influenced the increase in their numbers (figure 11.3).

As it was now possible to forego the building of a splendid entrance to the synagogue on the facade facing Jerusalem, the entrance was shifted to the wall opposite the direction of prayer. On the wall toward Jerusalem a round or square apse was installed, in which the Holy Ark was situated on a raised *bîmâ*. The inner row of columns found in the early synagogues, built parallel to the rear wall and forming a sort of ⊓-shaped enclosure, was removed to facilitate entrance, further emphasizing the elongated character of the prayer hall. Hence, the synagogue plan of the second half of the fifth century C.E. and especially of the sixth and seventh centuries C.E. came to resemble the plan of the basilical churches (figure 11.4). Today it is often only the presence of specifically Jewish elements—symbols or inscriptions—or a building's orientation towards Jerusalem that allows us to positively identify the site as a synagogue rather than a church.

Scrutiny of the synagogue plan at Bêt 'Alpā' (sixth century C.E.)—a classical example of the "later" synagogue—reveals a close similarity to the church plan (Sukenik 1932: figure 11.5). It had a forecourt or atrium in front of its facade, with a cistern in the middle. Between this courtyard and the prayer hall was an entrance corridor the width of the facade, called the narthex. The hall proper was divided by two rows of columns into a nave and two flanking aisles, above which, apparently, there were balconies, possibly serving as the women's galleries. This arrangement is similar to that of the Christian basilica. Even the wooden-beam construction of the roof was typical of churches. At the southern end of the prayer hall, the end facing Jerusalem, there was a raised *bîmâ* and an apse containing the Holy Ark.

Although Christian influence was prevalent, it did not dictate the use of elements unsuitable to Jewish concepts and ritual. The church narthex, for example, was occupied by the catechumens, along with those not considered worthy of being present during the liturgy of the Eucharist. Such a space served no purpose in Judaism, so the synagogue narthex served merely as a partition between the holy and the profane, a sort of transitional space for the worshiper to adapt himself to the holy atmosphere prior to entering the prayer hall. The *bîmâ* and apse of the main hall served to emphasize the status of the Holy Ark, as did the chancel screen, which set off the *bîmâ* from the hall proper. The *bîmâ*, apse, and chancel screen were not imbued with special status, as they were in the church, where they were reserved for the priesthood and for mystical and "awesome" rites that were hidden from the lay worshipers.

The most distinctive feature of the synagogue is that the shape of the prayer hall approaches a square rather than the elongated rectangle characteristic of the church.[7] This square plan is typical of most prayer halls of the later synagogues. The longitudinal arrangement of the church enabled the congregation to concentrate and focus, from the moment of its entrance, upon the *bîmâ* and the altar where the mystical rites were conducted. This, together with the hall's dimness and the incense, created an atmosphere necessary for the mental preparation of their adherents.

Judaism, however, has long been outstanding for its direct, intellectual approach and has sought to attain the loyalty of each member of the community through individual prayer and study.[8] Thus, the synagogue building, though pleasing in itself, omitted any ornamentation that might have augmented tendencies toward the mystical. The architect's intent was to promote closeness and attentiveness between the individual worshiper and the public reader of the Torah, disdaining any hierarchy between reader and worshiper. (An identical approach is found in Islam, during the later period, which dictated the building of relatively broad mosques.)

The common background of the Jewish and Christian communities, and the day-to-day contacts between them, finds its expression in the detailed construction, ornamentation, furnishing, stone-carving, and mosaics of their respective houses of worship in the Byzantine period. The stone chancel screens of the churches and synagogues were often made by the same artisan, and distinction between them is possible only on the basis of inscriptions or symbols incised upon them. Metal lamps used in the churches were ornamented with crosses, and identical ones found in the synagogues bore the menorah motif. Also, mosaic pavements of almost identical styles have been found in synagogues and churches[9] (figure 11.6). If within the Holy Land there was considerable mutual influence between Jews and Christians, the Christian artistic and architectural tradition certainly dominated the Byzantine Empire as a whole, and the Jews adapted themselves to it and partook selectively of the cultural harvest it engendered.

Throughout this process, the Jews (and the Samaritans, if indeed the northern synagogue at Bêt Šě'ān is Samaritan) successfully preserved their identity as defined by Jewish religious tenets and an indigenous Jewish culture and religion. This is evidenced by depictions of the menorah and the Holy Ark, Jewish inscriptions, and the considerable freedom they allowed themselves—even more than the Christians—in depicting biblical scenes on the mosaic pavements of their synagogues.

The difference between synagogues and churches is even more apparent when we consider the function of many churches as memorial monuments for holy relics or holy places—the numerous *loca sancta* of Palestine. These churches, known as *memoria* or *martyria*, were built with a concentric ground plan that was round, octagonal, or cross-shaped (Grabar 1946; Tsafrir 1984: 223–64; figure 11.7). The holy place or the holy relic was enclosed by a dome or conical roof meant to resemble a monumental canopy above the holy object. Other churches contained crypts. The idea of loca sancta and holy relics was foreign to the main stream of Jewish thought, and there are, therefore, no remains of a synagogue with a centralized plan or a crypt. The common elements of synagogues and churches were thus limited to the genus of congregational cult houses—that is, to the basilical type of churches.

The conclusions are clear: When there were differences or contradictions in principles of faith or in liturgical functions, the two religions found individual and independent solutions. But both religions shared the same architectural concepts and means of expression. Christianity was the leading power in the Byzantine Empire, and Christian architects determined the prevalent architectural styles. It was in a Christian-Byzantine cultural setting that the Jews originated a dialogue of adoption and adaptation. They could assimilate to or struggle against this environment, but they could not remove themselves from it.

The answer to our initial question is yes. We can date a synagogue to the Roman or Byzantine period by its architecture, even when there are no clear archaeological data.[10] This article has tried to show the different character of the two periods, through consideration of sacral architecture. In general terms, it was against the nature of architecture to continue the building of the "Roman type" at a time when the whole cultural setting became "Byzantine."

Notes

1 This article is based, in part, on a wealth of detailed discussion published in Hebrew (Tsafrir 1981: 29–46; 1984: 165–89, 285–300).

2 One specific case is the debate of the dating of the synagogue at Capernaum. It was originally dated to the second or third century on the basis of its style and architecture. The excavators, Virgilio Corbo and Stanislao Loffreda, suggested a much later date on the basis of stratigraphy, numismatics, and ceramics (Corbo 1975: 113–70; Loffreda 1979: 215–20). According to Loffreda, "After ten years of excavations, more than twenty thousand Late Roman coins were found in the synagogue of Capharnaum. After a preliminary study of all of them, we realized one important fact: the latest coins, coming from the sealed levels, belong to Emperor Leo I, down to a date around 474 A.D. This is—in our opinion—the terminal date for the construction of the synagogue. The numismatic evidence is in line with the potsherds under review" (Loffreda 1979: 218). Similar dating was suggested by Ma'oz (1981: 98–115) for the synagogues in the Golan. Note especially the dating of the synagogue at Ḥôrḇat Kanef to the early sixth century (Ariel 1980: 59–62). As the synagogue at Capernaum is the most prominent among the Galilean synagogues, its dating becomes a test case for the dating of other synagogues of the same type. I agree with the scholars who, despite the new data, continue to date the Capernaum and other "Galilee-type synagogues" to the third century or, at the latest, to the first part of the fourth century, and who explain the finding of fifth-century coins as the result of a later intrusion during reconstruction of the synagogue floors. See the detailed discussions in Tsafrir (1984).

3 The dates suggested by excavators for the foundation of the Galilean synagogues of Gûš Ḥālāḇ, Mêrôn, and Nabratein are in the second half of the third century (E. Meyers, Strange, and C. Meyers 1979: 33–58; 1981; Meyers 1982: 77–81). In the latter site, an earlier edifice, smaller and of single plan, was discovered beneath the synagogue, and may well be an early synagogue (a "domus ecclesia" type?) of the first half of the third century. The synagogue at Ḥôrḇat Ha-'Ammûdîm is dated to around 300 C.E. (Levine 1982: 1–12). The "transitional" type synagogue at Ḥôrḇat Šema' was founded, according to the excavators, between 286 and 306 (Meyers, Kraabel, and Strange 1976: 33–102). The monumental building at Ḥôrḇat Qatsion, the architectural sculpture of which inspired the builders of the neighboring, later synagogue of Ḥôrḇat Marûs (Ilan and Damati 1984: 265–68), was dedicated, according to a dedicatory inscription, in 197–198 C.E. If this building was indeed a synagogue, as some scholars suggest, it is the only one dated to the second century, albeit to the latter part of it (Kohl and Watzinger 1916: 209–10).

4 Compare the "Christian Building" at Dura Europos (Hopkins 1934: 238–53; Kraeling 1967), whose plan is similar, from the functional point of view, to that of the synagogue at the same site; both were built in the middle of the third century. See also the "House of Peter" at Capernaum (Corbo 1975: 59–74).

5 See especially the detailed analysis of each individual synagogue in Foerster 1972.

6 The Jewish tendency to absorb pagan architectural forms probably was possible because of Jewish self-confidence in the face of declining classical paganism, especially in the third century. This most likely is the background for the tolerant approach to figural art. See discussion in Tsafrir 1984: 186, 215–17, and bibliography.

7 The proportion of length to width of the main hall at Bêt 'Alpā' is around 1:0.85; at Bêt Šě'an (north), Mā'ôz Ḥayyîm, Rěḥôḇ, and Gaza it varies between 1.1–1.2:1; at Mā'ôn-Nîrîm it is slightly larger than 1.2:1; at Jericho 1.3:1, and at Na'arān, it is around 1.4:1 (dimensions in Chiat 1982). These synagogues are typical "later" synagogues. Most of the "transitional" type synagogues are broadhouses. The Galilean synagogues are, in general, a little longer than the "later" synagogues (compare Chen 1978: 193–202; 1980: 255–58). Most of the basilical churches are much longer, relatively, in their proportions, although a few have a "square" plan (compare Ovadiah 1970).

8 Mysticism and the practice of magic were recognized elements of Judaism and were

reflected in Jewish art of the Byzantine period (Levine 1981: 7–10); the most explicit and extreme discussion concerning Jewish mysticism and its influence on art is found in Goodenough 1953–58. Still, the reflection of Jewish mysticism in literature and art, or even in prayers and *piyyûṭîm*, may by no means be compared with the strong mystical character of the Christian liturgy. Nothing in Judaism is similar, for example, to the Christian concept of baptism as a symbol of rebirth or the offering of bread and wine as the flesh and blood of the Lord.

9   Compare, for example, the mosaic design of the synagogue at Gaza with those of several churches in southern Palestine (Avi-Yonah 1981), and the mosaic design at the synagogue of Naʿarān with that of the church at Ḥôrḇat Běraḵôt (Tsafrir and Hirschfeld 1979: 305–8).

10   The classification of a synagogue should be determined by the whole character of the building and not by single elements. The use of mosaic floors was once accepted as typical of the "transitional" or "later" groups, but this has changed since the discovery of a mosaic floor in a typical "earlier" synagogue at Ḥôrḇat Ha-ʿAmmûdîm (Levine 1982). Rebuilding of an "earlier" synagogue took place in Nabratein in the sixth century (Meyers 1982) and, according to an opinion I share, also in Capernaum (probably during the fifth century). A synagogue at Ḥôrḇat Marûs (ancient Meroth), dated by the excavators to the fifth century (Ilan and Damati 1984), resembles the "earlier" synagogues in its ground plan. Yet the general character of the building—whether or not it was "extroverted" or "introverted"—is not yet clear. A mosaic was found in one of its wings, and the architectural details seem to be an imitation of those of the early monumental building at the neighboring Ḥôrḇat Qatsion. It is, however, much inferior and fits its fourth- to fifth-century date. The whole structure seems to be a good example of the "transitional" type.

Bibliography

Ariel, D. T.
   1980   Coins from the Synagogue at Ḥorvat Kanef–Preliminary Report. *Israel Numismatic Society Journal* 4: 59–62.
Avigad, N.
   1981   The "Galilean" Synagogue and Its Predecessors. In *Ancient Synagogues Revealed*, edited by L. I. Levine, pages 42–44. Jerusalem: Israel Exploration Society.
Avi-Yonah, M.
   1959   Ancient Synagogues. *Qadmôniôt ʾArṣēnû*, edited by S. Yeivin and M. Avi-Yonah, volume 2, pages 220–36. Tel-Aviv: Hakibbutz Hamě̂ʾûḥād (Hebrew).
   1961   Synagogue Architecture in the Classical Period. In *Jewish Art*, edited by C. Roth, pages 157–90. New York: McGraw-Hill.
   1973   Ancient Synagogues. *Ariel* 32: 32–33.
   1981   *Art in Ancient Palestine.* Jerusalem: Magnes.
Chen, D.
   1978   Design of the Ancient Synagogues in Galilea. *Liber Annuus* 28: 193–202.
   1980   Design of the Ancient Synagogues in Galilea. *Liber Annuus* 30: 255–58.
Chiat, M. J. S.
   1982   *Handbook of Synagogue Architecture.* Series: Brown Judaic Studies 29. Chico, Calif.: Scholars Press.
Corbo, V.
   1975   *Cafarnao I. Gli edifici della Città.* Jerusalem: Franciscan Press.

Foerster, G.
   1972   *Galilean Synagogues and Their Relation to Hellenistic and Roman Art and Architecture.* 2
            parts. Ph.D. dissertation. Jerusalem: Hebrew University (Hebrew).
Goodenough, E. R.
   1953–58 *Jewish Symbols in the Greco-Roman Period.* 13 volumes. New York: Pantheon.
Grabar, A.
   1946   *Martyrium, Recherches sur le Culte des Reliques et l'Art Chrétien Antique.* 2 volumes.
            Paris: Collège de France.
Hopkins, C.
   1934   The Christian Church. In *The Excavations at Dura Europos, 5th Season,* edited by
            M. Rostovtzeff, pages 238–53. New Haven, Conn.: Yale University Press.
Ilan, Z., and Damati, I.
   1984   Notes and News. Kh. Marus, 1983 and 1984. *Israel Exploration Journal* 34: 265–68.
Kloner, A.
   1981   Ancient Synagogues in Israel: An Archaeological Survey. In *Ancient Synagogues
            Revealed,* edited by L. I. Levine, pages 11–19. Jerusalem: Israel Exploration Society.
Kohl, H., and Watzinger, C.
   1916   *Antike Synagogen in Galilaea.* Leipzig, W. Ger.: Hinrichs.
Kraeling, C. H.
   1967   *The Christian Building. The Excavations at Dura Europos, Final Report,* volume 8, part
            2. New Haven, Conn.: Yale University Press.
Levine, L. I.
   1981   Ancient Synagogues—A Historical Introduction. In *Ancient Synagogues Revealed,*
            edited by L. I. Levine, pages 7–10. Jerusalem: Israel Exploration Society.
   1982   Excavations at the Synagogue of Horvat 'Ammudim. *Israel Exploration Journal* 32:
            1–12.
Loffreda, S.
   1979   Potsherds from a Sealed Level of the Synagogue at Capharnaum. *Liber Annuus*
            29: 215–20.
Ma'oz, Z.
   1981   The Art and Architecture of the Synagogues of the Golan. In *Ancient Synagogues
            Revealed,* edited by L. I. Levine, pages 98–115. Jerusalem: Israel Exploration
            Society.
Meyers, E. M.
   1982   The Ark of Nabratein. *Qadmoniot* 15: 77–81 (Hebrew).
Meyers, E. M.; Kraabel, A. T.; and Strange, J. F.
   1976   *Ancient Synagogue Excavations at Khirbet Shema', Upper Galilee, Israel 1970–1972.*
            Durham, N.C.: Duke University Press.
Meyers, E. M.; Strange, J. F.; and Meyers, C. L.
   1979   Preliminary Report on the 1977 and 1978 Seasons at Gush-Halav (el-Jish),
            Upper Galilee, Israel. *Bulletin of the American Schools of Oriental Research* 233:
            33–58.
   1981   *Excavations of Ancient Meiron, Upper Galilee, Israel, 1971–1972, 1974–1975, 1977.*
            Cambridge, Mass.: American Schools of Oriental Research.
Netzer, E.
   1981   The Herodian Triclinia—A Prototype for the "Galilean Type" Synagogues. In
            Ancient Synagogues Revealed, edited by L. I. Levine, pages 49–51. Jerusalem: Israel
            Exploration Society.
Ovadiah, A.
   1970   *Corpus of the Byzantine Churches in the Holy Land.* Bonn, W. Ger.: P. Honstein.

Sukenik, E. L.
  1932 *The Ancient Synagogue of Beth Alpha.* London: Oxford University Press.
Tsafrir, Y.
  1981 On the Architectural Origins of the Ancient Galilean Synagogues—A Reconsideration. *Cathedra* 20: 29–46 (Hebrew).
  1984 *Archaeology and Art.* Volume 2 of *Eretz Israel from the Destruction of the Second Temple to the Muslim Conquest.* Jerusalem: Yad Ben-Zvi (Hebrew).
Tsafrir, Y., and Hirschfeld, Y.
  1979 The Church and Mosaics at Horvat Berachot, Israel. *Dumbarton Oaks Papers* 33: 305–8.
Zevi, B.
  1957 *Architecture as Space.* English edition. New York: Horizon.

12. Pagan and Christian Evidence on the Ancient Synagogue

Shaye J. D. Cohen

The historian Socrates reports that the Jews of Alexandria in 412 C.E. spent their Sabbaths not in the synagogue but in the marketplace: "On the day of the Sabbath the troop of dancers would collect greater crowds than normal because the Jews, idle on that day, devote their attention not to the hearing of the Law but to theatrical amusements. Consequently the day became the cause for disorder among portions of the populace" (*History of the Church* 7.13 = PG 67: 761).[1] Not all Jews in antiquity, it seems, appreciated the spiritual worth of the synagogue. In many ways Socrates's report exemplifies the Greco-Roman and patristic references to the synagogue. It reveals interesting details, but it does not address the fundamental questions that need to be answered for an understanding of the ancient synagogue: what was the nature of the institution and what were the stages of its development? Who were its leaders? What prayers did the Jews recite and how did they study the Scriptures? In sum, what kind of Judaism was practiced within the synagogue's walls? To answer these questions, modern scholars (for example, Moore 1927: 281–307; Schürer 1979: 423–63) have generally based their accounts almost exclusively on the evidence provided by archaeology (the material remains of ancient synagogues, notably inscriptions) and Jewish literature (especially the rabbinic). Greco-Roman and Christian literary sources are not nearly as informative, but their testimony should not be overlooked.

In this essay my concern is both historiographical (how did non-Jews view the synagogue?) and historical (what information about the ancient synagogue can be gleaned from non-Jewish literary sources?). I am especially interested in the degree to which these sources confirm, contradict, or supplement the testimony of Jewish texts.[2] The number of sources to survey is vast, and many of them are still uncharted.[3] I do not claim to have mastered all, or even most, of them. I shall first make some general observations about the material and then turn to three specific issues that are illuminated modestly by these sources—synagogues as "temples," rituals and practices, and patriarchal control.

The Evidence as a Whole

The cult of the synagogue consists of the public worship of God through prayer and study. In their philosophical schools, the Greeks and Romans studied the definition of virtue and the knowledge of the gods; in their temples, they offered prayers on various occasions. They had, however, no institution that approximated the synagogue. Many modern writers (for instance, Moore 1927: 284–85) have observed the uniqueness of the synagogue and its formative influence on Christianity and Islam. The invention of the synagogue was a revolutionary step in the development of ancient Judaism, indeed, of ancient religion generally. The fact that the rabbis paid little attention to this revolution is not particularly remarkable, given their ahistorical thinking and their tendency to harmonize the oral law with the written. The fact that the pagans, too, however, paid little attention to this revolutionary institution is remarkable. Pagan authors commented on many of the beliefs and practices of Judaism—notably circumcision, the Sabbath, the fasts, the food laws, the avoidance of images, and the ethos of separation —but none of them commented on the synagogue, and only a few of them even bothered to mention it.[4] We might conclude from this silence that pagans were not admitted into the synagogue, but, as is well known, the contrary was the case. Why then do pagan authors seldom mention the synagogue? The answer is unclear.

Christian authors, of course, mention the synagogue much more frequently. *Synagoga* becomes a symbol of Judaism itself, in contrast to *ecclesia*, the symbol of Christianity.[5] The early fathers, however, only rarely talk about the contemporary synagogue. Echoing various gospel references, they refer to the synagogues as *fontes persecutionum* (Tertullian, *Scorpiace* 10) and describe the curses that the Jews daily hurl upon Christ (Justin, *Dialogue with Trypho* 137.2). It is only in the latter part of the fourth century that patristic writers, notably Chrysostom and Jerome, discuss the contemporary synagogue. Abundant synagogue remains date no earlier than the fourth century and it is also in the fourth century that the legal status of synagogues became the subject of imperial legislation.

The congruence between the archaeological evidence and the non-Jewish literary evidence is too close to be coincidental. From the last centuries B.C.E. and the first century C.E. we have scattered references to synagogues in Jewish and non-Jewish sources and scattered archaeological remains of synagogues. In the second and early third centuries C.E. the number of literary references (even in rabbinic sources) declines and archaeological remains from that time are also scarce.[6] Late third-century, and fourth- to fifth-century (and later) literary and archaeological attestations are more numerous. This congruence suggests that synagogues did not attain institutional prominence until the very period in which the patriarch first attained prominence outside the Land of Israel. I shall return to this suggestion later.

Synagogues as "Temples" and Loca of Sanctity

Agatharchides (middle or late second century B.C.E.) is the earliest extant pagan author to refer, even if ambiguously, to synagogues:

> The people known as Jews . . . have a custom of abstaining from work every seventh day; on those occasions they neither bear arms nor take any agricultural operations in hand, nor engage in any other form of public service, but pray with outstretched hands in the temples until the evening. Consequently, because the inhabitants, instead of protecting their city, persevered in their folly, Ptolemy, son of Lagus, was allowed to enter with his army. (Josephus, *Against Apion* 1.22 [209–10] in Stern 1974: number 30a)

Agatharchides seems to say that, already in the time of Ptolemy I Soter, the Jews celebrated the Sabbath by praying in their "temples," but this interpretation mistakes Agatharchides's intent. His main point is that Jerusalem fell to Ptolemy Soter because the superstitious Jews refused to fight on the seventh day (Josephus, *Antiquities* 12.1.1 [6] in Stern 1974: number 30b). As further testimony to their unreasonable behavior, he adduces that instead of engaging in any form of work they spend the entire day ("until evening") praying in their "temples." This part of Agatharchides's report may well derive from his observation of Jews in the second century rather than from his source for fourth-century Jewish history. In any case, what does he mean by "temples" (*tois hierois*)?

There are two possibilities. Either Agatharchides is referring to the Temple in Jerusalem or he is not. If he is, the plural *hierois* must be regarded as a simple mistake by a Greek who believed that the Jews, like the Greeks, had many temples.[7] If he is not, the noun must mean *synagogues* (that is, places of prayer) since it is unlikely that there were many *temples* (that is, places of sacrifice) in the Jerusalem of the fourth or the second century B.C.E.[8] I see no sure way to choose between these possibilities since the gesture that Agatharchides ascribes to the Jews ("with outstretched hands") characterizes the prayer of both the Temple and the synagogue, and of both Jews and gentiles (1 Timothy 2:8 with the commentaries; Gruber 1980: 22–89). All in all, however, I think that *synagogues* is the more likely alternative.

The assimilation of the synagogue to the temple is more explicit in the following excerpt from book 3 of Apion's *History of Egypt*:

> Moses . . . was a native of Heliopolis, who, being pledged to the customs of his country, erected prayer-houses, open to the air [*aithrious proseuchas anēgen*], in the various precincts of the city, all facing eastwards [*pros apheliōtēn*, literally, the east wind]; such being the orientation also of Heliopolis. In place of obelisks he set up pillars, beneath which was a model of a boat; and the shadow cast on this basin by the statue described a circle corresponding to the course of the sun in the heavens. (Josephus, *Against Apion* 2.1 [10–11] in Stern 1974: number 164)

"*[A]ithrious proseuchas anēgen*" might mean "he offered prayers out of doors," but this translation is excluded by the next clause, "*pros apheliōtēn de pasas apestrephen.*" As is well known, the term *proseuchē* was used by the Jews of the Diaspora to mean prayer house, and there can be little doubt that this was Apion's intent. According to Apion, the prayer houses erected by Moses were open to the air, scattered throughout Jerusalem ("the city" means Jerusalem, not Heliopolis), oriented to the east, and marked by pillars with a sundial in the form of a boat or basin (*skaphē*). Although Apion was describing Jewish prayer houses, the first and last characteristics pertain to the Temple, the first to the Temple of Herod and the last to the Temple of Solomon. The pillars were the *Yākîn* and *Bō'az* of the Solomonic Temple, and the basin sundial was perhaps the bronze "sea" mounted on twelve oxen (Reinach 1930: 61, note 1).[9] The reference to prayers offered under the open sky probably refers to a practice in the Herodian Temple, where the people assembled in large courtyards on various occasions. These court-yards led Dio Cassius to describe the Herodian Temple as *anōrophos*, roofless (Stern 1980: number 406). Tertullian mentions that on fast days the Jews abandoned their "temples" (*templis omissis*), that is, their synagogues, and prayed outdoors near the shore, a practice that conformed to the prescriptions of Mishna Ta'anît, but neither Tertullian nor the Mishna refers to prayer in an unroofed building (Krauss 1922: 272–73 and 330; Schürer 1979: 444–45).

The eastern orientation is more elusive. Perhaps it is indeed a transferral from the temples of Heliopolis (including its Jewish temple?) to the prayer houses of Judea. Or perhaps Apion had somehow heard of the worship of the rising sun by various Jews (Smith 1982). S. Krauss has suggested that Apion's remark be juxtaposed to T Měgîllâ 4,22,[10] which enjoins that "the entrances of a synagogue are to be opened only in the east" in imitation of the entrances to the wilderness tabernacle. When describing the tabernacle, Josephus says, "Moses set [it] . . . facing eastward (*tetrammenēn pros tas anatolas*), in order that the sun, at its rising, should shed its first rays upon it" (*Antiquities* 3.6.3 [115]).[11] Archaeology has revealed synagogues in which the doors did, in fact, face east (Krauss 1922: 323–26; Landsberger 1957; Chiat 1982: 402). The portals of these synagogues, of the temple, and of the tabernacle, were in the east, but the focal point was to the west (unless we are to imagine, as some scholars have suggested, that after entering these synagogues the people turned around and directed their prayers eastward through the doors). Apion's intent is unclear.

Agatharchides and Apion, the two earliest authors to refer to synagogues, transfer to the synagogue some of the features of the Temple of Jerusalem, a practice that was continued by both pagan and Christian writers. Like Agatharchides, some authors called the synagogue a *hieron* (or, in Latin, *templum*).[12] The Christians of Antioch, who thrilled to the oratory of John Chrysostom, believed, at least until they were corrected, that the synagogues of the Jews were temples like the Temple in Jerusalem (*Against the Jews* 6.7.5–7 = PG 48:915). Apion transferred to the synagogue some of the architectural motifs of the Temple of Jerusalem; centuries later a Syriac life of Barsauma claimed that the saint destroyed a synagogue in Rabat Moab that was a replica of the Temple of Solomon (Juster 1914: 500; Krauss 1922: 228). Three fourth-century sources refer to "priests" who serve in synagogues or occupy some other posts of authority within the Jewish community.[13] The transferral of the nomenclature, holiness, architecture, and prerogatives of the Temple of Jerusalem to the synagogue was not the work of gentile observers alone; rabbinic and archaeological evidence demonstrates that the Jews were implementing the same transference at least from the second century C.E. onwards (Krauss 1922: 93–102; Hengel 1966: 173–76; Cohen 1984). Some Jews offered sacrifices or ate communal meals in their assemblies, thereby blurring even further the distinction between synagogue and temple (see below). In sum, the gentile interpretation of the synagogue as *a* temple or as a representative of the Temple in Jerusalem was the natural, perhaps inevitable, way for an outsider to understand this Jewish institution; but by the fourth century, if not earlier, it probably reflected the views of the Jews themselves. A full study of this issue is needed.

Like any temple, the synagogue was sacred space. In the inscriptions (Naveh 1978; Lifshitz 1967) the synagogue is sometimes called an *'atrâ qadîšâ* or is described in terminology borrowed from the temple (house, house of God, and so on). Amoraic literature also attributes sanctity to the synagogue, even arguing that the *šĕkînâ* dwells in synagogues just as it had in the Temple of old.[14] Many Christians of the fourth century accepted the synagogue's claim to sanctity. Valentinian I (about 370 C.E.) declared synagogues to belong to the class of *religionum loca* and thereby off limits to soldiers seeking *hospitium* (Linder 1983: number 14 = CT 7.8.2).[15] From 393 to 428 C.E., the emperors repeatedly prohibited the molestation of synagogues (Linder 1983: numbers 21, 25, 40, 46, 47, 48, 49, and 54), perhaps because they believed them to be holy. Of course those Christians who were molesting them did not share this attitude.

Many Christian writers, from the second century onwards, referred to the presence of sacred scrolls in the synagogue,[16] but only one author, John Chrysostom, felt it necessary to combat the belief that the scrolls rendered the synagogue holy. The sacred books, Chrysostom argued, cannot render synagogues holy any more than they can render pagan temples holy. Furthermore, he asked, "what sort of ark [*kibōtos*] is it that the Jews now have, where we find no propitiatory, no tables of the law, no holy of holies, no veil, no high priest, no incense, no holocaust, no sacrifice, none of the other things that made the ark of old solemn and august?"[17] *Kibōtos* is the Septuagint's translation (followed by Philo, Josephus, the Church Fathers, and the Peshitta) of the biblical *'ārôn*, and Chrysostom's use of this term is further testimony to the transferral, probably by the Jews of Antioch, of the ideology of the temple to the synagogue (Krauss 1922: 366; Goodenough 1954: 115–16; Schürer 1979: 524, note 83).

The position against which Chrysostom argued does not appear in the writings of any previous Christian author or in rabbinic literature. It does not even appear in Aphrahat's work, though he rebuked the Jews for "making the ark [*'ārnā'*] and the testament of the covenant" (Aphrahat, *Demonstration* 12.11; Neusner 1971: 39; Lieberman 1970: 24). The sole pagan text that refers to the presence of sacred scrolls in the synagogue, a decree of the emperor Augustus issued on behalf of the Jews of Asia Minor, clearly implies that the scrolls were sacred but that the building itself was not. Here is the relevant portion of the decree:

> And if anyone is caught stealing their sacred books [*tas hieras biblous*] or their sacred monies [*ta hiera chrēmata*] from a sabbath-house [*ek sabbateiou*] or a banquet-hall [*ek andrōnos*], he shall be regarded as sacrilegious, and his property shall be confiscated to the public treasury of the Romans. (Josephus, *Antiquities* 16.6.2 [164])

Augustus referred to the *sabbateion*, sabbath-house, a term attested later in both Greek and Syriac (Krauss 1922: 25–27; Tcherikover 1964: 46), and the *andrōn*, a common term for the meeting places or collective meals of clubs and citizen associations (Nock 1936: 47–48 and 1972: 896).[18] The sacred books were the scrolls used for the public reading of the Torah; presumably they were stored in the *sabbateion*. The sacred monies were the funds collected either for the Temple in Jerusalem (Josephus, *Antiquities* 16.6.4 [167]; Philo, *Embassy to Gaius* 156, 311, and 315; and elsewhere) or for the communal meals in the banquet hall.[19] In the eyes of the emperor the monies and the books were sacred, but the *sabbateion* and the *andrōn* were not. Whence the Christians of Antioch derived the idea that the synagogue was holy because of the presence of the scrolls is not clear. Perhaps they transferred to the synagogue the Christian idea that a church must be equipped with relics if it is to be sacred space.

Rituals and Practices

The pagan and Christian literary evidence regarding rituals and practices in the ancient synagogue is particularly sparse. Only a few passages merit extended discussion.

In Greek, *synagōgē* means association, session, or meeting, and in the eyes of the Romans the right of Diaspora Jews to assemble for worship was governed by the law that determined the rights of all associations (Juster 1914: 409–13; Smallwood 1981: 120–43). In a decree concerning the Jews of Delos, Julius Caesar indicated his displeasure that the Jews there had been prevented from "living according to their customs and contributing money for common meals and sacred rites" when even in Rome the Jews were permitted to engage in these activities. All other *thiasoi* were prohibited from assembling, but the Jews had to be allowed to collect money and to "assemble and conduct their communal meals [*sunagesthai te kai hestiasthai*] in accordance with their ancestral customs and practices" (Josephus, *Antiquities* 14.10.8 [214–16]). In contrast to a contemporary decree of Halicarnassus, which permitted the Jews to "offer prayers [*tas proseuchas poieisthai*] by the sea in accordance with their ancestral custom" (Josephus, *Antiquities* 14.10.23 [258]),[20] Caesar's decree omitted prayer. In contrast to the statement of the Jews of Rome in 200 C.E. that "the Romans permitted us to read publicly our ancestral laws" (Hippolytus, *Refutation of all Heresies* 9.12.8 = GCS 26.247),[21] this decree omitted the study of Torah. In contrast to many decrees that permitted the Jews to collect money to be sent to Jerusalem, this decree referred to the collection of money for the use of the Jews of Delos. According to this decree, the essence of the Jewish cult, the major ritual necessitating public assembly and the public collection of money, was communal feasting.

The nature of these communal meals is unknown (Nock 1972: 896). Were they sacred or secular? A resolution of the city of Sardis, passed in response to a request by the Jews, implies the former. The Jews requested:

> [T]hey may, in accordance with their accepted customs, come together [*sunagontai*] and have a communal life and adjudicate suits among themselves, and that a place be given them in which they may gather together with their wives and children and offer their ancestral prayers and sacrifices to God [*epitelōsi tas patrious euchas kai thusias tōi theōi*].

The city responded:

> Permission shall be given them to come together on stated days to do those things which are in accordance with their laws, and also that a place shall be set apart by the magistrates [*strategōn*] for them to build and inhabit, such as they may consider suitable for this purpose, and that the market-officials [*agoranomoi*] of the city shall be charged with the duty of having suitable food for them brought in. (Josephus, *Antiquities* 14.10.24 [260–61])

The Jews make three requests: the right of association, judicial autonomy, and a place (*topos*) in which to conduct their ancestral practices. They obtained their first and third requests; their petition for judicial autonomy had to be renewed on another occasion (Josephus, *Antiquities* 14.10.17 [235]—a document that also refers to a *topos* but that calls the community a *sunodos*, avoiding the verb *sunagein*). What is striking here is the Jews' own description of their ancestral practices: prayers and sacrifices. The reading of the Torah was omitted. The simplest explanation of these sacrifices is that they were identical with the communal meals that figured so prominently in Caesar's decree about the Jews of Delos.[22] This explanation would account for the reference to the *andrōn*, banquet-hall, and, perhaps, to the sacred monies in the decree of Augustus concerning the Jews of Asia Minor. What the priests of Jerusalem thought of these sacrifices, we do not know. The Jews of Sardis, at least, whatever their sacrifices may have been, collected money for the Jerusalem Temple (Josephus, *Antiquities* 16.6.6 [171] and compare Philo, *Embassy to Gaius* 315).[23] But the sacrifices of Sardis, the communal meals of Delos, and the banquet-hall of Asia Minor show that some Jews of the Greek Diaspora in the first century B.C.E. had synagogues that did not resemble those of Rome, Alexandria, or Palestine.[24]

Diversity in synagogue practice is even more clearly documented in the fourth century. In his *Against the Jews* (recently translated by Harkins 1979 under the ecumenical title *Against the Judaizing Christians*), eight sermons delivered in Antioch in the 380s, John Chrysostom rebuked the members of his flock who had "Judaized." Chief among their sins was the veneration of the synagogues and the festivals of the Jews. These orations reveal several things about the synagogue.

First, gentile Christians found the synagogue attractive and, as a result, regularly attended its services and entered its precincts (passim). The *Apostolic Constitutions*, likewise a document of Syrian Christianity, documents the same attraction (8.47.65 and 71). According to the book of Acts, gentiles crowded into the synagogues of Asia Minor in the first century. If the synagogue attracted gentiles, we may presume that its language was Greek. The liturgy of the rabbinic synagogue was entirely in Hebrew; the prayers composed by the talmudic rabbis and the early medieval poets (*paytānîm*) do not contain a single Greek or Latin word.[25] The rabbis translated Scripture into Aramaic and gave sermons in that language, but did not accord Greek any liturgical function. How many synagogues in Israel adhered to this rabbinic regimen is not known; the Palestinian Talmud refers to a synagogue in Caesarea in which the *Šĕmaʿ* was recited in Greek, and the synagogue inscriptions of Israel are divided between Aramaic and Greek. But in the synagogues of the Roman Diaspora, as the epigraphical evidence amply testifies, Greek was predominant.[26] Almost two centuries after Chrysostom, Justinian's Novella 146 demonstrated the vigor of Greek-speaking Jews who preferred Greek to Hebrew for the reading or translation of Scripture. Chrysostom's testimony also implies that the gentile Christians were welcomed into the synagogues by the Jews. There is no reference to active proselyting (Wilken 1983: 91), but there also is no reference to the daily cursing of Christ and Christians. (Of course, it is possible that the wily Jews of Antioch successfully concealed their cursing from the none-too-learned Christians, but I consider this unlikely.) There is no need to enter into the tortuous history of the *Birkat Ha-Mînîm* (Kimelman 1981a), but note that the four patristic authors who claim that the Jews cursed Christ or Christians—Justin, Origen, Epiphanius, and Jerome—had strong connections with Palestinian Judaism. Fathers, like Chrysostom, who had little or no familiarity with Palestine knew nothing of this tradition.

Second, Chrysostom implies that Christians were attracted to the synagogue by the sheer theatricality of the synagogue rituals. He accuses the Jews of bringing troops of actors, dancers, and harlots into the synagogue for the festivals; in fact, there was little difference, he argues, between a synagogue and a theater (1.2.7 = PG 48.847; 2.3.4 = PG 48.861; 4.7.3 = PG 48.881; 7.1.2 = PG 48.915). What truth, if any, lurks behind these statements is hard to discern, but Chrysostom's polemic implies that the synagogue services in Antioch were spectacular events. In one passage, he says that the ceremonies were accompanied by drums, lyres, harps, and other instruments (1.7.2 = PG 48.853), but perhaps he is talking about the Temple in Jerusalem, not the synagogues of Antioch. As far as I know, these are the only passages from antiquity that refer to the synagogue's capacity to entertain.

Third, Christians were attracted by the synagogue's numinous quality. This attitude resulted from a general veneration of Judaism and Jewish rituals and from the specific belief that the synagogue was sacred because it was the repository of the sacred scrolls. In addition, the sanctity of the Jerusalem Temple adhered residually to the synagogue. As a result, oaths taken in the synagogue were more fearsome than those taken in the church (Wilken 1983: 79–83). These ideas have been treated above.

Fourth, Christians who needed healing went to the synagogue because they were sure that the Jews would make them well by using incantations and amulets (8.5.6 = PG 48.935 and 8.8.7–9 = PG 48.940–41). The synagogue of Matrona at Daphne, a suburb of Antioch, employed a different technique. There Christians would incubate overnight, just as they might have done at a shrine of Aesculapius (1.6.2–3 = PG 48.852 and 1.8.1 = PG 48.855). Many ancient texts illustrate the Jews' proficiency in magic and medicine, but the localization of this magical activity in the synagogues is documented nowhere but in Chrysostom's *Against the Jews*.

Finally, some time during the fourth century, an Antiochene synagogue built upon the supposed remains of the Maccabean martyrs passed from Jewish to Christian control. The seizure of the synagogue was prompted by many Christians' veneration of these relics, and the Christian authorities obviously believed the cause of truth would be better served if they were under Christian control. Our information about this synagogue and its usurpation by Christians derives from John Malalas and scattered references in Syriac, Arabic, and Hebrew texts. The trustworthiness of these sources is not above question, but the basic facts seem to be correct (Obermann 1931; Bickerman 1951; Hadas 1953: 109–13). Although Chrysostom's orations against the Jews do not mention either the Maccabean martyrs or the synagogue/church erected in their honor, Marcel Simon has suggested that the Christian veneration of the laws of the Jews, the prime target of Chrysostom's abuse, was fueled by the Christian veneration of the relics of those who died in order to uphold those laws. In a separate set of orations delivered in honor of the Maccabean martyrs, Chrysostom (and other fathers) stressed that the Maccabees were Christian martyrs, forerunners of Christ, who martyred himself on the cross. The orations against the Jews provide the other half of the message: do not venerate the Jews or their laws (Simon 1962: 140–53).

What sort of synagogue was this, built over the remains of martyrs? No other ancient synagogue either in the Diaspora or in Israel was a shrine to the dead. The Jews who worshiped in it had a very different conception of corpse uncleanness from that held by the talmudic rabbis and mentioned in the book of Leviticus. Here the dead served not as sources of impurity but as intermediaries between the earthly and the heavenly realms. Here the dead were not removed from the perimeters of society but were placed in a central position in the cult (Brown 1981: 1–22; Lightstone 1984: 57–87). The idea is basic to Christianity but peripheral to rabbinic Judaism.[27] Catacomb 14 at Beth Šeʿārîm, the supposed permanent resting place of the patriarchal family, was topped by a theaterlike structure that was used, perhaps, for communal study or prayer at the tomb of the holy ones (Avigad 1976: 42–65; Cohen 1981: 67, note 23). Almost adjacent to the synagogue of Ḥîrbet Šemāʿ is a large mausoleum of uncertain date (Meyers 1976: 119–22). T ʾÔhālôt 4, 2 (Zuckermandel 1963: 600) narrates that in the time of Rabbi ʿAqîḇāʾ a collection of bones was brought from a certain village and deposited in the synagogue of Lod. Rabbi ʿAqîḇāʾ and his colleagues declared that the bones did not impart impurity, but the text does not tell us why the villagers brought the bones into the synagogue in the first place. By the sixth century at the latest, Jews were praying at the *Makpēlâ* cave in Hebron, and in later centuries many shrines were located at the tombs of the Jewish saints (Bickerman 1951: 74–76; Simon 1962: 146–47). This evidence might indicate that Palestinian Jews, too, were developing a cult of the dead at approximately the same period as their Antiochene brethren. But it is in Antioch, not Palestine, that the cult of the dead for the first time was clearly associated with a synagogue.

I close this section with a discussion of an insignificant but intriguing passage from the *Life of Isidore* by Damascius, a Neoplatonist of the first half of the sixth century:

> Zeno, an Alexandrian born a Jew, renounced in public the nation of the Jews in the way usual among them, driving [or: riding, *elasamenos*] the white ass through their so-called synagogue on the day of rest. (Stern 1980: number 550)

Damascius reports that driving (or riding) a white ass through the synagogue[28] on the Sabbath was the customary ritual of the Jews by which a Jew, in this case Zeno the Neoplatonist, indicated his apostasy. At first glance, this is not very plausible, because Jewish apostates usually do not bother to perform Jewish rituals. (Or was the purpose of the ceremony to prevent the Jewish community from taxing the apostate as a Jew?) In any case, this passage is illuminated by several rabbinic texts. Stern cites the incident of Ělîšāʿ ben ʾAbûyâ who was riding his horse near the synagogue of Tiberias on the Sabbath when he met Rabbi Mēʾîr (J Ḥagîgâ 2.1.77b). Several other rabbinic stories talk about apostates riding horses on the Sabbath.[29]

Damascius, however, refers not to a horse but to a white donkey, perhaps in imitation of the mount of the arch-heretic Jesus. (Matthew 21:2–7; but was the donkey white?). The following story may be relevant:

> Ḥanînâ, the son of the brother of R. Yĕhôšū'a, came to Capernaum and the *mînîm* worked a spell on him, and set him riding on an ass on the Sabbath. He came to Yĕhôšū'a his friend and he put ointment on him and he was healed. (Ecclesiastes Rabbâ 1.8, p. 4b Vilna edition = Herford 1903: number 78)

Heretics employed magic to set Rabbi Ḥanînâ upon an ass on the Sabbath. But this story does not mention the synagogue, and none of these rabbinic stories describes a ritual. The background and meaning of Damascius's report remain elusive.

Patriarchal Control

Who controlled the synagogues of antiquity? Before the work of E. R. Goodenough, scholars had little doubt that synagogue piety was synonymous with rabbinic piety and that the synagogues of the Greco-Roman Diaspora were under the firm control of the patriarch, the "chief rabbi" of the West. Although most of the evidence about the patriarchate is of fourth-century origin, until recently scholars (for example, Mantel 1965: 175–253) have assumed that what was true of the patriarchate in the fourth century was also true generations earlier. Since fourth-century sources state explicitly that the patriarch collected money from, and sent emissaries ("apostles") to, the Jews throughout the empire, these scholars assumed that the patriarch was doing these things already in the second century. Furthermore, according to this traditional view, the demise of the patriarchate in the second decade of the fifth century did not affect rabbinic control of the synagogues, since the vast majority of Jews were delighted to support what they knew to be true. Since Goodenough's work most scholars are convinced that the situation was far more complex and that the degree of rabbinic control, especially in the Diaspora, was much less complete than had been thought previously. Rather than produce a full discussion of the patriarchate and its history, I shall try to demonstrate that pagan and Christian sources document the dramatic growth of patriarchal power from the third century to the last quarter of the fourth century C.E. The sources must be read in chronological sequence and must not be forced to fit a preconceived scheme.

In a passage often quoted by modern scholars, Origen says that the patriarch (whom he calls the *ethnarch*) ruled the Jews like a veritable king or emperor, and decided legal cases, even those entailing a death penalty

(*Epistle to Africanus on the Story of Susanna* in PG 11.81 and 84). Origen claims that he personally witnessed the power of the patriarch in the country of the Jews. In another passage he states that the Jews rejected the Christian interpretation of Genesis 49:10 by arguing that the existence of the office of the patriarch (again called *ethnarch*) demonstrated that the scepter had not yet departed from the tribe of Judah (*De Principiis* 4.3 = PG 11.348). But in neither passage does Origen hint that the patriarch had any power either over synagogues or outside of the Land of Israel. For Origen, the patriarch was a powerful but local figure.[30] Two generations later Eusebius mentioned the Jewish "apostles" but did not connect them specifically with the patriarch. He writes, "Even now the Jews still customarily call 'apostles' those who bear encyclical letters from their rulers" (commentary on Isaiah 18:1 = PG 24.212).[31] He says nothing about their power over synagogues. In another passage Eusebius explains that the prophecy of Isaiah 3:4–5 ("I shall make boys their rulers, and babes shall govern them. So the people shall oppress one another . . . the young shall bully the old") was fulfilled in the patriarchs of the Jews who were "unfinished (*ateleis*) in their souls and deficient in their minds" (commentary on Isaiah 3:4–5 = PG 24.109).[32] Clearly the patriarchate was a powerful office in Eusebius's eyes, but he gives no specific facts about its power.

Amnon Linder argues that patriarchal supervision of the synagogue was assumed by a law of Constantine the Great enacted in late 330 or 331 C.E. (Linder 1983: number 9), but the point is debatable. The law appears to have been enacted in two versions, Theodosian Code (= CT) 16.8.2 and 16.8.4. The first, dated 29 November 330 C.E. and addressed to the praetorian prefect, runs as follows:

> Qui devotione tota synagogis Iudaeorum patriarchis vel presbyteris se dederunt et in memorata secta degentes legi ipsi praesident, inmunes ab omnibus . . . muneribus perseverent . . .

In this law Constantine granted to synagogue functionaries the same privileges accorded to church functionaries (see also the legislation of Theodosius quoted below). The synagogue was not merely tolerated by the state, as it had been before, but was recognized as the official institution of Jewish communal identity.

In this law, what was the relationship of the patriarchs and elders to those "who dedicate [literally, surrender] themselves to the synagogues"? Unfortunately syntax and meaning are obscure. Adopting O. Seeck's emendation of *patriarchis vel presbyteris* to *patriarchae vel presbyteri*, C. Pharr translates the law as follows:

> If any persons with complete devotion should dedicate themselves to the synagogues of the Jews as patriarchs and [*sic*] priests [*sic*] and should live

in the aforementioned sect and preside over the administration of their law, they shall continue to be exempt from all compulsory public services. (Pharr 1952)

According to this translation, Constantine referred not to patriarchs who were the leaders of Palestinian or imperial Jewry, but to patriarchs, apparently equivalent to *archisynagogae*, who were the leaders of local synagogues. If this is correct, the text tells us nothing about the power wielded by the central Jewish authority.

If we follow Mommsen, the editor of the standard edition of the *Codex Theodosianus*, and do not accept Seeck's emendation, the text can be translated in only two ways. Either "Those who, through total devotion to the synagogues of the Jews, have dedicated themselves to the patriarchs or to the elders . . ." or "Those who through total devotion have dedicated themselves to the synagogues of the Jews, the patriarchs, or the elders . . ." According to the first translation, the law addresses two categories of people and assumes that those who served synagogues ipso facto served patriarchs and elders. According to the second translation, the law addresses three categories of people and implies that those who served synagogues did not ipso facto serve patriarchs and elders. Both of these translations are problematic, and perhaps the only secure way to choose between them is to study the use of *vel* in the *Codex Theodosianus* in general and in the laws of Constantine in particular. In the absence of such a study I find the second translation preferable for three reasons. First, two laws of Theodosius refer to persons who were subject to the patriarch, and in those laws, unlike here, the relationship is stated clearly (CT 16.8.13 = Linder 1983: number 27 and CT 16.8.15 = Linder 1983: number 32). Second, no other law refers to people who were subject to the elders. Third, the alternative version of this law (or, perhaps more accurately, the second law of Constantine on the subject), *Codex Theodosianus* 16.8.4, dated 1 December 331, confirms the privileges of "priests, archisynagogues, fathers of synagogues, and others who serve synagogues" (*et ceteros qui synagogis deserviunt*) but completely omits patriarchs and elders. I assume that these considerations impelled Mommsen to suggest that *patriarchis vel presbyteris* be deleted from 16.8.2. I conclude that this law of Constantine is not reliable evidence for patriarchal jurisdiction over synagogues.[33]

Nevertheless, the period of Constantine provides the earliest possible evidence for patriarchal involvement in the life of the Diaspora synagogue. The evidence comes not from an imperial law but from the synagogue inscription at Stobi (Lifshitz 1967: number 10). Claudius Tiberius Polycharmus demanded that he who violated the terms of his testament should pay the patriarch "250,000 denarii." I assume, for the sake of argument, that "the patriarch" was indeed the patriarch of Israel and not some local official. The penalty was exorbitantly high, even for the inflationary late third century, the period to which this inscription is usually ascribed (Hengel 1966: 158–59). In a note to me, the late Elias Bickerman suggested that the inscription was written toward the end of the reign of Constantine, when 250,000 denarii was worth one gold *solidus*, still an impressive amount but neither exorbitant nor unparalleled. I am not competent to assess Bickerman's numismatic argument, and it is most unfortunate that the date at the beginning of the inscription is all but illegible (Lifshitz 1975: 76–77).[34] In any case, the inscription attests to the readiness of the Jews of Stobi to pay money to the patriarch, indicating that he was for them a revered figure. Their readiness may also indicate that they were already in the habit of paying him the *apostolē* or *aurum coronarium*.

When Diaspora Jews began these payments is not clear. In Origen's time the Jews were still paying their *didrachmon* to the Romans, not to the patriarch. The first certain evidence of these payments is in the letter addressed "to the community of the Jews" by the emperor Julian (Stern 1980: number 486a). For reasons that need not be pursued here, Julian wanted the patriarch Ioulos to abolish the collection of the *apostolē*, a tax that, Julian claims, the Jews found onerous. Chrysostom says that the patriarch at the time of Julian was growing rich from the levies that he received from Diaspora Jews (*Contra Judaeos et Gentiles* 16 = PG 48.835). Julian's letter presumes that the patriarch had been collecting this tax for some time, and I suggest that it was Constantine who first authorized this tax, thus putting the patriarch on the legal map. Whatever the virtues of this suggestion and whatever the success of Julian's initiative, by the 380s the patriarch was collecting the tax again. It became the subject of legislation again in 399 (CT 16.8.14 = Linder 1983: number 30) and 404 C.E. (CT 16.8.17 = Linder 1983: number 34), and was finally abolished in 429 C.E. (CT 16.8.29 = Linder 1983: number 53). These laws assume that the tax was collected by the patriarch from the synagogues, through either the archisynagogues or the emissaries of the patriarch. This system is, perhaps, already presumed by the Stobi inscription.

From collection of taxes to outright control was a small but significant step that can be dated to the second half of the fourth century. A letter from Libanius (Stern 1980: number 504) to his friend Priscianus in 364 C.E. may imply that the chief archonship of the Jews of Antioch was at the disposal of the patriarch in Israel, but the interpretation of the letter is disputed and, in any case, the text does not refer to synagogues specifically. By the last quarter of the century, however, patriarchal power was unmistakable. In the 370s Epiphanius wrote that the *apostolos* of the patriarch had the authority to remove "archisynagogues, priests, elders, and *ḥazzānîm*" (*Panarion* 30.11.4 = PG 41.424 = GCS 25.346).[35] Jerome, writing in 387, stated that the patriarchs sent out apostles who instructed the Jews how to behave (commentary on Galatians 1:1 = PL 26.335). The patriarch emerged into literary prominence in the 380s with references in the correspondence of Libanius (Stern 1980: numbers 496–503) and in the *Historia Augusta* (Stern 1980: numbers 521 and 527). In his *Dialogue on the Life of John Chrysostom* (PG 47.51), written in the first decade of the fifth century, Palladius claims that, as a result of bribery, the patriarch changed archisynagogues every year or two (Juster 1914: 452, note 5).

The new status of the patriarch was recognized by Arcadius in 397 (CT 16.8.13 = Linder 1983: number 27). Those privileges bestowed on the chief Christian clerics were to be bestowed also upon those Jews "who [were] subject to the power of the illustrious patriarchs" (*qui inlustrium patriarcharum dicioni subiecti sunt*), namely, upon *archisynagogis patriarchisque ac presbyteris ceterisque qui in eius religionis sacramento versantur.* In 361 C.E. Julian called Ioulos "the most venerable patriarch" (*ton aidesimōtaton patriarchēn*). In 392 Theodosius I called the patriarch "illustrious" (CT 16.8.8 = Linder 1983: number 20), a definite promotion and a sign of his new status. The same title appears in a law of Arcadius in 397 (and in an inscription from a synagogue in Tiberias; Lifshitz 1967: number 76). What is new here is the clear statement that archisynagogues, "patriarchs" (local patriarchs? a corruption of *patribus?*), elders, and others who were engaged in the rites of Judaism were subject to patriarchal jurisdiction. In Constantine's time those who dedicated themselves to synagogues were not subject to the patriarch; by the end of the fourth century they were.

I conclude from this survey of pagan and Christian sources that the patriarch did not have theoretical power over the synagogues of the Diaspora until sometime in the fourth century, probably the latter part of that century (Goodman 1982: 111–18). To what extent his theoretical control was applied in practice—John Chrysostom says nothing of it in his *Against the Jews*[36]—and to what extent the synagogues of antiquity were "rabbinic" institutions, are questions I will not pursue here. Jerome knew (*Epistle* 121.10.19–20 = CSEL 56.48–49) that the Jews had *praepositi sapientissimi* in charge of their synagogues whose task it was to instruct the Jews in the intricacies of the traditions of the Pharisees (*traditiones pharisaeorum quas hodie deuteroseis vocant*). He also claimed (commentary on Isaiah 59:15 = PL 24.581 = CChr 73a.686) that those Jews who did not accept the Pharisaic traditions were liable to attacks and persecutions, akin to that suffered by the man blind from birth who recovered his sight (John 9).

Whether rabbinic evidence will confirm this picture of a developing patriarchate is another question that awaits investigation. Most of the rabbinic references to the patriarch derive from the third century, precisely the period when the external evidence is nearly silent (Levine 1979; Kimelman 1981b), but these references do not claim that the patriarch controlled Diaspora synagogues or collected taxes from them. In fact, rabbinic literature says little of patriarchal control over Palestinian synagogues.

Conclusions

This survey of pagan and Christian evidence on the ancient synagogue has led in many directions and raised many unanswered questions. The common threads are complexity and diversity. From the synagogues of Asia Minor in the first century B.C.E., which had sacrificial feasts, to the synagogue of Antioch erected over the tomb of the Maccabean martyrs, the evidence provided by outsiders yields a complex portrait of the ancient synagogue. Indeed, repeated use of the term *synagogue* results from the erroneous view that there was a single phenomenon that can be designated by this term. All ancient synagogues had a cult based on communal study or prayer, but the diversity possible within this general definition was so great that the term is not always helpful. The complexity of ancient Judaism is faithfully mirrored in the complexity of the ancient synagogue.

Notes

1 The abbreviation PG in this article refers to the *Patrologiae Cursus Completus: Series Graeca*, published in Paris by J.-P. Migne in 1857–1866.

2 I do not treat the New Testament because it has been studied frequently in this connection and because I cannot determine which parts of it are "non-Jewish." Other topics not treated here are the relics of Jewish liturgy in Christian sources, the structure of the ancient Jewish community, and the rabbinic and Christian evidence for the participation of outsiders in Jewish rituals.

3 Patristic references to contemporary Jews and Judaism remain uncollected. In spite of the recent works of Neusner (1971), de Lange (1976), Schreckenberg (1982), and Wilken (1983), the pioneering essay by Krauss (1893–94) remains fundamental. Detailed studies of Jerome, Epiphanius, and the Syriac fathers would be especially valuable.

4 References to *proseuchae*: Apion (discussed below); Juvenal 3.296 (Stern 1980: number 297); Cleomedes (Stern 1980: number 333); Artemidorus, *Oneirokritikon* 3.53 (Stern 1980: number 395). Reference to *synagogae*: Damascius (Stern 1980: number 550). References to *hiera*: Chrysostom, *Against the Jews* (Krauss 1922: 24); Josephus, *War* 7.3.3 [45].

5 This usage first appears in Justin, *Dialogue with Trypho* 134.3.

6 Synagogues are almost invisible in the Mishna and tannaitic literature generally (Cohen 1984). The talmudic and midrashic references to synagogues have not yet been catalogued according to the generation and place of their attestation.

7 Can *tois hierois* mean "precincts of the temple"? I have not found a precise parallel to this usage; *hieron* in the singular often means "the temple and its enclosures."

8 Compare Tacitus, *Histories* 5.5.4 (Stern 1980: number 281), *igitur nulla simulacra urbibus suis, nedum templis sistunt*, and Minucius Felix, *Octavius* 33.2–4 (compare 10.4), where the

spokesman for paganism states, *sed Iudaeis nihil profuit quod unum et ipsi deum aris atque templis maxima superstitione coluerunt.*

9 Apion's account is not based on the Septuagint version of 1 Kings 7:21–26 (which has *stylous* instead of Apion's *kiōnas*, and *thalassa* instead of Apion's *skaphē*).

10 For those general readers who are unfamiliar with rabbinic literature, there are many good books on the subject; see, for example, Strack 1969.

11 Thackeray's alternate translation "in the eastern portion" seems unlikely. Troiani's commentary (1977) does not elucidate the texts of either Agatharchides or Apion.

12 Use of *hieron*: Krauss 1922: 24 (citing Chrysostom, *Against the Jews* 1.6.3 = PG 48:852, and Josephus, *War* 7.3.3 [45]). See, too, Josephus, *Antiquities* 13.3.1 [66] (or does Onias mean that the Jews of Egypt have real temples?), the passage of Agatharchides, and the various inscriptions mentioned below. Use of *neos*: Krauss 1922: 24 (citing Procopius, *De Aedificiis* 6.2). Use of *templum*: Krauss 1922: 28–29, note 3 (citing Tacitus, *Histories* 5.5.4 in Stern 1980: number 281). Also see Minucius Felix, *Octavius* 33.2–4 and 10.4.

13 CT 16.8.4 (Constantine, 330–331) = Linder 1983: number 9; *Historia Augusta, Life of Alexander Severus* 45.6–7 in Stern 1980: number 523, and compare 28.7 in Stern 1980: number 521 (Severus was called a *Syrus archisynagogus et archiereus*); and Epiphanius, *Panarion* 30.11.4 = PG 41.424 = GCS 25.346. Juster (1914: 453, note 7), copied by Krauss (1922: 168), cites John Chrysostom, *Oratio in eos qui conventum eccl. deserviunt*, but I have not been able to verify the reference. In all of these passages "priest" probably is not the technical title for "descendant of Aaron the High Priest" but the generic title for a functionary or high official; see Linder 1975: 122–24. Only two synagogue inscriptions mention priests and in each the meaning probably is "descendant of Aaron"; see Lifshitz 1967: numbers 79 (Theodotus of Jerusalem) and 100 (Berenike). For other epigraphical references to priests, see Brooten 1982: 95–98. On Julian's reference to the Jewish priests, see Stern 1980: number 481a.

14 B Měgîllâ 29a; B Běrākôt 6a–b; Pěsîqtā' dě-Rab Kahanā' 28,8 in Mandelbaum 1962: 431–32.

15 Juster (1914: 459–62), followed by Krauss (1922: 417–19), argues that synagogues were *aedes sacrae* in Roman law, but this is wrong; see Rabello 1980: 723.

16 Justin, *Dialogue with Trypho* 72.3; pseudo-Justin, *Exhortation to the Greeks* 13 = PG 6: 268.

17 John Chrysostom, *Against the Jews* 1.3.3 (PG 48.847), 1.5.2 (850), 6.6.8 (913), and 6.7.2 (914), which is the text quoted.

18 It does not mean "the men's section," a suggestion advanced by Juster (1914: 458) and Krauss (1922: 25). Instead of *ek andrōnos*, the unanimous testimony of all the manuscripts, the Loeb edition (Marcus and Wikgren 1963) accepts the emendation *ek aarōnos*, "from an ark (of the Law)." This is impossible. Augustus would not have used the Hebrew term *'ārôn* without some word of explanation (see Josephus, *Antiquities* 3.6.5 [134]). Furthermore, the term *'ārôn* is not used to mean a synagogue ark until the third century (see Aphrahat; B Šabbāt 32a; and Naveh 1978: number 90, an Aramaic inscription from the Dura synagogue). Correct accordingly Wikgren's note ad loc in the Loeb edition.

19 Section 163 refers explicitly to the "sacred items" (*ta hiera*) that are inviolable and sent to Jerusalem. Several scholars, supposing that the *ta hiera* of section 163 are identical with the *ta hiera chrēmata* of section 164, have proposed emending section 163 to read *ta hiera [chrēmata]*. We cannot be certain, however, that they are identical.

20 The translation of *tas proseuchas poieisthai* is debated; "to build synagogues" is possible but is less likely than "to offer prayers" (against Schürer 1979: 441, note 65 and Hengel 1971: 176). The three requests of section 257 are balanced by the three grants of section 258 (although not in the same order). The Jews request the right to worship God (*hai eis*

ton theon hieropoiiai) and receive the right to conduct their sacred rituals (*ta hiera suntelein*); the Jews request the right to observe their customary festivals and are granted the right to observe the Sabbath; the Jews request the right to maintain their assemblies (*sunodoi*) and are granted the right *tas proseuchas poieisthai*, which must mean "to offer prayers in public." In the Roman decree sent to Sardis (Josephus, *Antiquities* 14.10.17 [235]) *sunodon* means "community" (as it does in Philo, *Embassy to Gaius* 312 and elsewhere); it does not refer to a building.

21 Philo, *Embassy to Gaius* 156–157, attributes such a permission to Augustus.

22 Marcus suggests that *thusiai* be understood to mean "offerings." The Septuagint often uses *thusia* to translate *zebaḥ* in the sense of "feast"; see, for example, 1 Samuel 20:6, 9. See also *Antiquities* 18.9.5 [345].

23 That *thusiai* in *Antiquities* 14.10.24 [260] also refers to "[money for] sacrifices [in Jerusalem]" is unlikely; compare the phraseology of *Antiquities* 14.10.12 [227].

24 To what extent the sacrificial cult was practiced outside of Jerusalem during the Second Temple period (see Valerius Maximus, Stern 1974: number 147a), and whether it was practiced at all after 70 C.E. (see Julian, *Against the Galileans* 305E-306A in Stern 1980: number 481a [page 526 in Greek, page 542 in English; the passage is incorrectly paraphrased by Stern on page 504]) are questions that do not need to be pursued here. Perhaps we should distinguish the Jews of Sardis, who gave sacrifices, from the Jews of Ephesus, who gathered for the sake of "offerings for the sacrifices" (in Jerusalem?).

25 I owe this acute observation to Professor Moshe Bar-Asher.

26 The Greek of the synagogue is disparaged by Cleomedes in Stern 1980: number 333.

27 Bickerman (1951: 77) argues that the Jews who built this synagogue were influenced by Christian ideas. Lightstone (1984: 77–78) rejects this but fails to distinguish public cult from private devotions. Lightstone may be correct that the notion of the dead as mediators was part of Judaism from Hellenistic, if not biblical, times, but Bickerman may yet be correct that the Jews were inspired to give public expression to this idea only under Christian influence.

28 Damascius writes "their so-called synagogue" (*dia tēs kaloumenēs autōn synagogēs*). Socrates, *History of the Church* 7.13 (= PG 67.764) also is uncomfortable with the word "synagogue" (". . . the synagogues of the Jews, for thus they call their places of prayer . . .").

29 See Genesis Rabbâ 65,22 in Theodor and Albeck 1965: 742, with the apparatus and commentary (on Yaqîm of Zĕrôrôt), and B Sanhedrîn 46a ("one who rode a horse on the Sabbath during [the persecution by] the Greeks, and they brought him to the court and stoned him").

30 Elsewhere Origen mentions Ioullos (or Huillus) the patriarch (de Lange 1976: 23–25).

31 Compare Jerome's strictures against Eusebius' interpretation in PL 24.179 = CChr 73.190.

32 Compare Jerome in PL 24.64 = CChr 73.49.

33 Linder (1975: 125) argues that CT 16.8.2 recognizes the patriarch as the head of Diaspora synagogues, a tendency which he thinks was already evident in the law of 329 C.E. (CT 16.8.1 = Linder 1983: number 8), the first law to mention the patriarch. I am not convinced by Linder's interpretation of either law. Linder translates 16.8.2 in accordance with my second alternative but understands the law in accordance with my first alternative.

34 Lifshitz omits the date from his edition of the inscription.

35 Epiphanius claimed that he was narrating a story that he had heard during the reign of Constanius II (337–61) and that took place during the reign of Constantine. See Avi-Yonah 1976: 167.

36   The only place he mentions the patriarch is at 6.5.6 = PG 48.911, where Chrysostom
rejects the claims of the Jews that the patriarch fulfills the role of a high priest.

Bibliography

Avigad, N.
   1976   *Beth She'arim, volume 3: Catacombs 12–23.* New Brunswick, N.J.: Rutgers Univer-
         sity Press.
Avi-Yonah, M.
   1976   *The Jews of Palestine.* Oxford: Blackwell.
Bickerman, E.
   1951   Les Maccabées de Malalas. *Byzantion* 21: 63–83.
Brooten, B.
   1982   *Women Leaders in the Ancient Synagogue.* Series: Brown Judaic Studies 36. Chico,
         Calif.: Scholars.
Brown, P.
   1981   *The Cult of the Saints.* Chicago, Ill.: University of Chicago Press.
Chiat, M. J. S.
   1982   *Handbook of Synagogue Architecture.* Series: Brown Judaic Studies 29. Chico, Calif.:
         Scholars.
Cohen, S. J. D.
   1981   Patriarchs and Scholarchs. *Proceedings of the American Academy for Jewish Research*
         48: 57–85.
   1984   The Temple and the Synagogue. In *The Temple in Antiquity,* edited by T. Madsen,
         pages 151–74. Provo, Utah: Brigham Young University Press.
Goodenough, E. R.
   1954   *Jewish Symbols in the Greco-Roman Period,* volume 4. New York: Pantheon.
Goodman, M.
   1983   *State and Society in Roman Galilee, A.D. 132–212.* Totowa, N.J.: Rowman and
         Allanheld.
Gruber, M.
   1980   *Aspects of Non-Verbal Communication in the Ancient Near East.* Series: Studia Pohl
         12/1. Rome: Pontifical Biblical Institute.
Hadas, M.
   1953   *The Third and Fourth Books of Maccabees.* Philadelphia, Pa.: Dropsie College.
Harkins, P.
   1979   *Saint John Chrysostom: Discourses Against Judaizing Christians.* Series: The Fathers
         of the Church, volume 68. Washington, D.C.: Catholic University.
Hengel, M.
   1966   Die Synagogeninschrift von Stobi. *Zeitschrift für die Neutestamentliche Wissenschaft*
         57: 145–83.
   1971   Proseuche und Synagoge. In *Tradition und Glaube: . . . Festgabe für Karl Georg
         Kuhn,* pages 157–84. Göttingen, W. Ger.: Vandenhoeck & Ruprecht.
Herford, R. T.
   1903   *Christianity in Talmud and Midrash.* London: Williams and Norgate.
Juster, J.
   1914   *Les juifs dans l'empire romain,* volume 1. Reprint. New York: Burt Franklin.

Kimelman, R.

1981a *Birkat Ha-Minim* and the Lack of Evidence for an Anti-Christian Jewish Prayer in Late Antiquity. In *Jewish and Christian Self-Definition*, volume 2, edited by E. P. Sanders, et al, pages 226–44. Philadelphia, Pa.: Fortress.

1981b The Conflict between R. Yohanan and Resh Laqish on the Supremacy of the Patriarchate. In *Proceedings of the Seventh World Congress of Jewish Studies: Studies in the Talmud, Halacha and Midrash*, pages 1–20. Jerusalem: World Union of Jewish Studies.

Krauss, S.

1893–1894 The Jews in the Works of the Church Fathers. *Jewish Quarterly Review* 5: 122–57; 6: 82–99, 225–61.

1922 *Synagogale Altertümer*. Berlin/Vienna: Benjamin Harz.

Landsberger, F.

1957 The Sacred Direction in Synagogue and Church. *Hebrew Union College Annual* 28: 181–203.

Lange, N. R. M. de

1976 *Origen and the Jews*. Cambridge, Eng.: Cambridge University.

Levine, L. I.

1979 The Jewish Patriarch (Nasi) in Third Century Palestine. In *Aufstieg und Niedergang der römischen Welt*, part 2, volume 19.2, edited by W. Haase and H. Temporini, pages 649–88. Berlin/New York: de Gruyter.

Lieberman, S.

1970 *Yemenite Midrashim*. Second edition. Jerusalem: Wahrmann.

Lifshitz, B.

1967 *Donateurs et fondateurs dans les synagogues juives*. Paris: Gabalda.

1975 Prolegomenon to the reprint of J. B. Frey, *Corpus Inscriptionum Judaicarum*, volume 1. New York: Ktav.

Lightstone, J.

1984 *The Commerce of the Sacred*. Series: Brown Judaic Studies 59. Chico, Calif.: Scholars.

Linder, A.

1975 Roman Rule and the Jews during the Period of Constantine. *Tarbiz* 44: 95–143 (Hebrew).

1983 *Roman Imperial Legislation on the Jews*. Jerusalem: Israel Academy of Sciences and Humanities (Hebrew).

Mandelbaum, B., editor

1962 *Pesikta de Rav Kahana*. 2 volumes. New York: Jewish Theological Seminary.

Mantel, H. D.

1965 *Studies in the History of the Sanhedrin*. Cambridge, Mass.: Harvard University Press.

Marcus, R., and Wikgren, A., translators

1963 *Josephus VIII. Jewish Antiquities, Books XV–XVII*. Cambridge, Mass., and London: Harvard and Heinemann.

Meyers, E. M.; Kraabel, A. T.; and Strange, J. F.

1976 *Ancient Synagogue Excavations at Khirbet Shema*. Durham, N.C.: Duke University Press.

Mommsen, T.

1905 *Theodosiani Libri XVI*. Berlin: Weidmann.

Moore, G. F.

1927 *Judaism in the First Centuries of the Christian Era*, volume 1. Cambridge, Mass.: Harvard University Press.

Naveh, J.
1978   *On Stone and Mosaic: The Aramaic and Hebrew Inscriptions from Ancient Synagogues.* Jerusalem: Israel Exploration Society (Hebrew).
Neusner, J.
1971   *Aphrahat and Judaism.* Series: Studia Post-Biblica 19. Leiden, The Netherlands: Brill.
Nock, A. D.
1936   The Gild of Zeus Hypsistos. *Harvard Theological Review* 29: 39–88.
1972   *Essays on Religion and the Ancient World*, volume 2. Edited by Z. Stewart. Cambridge, Mass.: Harvard University Press.
Obermann, J.
1931   The Sepulchre of the Maccabean Martyrs. *Journal of Biblical Literature* 50: 250–65.
Pharr, C.
1952   *Theodosian Code and Novels and the Sirmondian Constitution.* Princeton, N.J.: Princeton University Press.
Rabello, A. M.
1980   The Legal Condition of the Jews in the Roman Empire. In *Aufstieg und Niedergang der römischen Welt*, part 2, volume 13, edited by W. Haase, pages 662–762. Berlin/New York: de Gruyter.
Reinach, T.
1930   *Flavius Josèphe Contre Apion.* Paris: Les Belles Lettres.
Schreckenberg, H.
1982   *Die christlichen Adversus-Judaeos-Texte.* Frankfurt, W. Ger.: Peter Lang.
Schürer, E.
1979   *The History of the Jewish People in the Age of Jesus Christ*, volume 2. Revised edition. Edited by G. Vermes and F. Millar. Edinburgh, Scotland: T. & T. Clark.
Seeck, O.
1919   *Regesten der Kaiser und Papiste.* Stuttgart, W. Ger.: J. B. Metzler.
Simon, M.
1962   *Recherches d'Histoire Judéo-Chrétienne.* Paris: Mouton.
Smallwood, E. M.
1981   *The Jews under Roman Rule.* Series: Studies in Judaism in Late Antiquity 20. Corrected reprint. Leiden, The Netherlands: Brill.
Smith, M.
1982   Helios in Palestine. *Eretz Israel* 16: 199*–214*.
Stern, M.
1974   *Greek and Latin Authors on Jews and Judaism*, volume 1. Jerusalem: Israel Academy of Sciences and Humanities.
1980   *Greek and Latin Authors on Jews and Judaism*, volume 2. Jerusalem: Israel Academy of Sciences and Humanities.
Strack, H. L.
1969   *Introduction to the Talmud and Midrash.* New York: Atheneum.
Tcherikover, V.
1964   *Corpus Papyrorum Judaicarum*, volume 3. Cambridge, Mass.: Harvard University Press.
Theodor, J., and Albeck, C., editors
1965   *Midrash Bereshit Rabba.* Jerusalem: Wahrmann.

Troiani, L.
1977 *Commento Storico al "Contro Apione" di Giuseppe.* Series: Biblioteca degli Studi Classici e Orientali 9. Pisa: Giardini.
Wilken, R.
1983 *John Chrysostom and the Jews.* Berkeley, Calif.: University of California Press.
Zuckermandel, M. S., editor
1963 *Tosephta.* Jerusalem: Wahrmann.

13. Pagan, Christian, and Jewish Elements in the Art of Ancient Synagogues

Bezalel Narkiss

The search for specific Jewish elements in the art of ancient synagogues leads necessarily to a comparison with other artistic expressions. In the syncretistic world of late antiquity, not only ideas and beliefs were fused, but artistic form, gesture, motif, style, and iconography flowed freely among the different pagan religions, and between them and the main monotheistic religions, Judaism and Christianity. The decline of the Roman Empire created an urgent need for security. Daily hazards hardly assured much safety and thus gave impetus to the development of ideas of spiritual and corporal salvation in "another world." Numerous sects within Judaism of the first centuries, of which Christianity was only one, stood side by side with scores of pagan sects that promised personal salvation to their members who underwent a mystical and secret initiation ceremony. Competition among the sects heightened the mutual borrowing of ideas and motifs and brought about a common expression in the sects' language and art.

One such motif, victory over death by the promise of eternal life in the next world, or resurrection in the future, was an idea common to Jews and Christians, as well as to other messianic sects with different outlooks and origins. Other groups such as the Mithraics and the Orphics put great emphasis upon salvation.

Orpheus, the Thracian singer who moved rocks and trees and tamed wild beasts with his music, was usually depicted as a young harp player wearing a Phrygian conical peaked cap, seated on a rock, and surrounded by animals that were charmed by his music. The numerous wall paintings, mosaic floors, and relief sculptures of Orpheus in this posture were, of course, only a symbolic allusion to his function as a savior who managed to enter the underworld and come out alive. The Orphic cult that was personified by this mystical image of personal salvation was widespread in the Roman Empire and included not only initiates of his cult but Jews and Christians as well. The many depictions in fourth-century Rome's early Christian catacombs (and later) of Orpheus charming the animals do not portray the Christians' belief in their salvation through Orpheus, but rather refer to Christ, who is disguised as the popular Orpheus.

This popular figure with all his attributes was depicted in early Jewish art as well. Orpheus wearing a Phrygian cap and playing a harp in front of some animals appears on the second stage of the main panel above the Torah Ark in the third-century synagogue of Dura Europos (figure 13.1). Here, too, the popular image of a musician was probably taken to represent King David, the harpist, the ancestor of the future Messiah, and the anointed king and savior of the Nation of Israel. Evidence for the existence of such a figure in Jewish art is found only later, in the beginning of the sixth century, in the mosaic floor of the synagogue at Gaza. There the harpist confronted by animals is crowned rather than donned with a Phrygian cap, and above his head is the Hebrew inscription "David" (figure 13.2).

Thus, the identification of a pagan cult image with a Jewish or a Christian messianic figure was very common in the syncretistic milieu of late antiquity and serves as but one example of the adoption by one cult of the pictorial symbolic language of another. The Orphic figure symbolized for the Jews an image of salvation and eternal life; it was legitimized by identifying him with David the musician, the Messiah to come. The Orphic salvation differed from that of the Jews mainly in assuring the initiates of Orphism a personal salvation, which, in fact, all other salvation sects, including the Pauline Christians, also claimed. Jewish redemption was a national one, and personal salvation could be found only in the salvation of the whole Nation. This special national Jewish redemption served as a guideline for all Jewish literary and artistic expression during late antiquity.

Therefore, most Jewish symbols and episodic depictions of this period bear a national rather than a personal character. For instance, the Temple facade served as a popular motif on some of the coins of Bar Kokhba (132–133 C.E.; figure 13.3), on the panel above the Torah Ark at the Dura Europos synagogue (figure 13.4), in fourth to sixth century synagogue mosaic floors, and in many minor objects such as clay oil lamps and gold glass plates. In fact, beyond the archaic meaning of "sacred portal," these late-antiquity facades are an abbreviated form of a Roman pagan temple featuring a cella surrounded by a colonnade. The closed door or a cult object, such as the Ark of the Covenant or the seven-branched Menorah, on the facade are what identify it as Jewish. They are substituted for an idol image identifying a temple as dedicated to a certain pagan god.

The walls of the synagogue at Dura Europos feature several depictions of a complete pagan temple that are symbolic of a Jewish sanctuary. These include the Tent of Meeting—the Tabernacle of the desert—occupied by Aaron the High Priest and some of the Tabernacle implements (figure 13.5), as well as the messianic Temple situated above the seventh heaven (figure 13.6). The Tent points to the use of a syncretic, symbolic, pictorial language that allowed commonly understood pictograms to denote holiness and hope of future redemption. The small temple on wheels on a relief at Capernaum symbolizes the destroyed Temple of Jerusalem, using a representation similar to those found in pagan Roman art.

In addition to the Temple and Tabernacle implements, other symbols that adorn the synagogues, appearing either in stone reliefs or in mosaic floors, can be identified as Jewish national symbols: the four or seven species symbolizing the Temple festival of Sukkoth (figure 13.7; Hammat Tiberias: whole floor); the lion of the tribe of Judah; the bull of Ephraim symbolizing the son of Joseph. On the other hand, the palm branches, the wreath of victory, the peacocks representing birds of paradise, the bird in a cage symbolizing the soul caged in the body, and, of course, the vine scroll are all pagan motifs translated into Jewish (figure 13.8; Nîrîm) and Christian religious pictorial language to adorn and give specific meaning to a synagogue or a church.

Jews and Christians have many times used the same symbolic pictorial language adopted from earlier pagan pictorial language. It is sometimes difficult to assess which of these two religions was the first to use it, and which borrowed and translated it according to its own needs. Orpheus as a savior was probably adopted simultaneously by Jews and Christians in the third century. The signs of the zodiac, a magical element in some pagan religions (including the Mithraics), used by both Jews and Christians in the beginning of the fourth century also was adopted simultaneously. The appearance of Helios as a victorious sun, on the mosaic floors of several synagogues (sometimes, as in pagan art, in a circular form with the deity in its center) is curious, though understandable in this syncretistic milieu. The rider on a quadriga was an ancient Greek symbol of victory in the hippodrome, on the battlefield, or over death. In the vault of the underground Christian mausoleum of St. Peter's in Rome, Helios riding his quadriga is a representation of the victorious Jesus. On sarcophagi and walls of the catacomb of Via Latina in Rome, Elijah, one of the prototypes of Jesus, appears riding a quadriga up to Heaven. It is not surprising, then, to find the apotheosis of a Roman emperor in a quadriga

on a consular diptych, housed by the British Museum, or on a medal of
Constantine the Great (figure 13.9) who was baptized into Christianity
while on his deathbed. This pagan motif may have been adopted first by
Christians, and only later, in the fourth century, by the Jews for the
synagogue of Hammat Tiberias.

Helios the victorious sun surrounded by the magical twelve signs of the
zodiac and the four seasons is also depicted in mosaic floors of synagogues
(figure 13.10; Bêt 'Alpā') and earlier has precedents in pagan art from all
over the Roman empire. The use of this composition in a Jewish context
need not presuppose biblical allusions. It may have represented for the Jews
the eternal movement of the sun, moon, and heavenly bodies, instigated by
the power of the one and only invisible God of the universe who, through
the covenant with Noah, promised that "while the earth remaineth, seed-
time and harvest, and cold and heat, and summer and winter, and day and
night shall not cease" (Genesis 8:22). Other biblical figures and episodes
may have been used by Jews before they were used by Christians.

Noah the righteous is one of many biblical figures depicted in the fifth-
century floor mosaic at the Gerasa synagogue. The remaining fragments
show the animals leaving the Ark in pairs next to Noah's three sons. The
floor mosaic of the enigmatic synagogue or church at Mopsuestia (today
the Turkish town of Misis) shows a small ark surrounded by animals. The
coin of Apamea Kibotos in Asia Minor, minted yearly since 193 C.E. in
honor of the equestrian games of the city, depicts at least three scenes of
Noah's life (figure 13.11): Noah and his wife in the Ark, the dove carrying
a branch, and the couple outside the Ark. It is possible that this detailed
three-episode depiction was fashioned after a similarly detailed wall painting in the synagogue at Apamea. Noah, Daniel, and Job were regarded
by the Jews (based on Ezekiel 14:14–20) as the most righteous people of
all times, and therefore were probably depicted in synagogues as interceders
before God for the members of the community. Daniel flanked by the lions
was represented on the mosaic floor of the sixth-century Naʿarān synagogue, and all three personnages were often depicted on the walls of the
Christian catacombs in Rome.

The way these three and other biblical figures were represented in Christian art points to a dependence on midrashic rather than biblical episodes
in Jewish art. Only the midrash can explain the nakedness of Daniel in the
lions' den, or the nakedness of Jonah after he was spewed out of the mouth
of the fish and while lying asleep under a creeping gourd (figure 13.12). It
is obvious that even the Evangelists did not understand Jesus' saying on
the "sign of Jonah"; Jewish pictorial models—some of which were incon-
gruous with any of the Gospels' interpretations of this saying (Matthew
12:38–42, 16:1–4; Mark 8:11–12; Luke 11:29–32)—were used to depict

the Jonah episodes in the catacombs. None alludes to the resurrection of Jesus "after three days," nor to the repenting Ninevites. Some details, such as the heat and the six-hundred thousand little fish in the belly of the large fish which devoured Jonah's clothes and caused him to repent and pray to God for salvation, are based on different midrashic sources. Jonah's repentance is related to the Jews' repentance on the Day of Atonement, when the book of Jonah is read as the haftarah before *Nĕ'îlâ*, the concluding prayer of the service. God's pardon of Jonah after he had "learned his lesson" is usually represented by Jonah, naked, lying blissfully asleep under a gourd for eternal life. The posture of the naked Jonah, with one hand supporting his head and the other over it, closely resembles that of the beautiful, young, and naked Endymion, the shepherd who was made to fall asleep for eternal life and remain young forever, so that his lover, the moon goddess Selene, could descend every night to embrace him. This same Endymion may have been the model used by Jewish artists in depicting the blissful eternal life of Jonah who, according to the midrash, is also the harbinger of the Messiah and the one who will bring to the table of the righteous the Leviathan on which they will feast. Although no depiction of Jonah in Jewish art has survived, Christian artists apparently used Jewish artistic representations, and not only midrashic texts, as their models.

Jewish midrashic representations appear on most of the walls of the mid-third-century Dura Europos synagogue. Examples are the identification of Yôkebed and Miriam, the mother and sister of Moses, with the midwives; the arms-bearing Israelites leaving Egypt; the crossing of the Red Sea in twelve paths (figure 13.13); the miraculous portable well in the desert; the legendary man who was to light the sacrifice of the Baal prophets being killed by a snake; and King Ahashverus seated on the miraculous throne of Solomon, together with Esther, in a posture resembling that of the local gods Haddad and Athargatis. In most cases these paintings were fashioned by artists who were well-versed in the current oral midrashic interpretations and who employed common pagan postures to render them. These midrashic interpretations were the main thematic source of Jewish art in late antiquity, whereas the style, gestures, and motifs were borrowed directly from general or regional contemporary art.

The combination of Jewish midrashic interpretation with contemporary local style was practiced in early Jewish art. For instance, a wall in Pompeii (figure 13.14) depicts Solomon aided in his judgement by two advisors, and not alone as stated in the Bible, since, according to halakhah, any lawsuit that may have resulted in punishment by death had to be heard by at least three judges. There is enough evidence to show that there were Jews in Pompeii before its destruction in 79 C.E. Although they themselves did not write any midrashim or targums, it is clear that an oral tradition of midrashic interpretation existed there. Moreover, since it is hard to believe that a complete series of biblical depictions based on midrashic interpretation would have been created in a border town under military pressure, such as Dura Europos, we may conclude that they were created in a more important Jewish center—possibly Rome, Antioch, or Alexandria in Egypt—where there were many Jews and several large synagogues. When these models reached Dura, the synagogue artists there may have modified the paintings to suit local needs and tastes.

Bibliography

Cumont, F.
   1922   *After-Life in Roman Paganism.* New Haven, Conn.: Yale University Press.
Eisler, R.
   1921   *Orpheus–The Fisher.* London: J. M. Watkins.
Goldman, B.
   1966   *The Sacred Portal.* Detroit, Mich.: Wayne State University Press.
Goodenough, E. R.
   1953–68 *Jewish Symbols in the Greco-Roman Period.* 13 volumes. New York: Pantheon.
Gutmann, J., editor
   1973   *The Dura-Europos Synagogue: A Re-Evaluation (1932–72).* Missoula, Mont.: Scholars.
Kraeling, C. E.
   1956   *The Synagogue, Excavations at Dura Europos, First Report,* volume 8, part 1. New Haven, Conn.: Yale University Press.
Narkiss, B.
   1979   The Sign of Jonah. *Gesta* 18/1: 63–76.
Roth C.
   1953   Jewish Antecedents of Christian Art. *Journal of the Warburg and Courtauld Institutes* 16: 24–44.
Weitzmann, K., editor
   1979   *Age of Spirituality.* New York: Metropolitan Museum of Art.

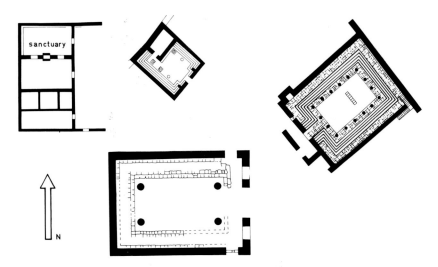

1.1   Plans of Second Temple synagogues at Delos (top left), Masada (top center), Gamla (top right), and Herodium (above).

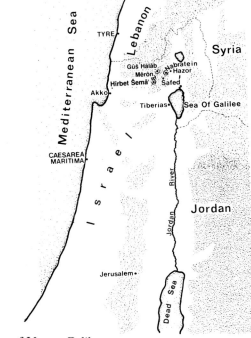

9.1   Map of Upper Galilee.

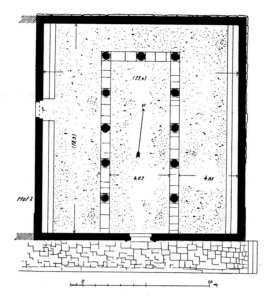

9.2   Ground plan of Gûš Ḥālāb according to Kohl and Watzinger 1916.

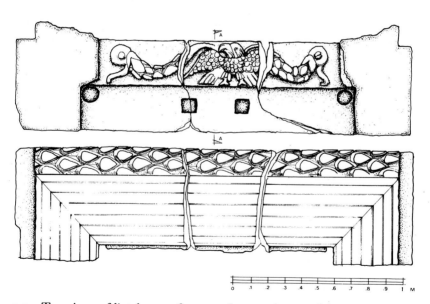

9.3   Two views of lintel stone from southern entrance of the synagogue at
       Gûš Ḥālāb. The top drawing shows the underside of the lintel,
       revealing the eagle that has been incised there. The bottom drawing
       shows a frontal view.

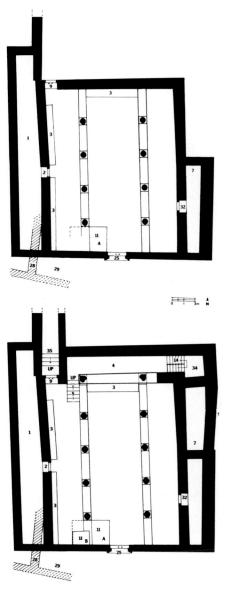

9.4 Two plans of the synagogue at Gûš Ḥālāb. Top: Synagogue without
gallery at north end. The southern entrance is 25; the *bîmâ* in the
third-century stage is 11; the large storeroom on the west is 1; and the
smaller storeroom on the east is 7. Bottom: Synagogue with gallery
(4) north of heart-shaped columns. Note the possible configuration
of room 7 on east and Byzantine stage of the *bîmâ* (11). The internal
space, except for the gallery, remains the same.

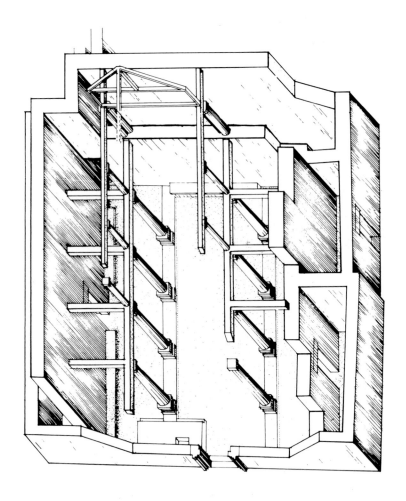

9.5   Isometric plan of synagogue at Gûš Ḥalāḅ.

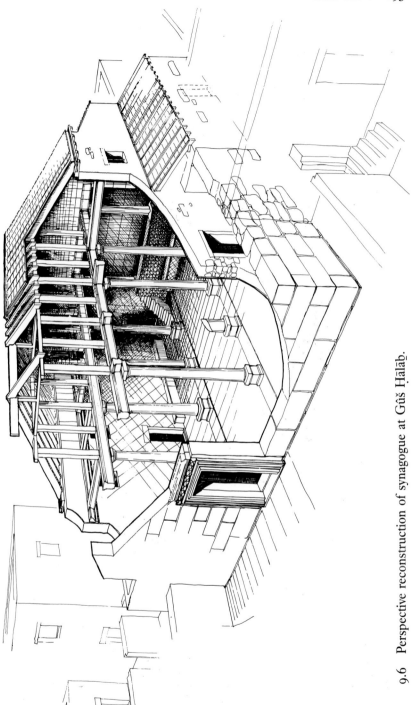

9.6 Perspective reconstruction of synagogue at Gūš Ḥalāb.

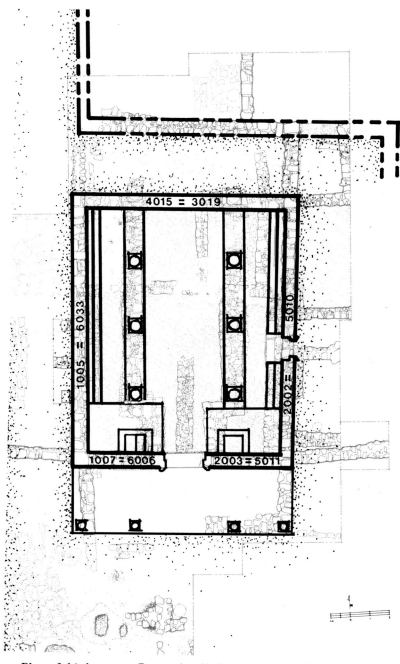

9.7   Plan of third-century Roman basilical synagogue at Nabratein.

9.8 Photograph of the pediment of Ark of Law found in the third-century building at Nabratein, with drawings that show an artist's reconstruction of the pediment stone and of the entire ark set on the *bîmâ*.

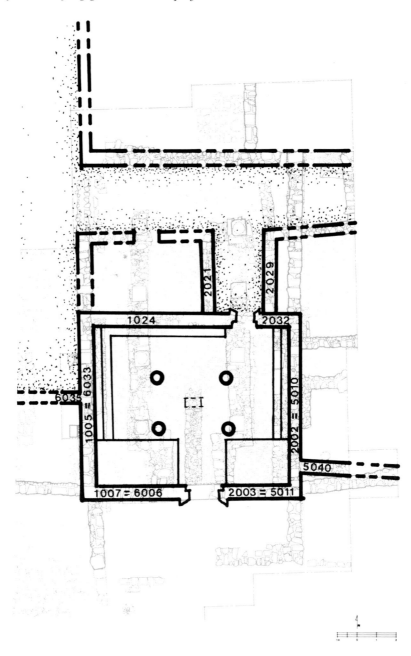

9.9   Plan of second-century broadhouse synagogue at Nabratein.

10.1 Facade of the synagogue at Mêrôn.

10.2 Interior of the synagogue at Capernaum.

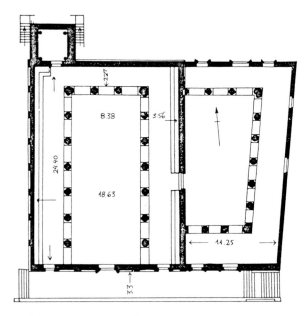

10.3   Plan of the synagogue at Capernaum.

10.4   Drawing of a synagogue window.

10.5   Lintel from synagogue at Capernaum. Now mutilated, it was originally decorated with garlands and supported by cupids, with an eagle in the center.

10.6   Lintel from synagogue at Gûš Ḥālāb. Soffit is decorated with eagle supporting garlands.

10.7   Frieze from synagogue at Capernaum decorated with acanthus scrolls and fruit.

10.8   Frieze from synagogue at Capernaum decorated with acanthus scrolls and geometrical designs.

10.9   Frieze from synagogue at Capernaum decorated with acanthus scrolls and geometrical designs.

10.10 Frieze from synagogue at Capernaum decorated with acanthus scrolls and geometrical designs.

10.11 Frieze from synagogue at Capernaum decorated with a "peopled" scroll. The animal is particularly mutilated.

10.12   Frieze from synagogue at Ḵôrāzîn decorated with "peopled" vine
scroll and vintage.

10.13   Cornice from synagogue at Ḵôrāzîn decorated with two eagles supporting a garland and capricorn.

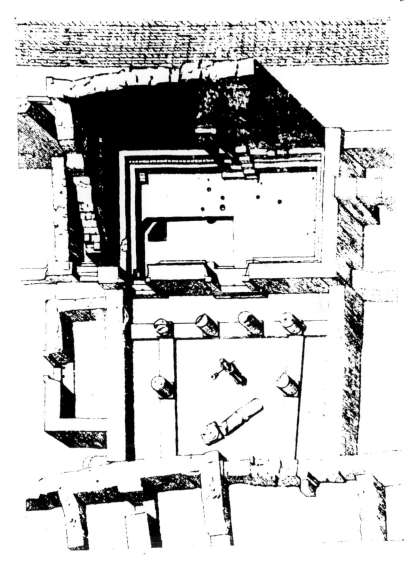

11.1a Isometric reconstruction of the second stage of the synagogue at Dura Europos. This structure, of the mid-third century, has a similar function to the Christian "domus ecclesiae" shown in figure 11.1b.

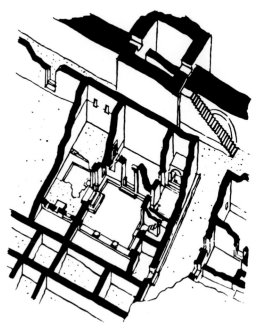

11.1b   Isometric reconstruction of the Christian "domus ecclesiae" at Dura
Europos. This structure, of the mid-third century, has a similar
function to the synagogue shown in figure 11.1a.

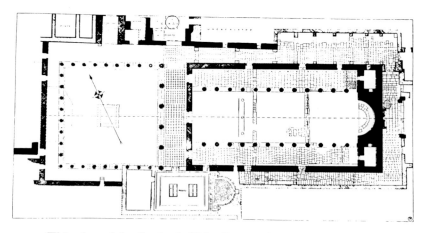

11.2   This plan of the "cathedral" in Gerasa, from the second half of the
fourth century C.E., shows a typically longitudinal Christian basilica
with atrium.

11.3 Reconstructions of two synagogues. Top: Typical "Galilean" synagogue at e-Dikke, with a monumental facade built of ashlars. Bottom: First stage of synagogue at Bêt 'Alp̱ā', with a rather modest facade covered with plaster.

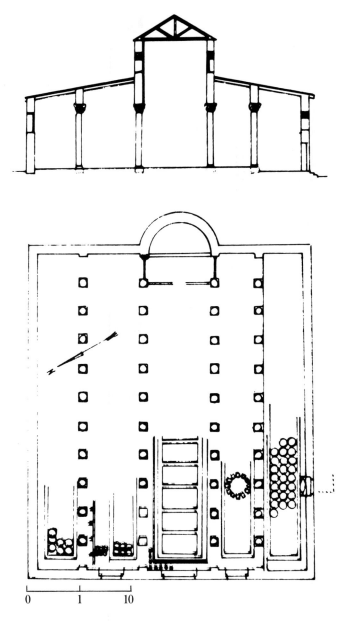

11.4   Basilical plan and elevation of the early sixth-century synagogue at
Gaza. The synagogue resembles a basilical church but is relatively
broad and has four rows of columns.

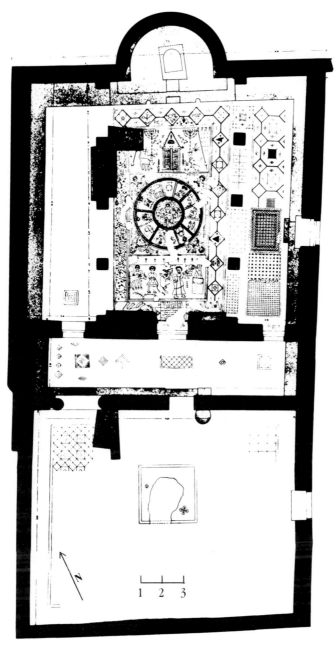

11.5   Ground plan of the synagogue at Bêt 'Alpā'.

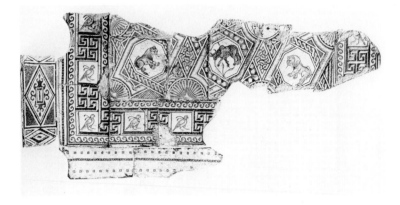

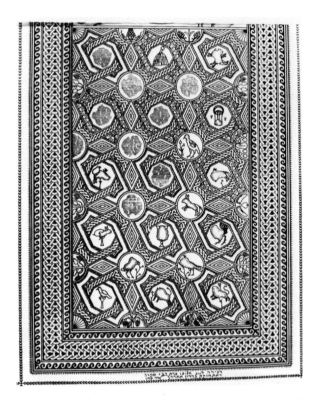

11.6   Mosaic compositions from the church at Ḥôrḇat Bĕrāḵôt (top) and the synagogue at Na'arān (below). Although the execution of the mosaic at Bĕrāḵôt is of much better artistic quality, their compositions are almost identical. (The mosaic at Na'arān suffered damage by iconoclasts in the early eighth century.)

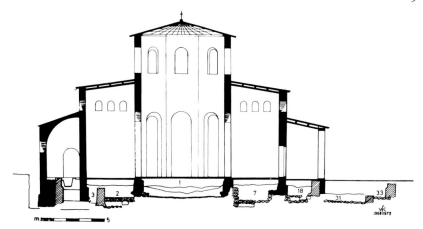

11.7   Elevation of a centralized "martyrium"-type church at Capernaum.

13.1   David-Orpheus in wall-painting from synagogue at Dura Europos. Damascus, National Museum.

13.2   David-Orpheus in floor mosaic from the synagogue at Gaza.

13.3   Temple facade on a coin of Bar Kokhba. Jerusalem, Israel Museum.

13.4 Temple facade in a wall-painting above the Torah Ark from the synagogue at Dura Europos.

13.5 The Tabernacle of the Desert in a wall-painting from the synagogue at Dura Europos. Damascus, National Museum.

13.6   The future Temple in a wall-painting from the synagogue at Dura Europos. Damascus, National Museum.

13.7   Floor mosaic from the synagogue at Ḥammat Tiberias.

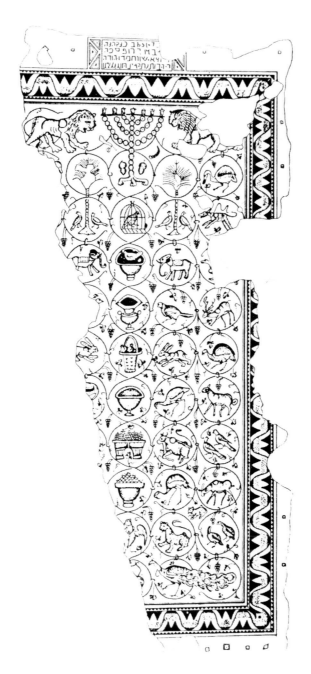

13.8 Floor mosaic from the synagogue at Nîrîm.

13.9   The Apotheosis of Constantine on a coin. Paris, Bibliothèque Nationale.

13.10   Floor mosaic from the synagogue at Bêt 'Alpā'.

13.11 Noah's Ark on a coin from Apamea Kibotos (in Asia Minor). Paris, Bibliothèque Nationale.

13.12 The story of Jonah on a wall-painting from the catacomb of St. Calixtus.

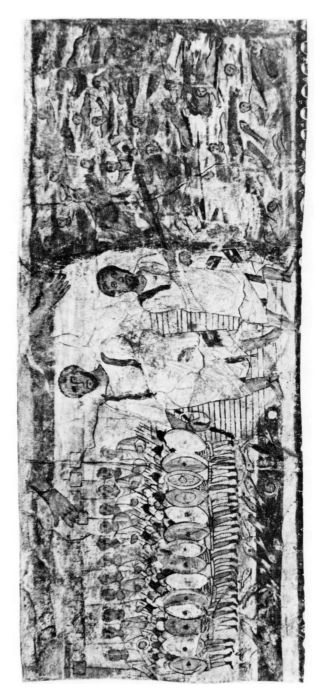

13.13 The Israelites crossing the Red Sea, shown in a wall-painting from the synagogue at Dura Europos. Damascus, National Museum.

13.14   The Judgement of Solomon, shown in a wall-painting from Pompeii.

Index

Illustration Credits

Chapter 9: All illustrations are by Larry Belkin, except for the reconstruction of the entire ark set on the *bîmâ* (9.8), which appears courtesy of the National Geographic Society, and the ground plan of Gûš Ḥālāb (9.2), which appears courtesy of Otto Zeller Verlag. **Chapter 10:** All figures, except 10.3, are used courtesy of the Institute of Archaeology at the Hebrew University of Jerusalem. Figure 10.3, the plan of the synagogue at Capernaum, appears courtesy of Oxford University Press. **Chapter 11:** Figure 11.1a appears courtesy of Harmondsworth Press, while figure 11.1b has been used courtesy of the Pontificio Istituto Biblico. Figure 11.2 appears courtesy of the American Schools of Oriental Research. Figure 11.3, top, appears courtesy of Otto Zeller Verlag; figure 11.3, bottom, is used courtesy of Oxford University Press. Figure 11.4 is used with permission from Lee I. Levine. Figure 11.5 is also used courtesy of Oxford University Press. Yoram Tsafrir consented to the use of figure 11.6. Figure 11.7 appears courtesy of the Franciscan Printing Press. **Chapter 13:** Figures 13.1, 13.4, 13.5, 13.6, and 13.13 all appear courtesy of Yale University Art Gallery. Figure 13.2 is used with permission from Lee I. Levine. Figure 13.3 appears with permission from Z. Radovan. Figures 13.7 and 13.11 appear with permission from Bezalel Narkiss. Figure 13.8 is used courtesy of Princeton University Press. Figures 13.9 and 13.10 are used with permission from Yoram Tsafrir. Figure 13.12 is used courtesy of Le Febvre & C.ⁱ, Librai-editori. Figure 13.14 appears courtesy of Museo Nazionale, Naples.

This book is typeset in Ehrhardt, a typeface of
classic European design exhibiting excellent readability.
Design and composition were by Marathon Typography Service, Inc., Durham, NC.
Printing was by PBM Graphics, Raleigh, NC,
on S.D. Warren's 70 lb.
Patina Matte.

DATE DUE

GAYLORD   PRINTED IN U.S.A.